Professional Issues for Primary Teachers

Professional Issues for Primary Teachers

Edited by
Ann Browne and Derek Haylock

P·C·P
Paul Chapman
Publishing

A SAGE Publications Company
1 Oliver's Yard
55 City Road
London EC1Y 1SP

SAGE Publications Inc
2455 Teller Road
Thousand Oaks, California 91320

SAGE Publications India Pvt Ltd
B-42, Panchsheel Enclave
Post Box 4109
New Delhi 100 017

Library of Congress Control Number 2003115342

A catalogue record for this book is available from the British
Library

ISBN 0 7619 4403 6
ISBN 0 7619 4404 4 (pbk)

Typeset by Dorwyn Ltd, Rowlands Castle, Hants.
Printed in Great Britain by T.J. International, Padstow

Contents

The Authors

Ann Browne is a senior lecturer in education at the University of East Anglia where she works with primary Postgraduate Certificate of Education (PGCE) students and practising teachers. She has written a number of books about teaching English in the early years, including *Developing Language and Literacy 3–8* (2nd edition, 2001), *A Practical Guide to Teaching Reading in the Early Years* and *Helping Children to Write*, all published by Paul Chapman Publishing, and *Teaching Writing at Key Stage 1 and Before*, published by Nelson Thornes (1999).

Derek Haylock is an author and educational consultant who has worked in primary teacher training for over 30 years. Until recently he was mathematics tutor and Co-Director of the Primary PGCE course at the University of East Anglia (UEA), Norwich. His books include *Mathematics Explained for Primary Teachers* (2nd edition, 2001), *Numeracy for Teaching* (2001), *Teaching Mathematics to Low Attainers 8–12* (1991) and (with Anne Cockburn) *Understanding Mathematics in the Lower Primary Years* (2nd edition, 2002), all published by Paul Chapman Publishing. He has also had published seven books of Christian drama and a Christmas musical.

Rob Barnes is a senior lecturer in education at UEA and teaches information and communications technology (ICT) and Art and Design on the primary PGCE. His books include *Teaching Art to Young Children 4–9* (2nd edition), *Art Design and Topic Work 8–13*, *Positive Teaching, Positive Learning* and *Successful Study for Degrees* (3rd edition).

Gill Blake has been Headteacher of Cringleford First and Middle School in Norwich for 14 years. She has spent 30 years teaching in a variety of primary schools and one year in which she was seconded to work as a tutor on the UEA Primary PGCE. She was a founding member of the UEA Primary Partnership Development Group.

Tony Blake has been the headteacher of St Mary's Middle School in Long Stratton, near Norwich, for the past 16 years. Prior to that he was a deputy and class teacher in Norwich and London. He is a member of the National Middle

Schools Forum Steering Group and has served on a number of local education authority (LEA) and university committees dealing with a wide range of educational issues. He was a founding member of the UEA Primary Partnership Development Group.

Helena Campion is a tutor in Education on the Primary PGCE course at the University of East Anglia. She has taught for 10 years across the primary school age range. Her research interests are in the fields of Information Technology and the learning environment.

Sue Cox is a Lecturer in Education at UEA. She contributes to the Primary PGCE and has joint responsibility for co-ordinating the continuing professional development programme for the school. She taught in primary schools for 12 years and has worked in teacher education for 18 years. Her publications include articles and chapters in books on primary curriculum and pedagogy, including the teaching of primary art and action research in teacher education.

Peter Gibley is headteacher of Nelson First School in Norwich. Before he came into teaching he was a baker and an actor. He taught British Forces children in Germany before taking over a tiny first school in rural Norfolk. He is now head of a large urban school. He is also a magistrate with a special interest in family work.

Sue Lawes is a recent entrant to the teaching profession, teaching in a Norwich Primary School. She trained on the UEA Primary PGCE course.

Ralph Manning is a tutor in primary teaching training at the University of East Anglia. Previously he taught in primary schools in Bedfordshire and Norfolk. He is a founding member of the General Teaching Council, to which he was elected by primary teachers in 2000. Prior to entering the teaching profession he worked in the computer industry for many years.

Ann Oliver is a Co-Director of the Primary PGCE course at the UEA. Prior to becoming a Primary PGCE science tutor she taught across Key Stages 1 and 2. She has researched teacher recruitment and attitudes towards science education. Her publications include articles about interactive science centres, teaching science through stories and chapters in *Teaching Children 3–11*, published by Paul Chapman Publishing.

Linda Rudge is the Director of the Keswick Hall Centre for Research and Development in Religious Education (RE) at the University of East Anglia. She teaches RE on the Primary PGCE programme and works with teachers on continuing professional development courses and in-service training. Her research interests and publications cover policy issues in RE, the professional needs of teachers, and the faiths, beliefs and values of teachers and their pupils.

Jenifer Smith is a tutor in Education at UEA, contributing to the English and drama curriculum components of the Primary PGCE. She has joint responsibility for co-ordinating the Continuing Professional Development programme for the school. She has worked as an English specialist adviser for Suffolk County Council and been actively involved in induction and in-service training for the teaching of English in schools. Her publications include a number of edited volumes of classic literature in the Cambridge Literature Series.

Fiona Thangata recently joined the Primary PGCE team at the University of East Anglia as a mathematics tutor. She has worked in England, Scotland, Namibia and the USA as a classroom teacher, curriculum developer, inservice provider and teacher trainer.

Barbara Vanlint is a primary school teacher and has taught at Mundesley Junior School on the Norfolk coast for the past 12 years. In 1999 she became a Farmington Institute Millenium Award holder, based at the UEA Keswick Hall Centre for RE, and wrote a paper entitled 'Children's spiritual development – why should we care?'.

Jacqueline Watson was an RE teacher for 10 years. She has been a research associate with the Keswick Hall RE Centre at UEA for the past six years, which have included research on citizenship and RE for a Farmington Fellowship. Her research interests include spiritual development, Religious Education and citizenship, and RE teachers' self-portrayals.

Maggie Woods is a School Development Adviser working with special schools and Education Support Centres in Hertfordshire. She has worked in special education for 18 years and has been headteacher of two special schools catering for pupils with moderate and severe learning difficulties. She has just completed her doctorate research at UEA looking at assessment and pedagogy for pupils in special schools in the context of RE.

Introduction

The influence of primary education on shaping our lives cannot be underestimated. Everyone remembers something from their early days in school. It might be the smell of polish or disinfectant, the sound of the bell or the sunlight filling the space in the hall as you walked into assembly. It might be feeling scared because you had to read a whole sentence in front of the class, or being milk monitor for the first time. It might be enjoying creative lessons, art, embroidery and cooking, or having a new exercise book in which to write. It might be playing or singing in a musical event or taking part in a dramatic production. It might be listening to your teacher read stories. It might be the pride associated with an unexpected achievement or the embarrassment of failure. The strength of these memories is an indication of the importance that those years in primary school have held for us as individuals. It is important, therefore, that all primary school teachers are dedicated to making that experience as effective and as happy as possible for all pupils. This involves being thoroughly professional. This book is intended to be a contribution to raising the awareness of primary teachers and trainee teachers as to what is involved in all the different professional dimensions of their work in schools.

Professional Issues for Primary Teachers is a companion volume to *Teaching Children 3–11* (edited by Anne Cockburn, also published by Paul Chapman Publishing). This new book also emanates from the primary team at the University of East Anglia, Norwich, but with significant contributions from a number of other colleagues who are associated in some way with the university.

Since our collective experience has been mainly in the UK, specifically in England, we inevitably draw on primary practice, legislation and government guidance in this country. Readers in other parts of the UK and oversees will nevertheless find that the principles dealt with here have a more general relevance.

The book deals with the key professional issues in primary teaching that are addressed in primary teacher training courses. It contributes specifically to the QTS Standards for Professional Values and Practice (DfES/TTA, 2002). The book aims to enable the reader to understand the nature of primary education in England and the professional demands made upon primary school teachers, including those from parents, the children themselves, the law, government agencies, society and the profession.

Some chapters are written by tutors on the primary PGCE course at UEA, others by practising headteachers or teachers in schools within the UEA primary partnership, and some by teachers or advisers undertaking educational research at UEA. This blend of authors is a feature of the book, providing what we hope is a useful mixture of demands upon the reader. We also hope that you will enjoy the opportunities to engage with some of the philosophical aspects of primary school teaching, that you will find your thinking about professional issues is given shape and that you get from this book the basic information you need to operate in your own professional context.

Each chapter contains an explanation and discussion of the issues, issues for reflection, a summary of key points and annotated suggestions for further reading. Tutors working with professional development groups of primary trainees will find the questions posed in the issues for reflection to be helpful starting points for discussions.

The Internet websites to which we refer in this book were consulted during the period April to August 2003. Addresses and details were correct at the dates of consultation but may have been subject to subsequent change.

Derek Haylock and Ann Browne
University of East Anglia, Norwich

Abbreviations and Acronyms

ACPC	Area Child Protection Committee
ADD	attention deficit disorder
ADHD	attention deficit hyperactivity disorder
ASD	autistic spectrum disorder
AST	advanced skills teachers
ATL	Association of Teachers and Lecturers
BESD	behavioural, emotional and social difficulty
CE	citizenship education
CEDP	Career Entry and Development Profile
DfES	Department for Education and Skills
DoH	Department of Health
EAL	English as an additional language
EAZ	Education Action Zone
EBD	emotional and behavioural difficulty
ESO	Education Supervision Order
GMC	General Medical Council
GTC	General Teaching Council
GTCE	General Teaching Council for England
GTCS	General Teaching Council for Scotland
GTCW	General Teaching Council for Wales
HMCI	Her Majesty's Chief Inspector of Schools
HRA	Human Rights Act
ICT	information and communications technology
IEP	individual education plan
ISCTIP	Independent Schools Council Teacher Induction Panel
ITT	initial teacher training
LEA	local education authority
LSA	learning support assistant
MLD	moderate learning difficulty
MSI	multi-sensory impairment
NACE	National Association for Able Children in Education
NASEN	National Association of Special Educational Needs
NASUWT	National Association of Schoolteachers Union of Women Teachers
NCC	National Curriculum Council

NQT	Newly-qualified teacher
NLS	National Literacy Strategy
NNS	National Numeracy Strategy
NUT	National Union of Teachers
OFSTED	Office for Standards in Education
PANDA	performance and assessment data
PcfRE	Professional Council for Religious Education
PD	physical difficulty
PE	physical education
PECS	picture exchange system
PEP	personal education plan
PGCE	Postgraduate Certificate of Education
PNI	physical and neurological impairment
PMLD	profound and multiple learning difficulty
PPA	planning, preparation and assessment
PR	parental responsibility
PSHE	personal, social and health education
PTA	parent–teacher association
QCA	Qualifications and Curriculum Authority
QTS	qualified teacher status
RE	religious education
SACRE	Standing Advisory Council for Religious Education
SCAA	Schools Curriculum and Assessment Authority
SEN	special educational need(s)
SENCO	special educational needs co-ordinator
SLD	severe learning difficulty
SpLD	specific learning difficulty
STRB	School Teachers' Review Body
TA	teaching assistant
TEACCH	Treatment and Education of Autistic and Related Communication Handicapped Children
TPLF	Teachers' Professional Learning Framework
TTA	Teacher Training Agency
UEA	University of East Anglia
VA	voluntary aided (school)
VC	voluntary controlled (school)
VLE	virtual learning environment

1
Primary Education in England

Ann Oliver

The following topics and issues are covered in this chapter:

- how we have got to where we are in current primary school practice;
- the emergence of distinctive primary practice;
- the increase in central control of education;
- the tension between progressive and traditional approaches;
- good primary practice and effective primary teaching;
- the diversity of primary schools, including alternative schools;
- the current primary school curriculum, including the National Curriculum, the Foundation Stage guidance, the National Literacy Strategy (NLS) and the National Numeracy Strategy (NNS);
- primary practice related to grouping by ability;
- national tests and their influence on the primary curriculum;
- the current promotion of excellence and enjoyment; and
- the importance of teachers focusing on the individual.

This chapter provides a brief overview of primary schooling in this country, setting the context for the discussion of professional issues in primary education in subsequent chapters. The main theme that emerges in this chapter is the ongoing tensions that confront primary school teachers within a culture of testing, raising standards, centralized control and accountability. I have included comments from practising primary school teachers to illustrate this theme and to show how these tensions impact on them.

The Development of Primary Education in England

The emergence of primary schools

The history of primary school education in England is comparatively recent. It was not until the mid-1960s that *all* children between the ages of 5 and 11 could be educated in schools specifically allocated to children within this age range. It is hard to believe that before 1944 there was not even a Ministry for Education. This was established through the 1944 Education Act. The main feature of this Act was the division of responsibility between central government, the LEAs, headteachers and schools' governing bodies. Primary education since then has seen many changes, with the autonomy of the headteacher and the local authorities gradually usurped by more and more directives and control from central government.

Today, parents in England have a legal obligation to ensure that their child is being educated. The LEA is required by law to make a place in a school available, although a significant proportion of parents choose to send their children to private fee-paying schools and a small number opt to teach their children at home. Children must start primary education no later than the term following their fifth birthday, though in most cases primary schools take children into their reception classes at age 4 and, increasingly, into their nursery classes when they are 3. Primary education officially ends after the school year in which the child turns 11.

There are about 4 million primary age children attending over 18,000 primary schools. On average children aged 5 to 11 find themselves in a school of 225 pupils with eight teachers, one of whom is the headteacher. There are 30 children in each class. Children are taught most of the curriculum by their class teacher, who is very likely to be female (OFSTED, 1999a). The largest primary schools have over 800 pupils. The smallest have fewer than 20 pupils, all of whom are taught by a single teacher.

Distinctive primary practice

The primary school curriculum and approaches to teaching and learning since 1944 have undergone remarkable changes. Primary practice in education in the 1950s was characteristically didactic, teacher-centred and narrowly focused on reading, writing and arithmetic. But more progressive influences were beginning to have an impact and to shift the focus towards the needs of the child. Froebel's theory and practice of natural development and spontaneity established the first kindergarten movement. Maria Montessori emphasized structured learning, sense training and individualization, based on the idea that teachers should listen to children in order to inform teaching. Alexander (2002) describes the relationship between primary education, education policy and society at that time as a mixture of nineteenth-century elementary education and a progressive counter-culture. 'The one sought to produce a workforce which was functionally literate and numerate but socially

conformist and politically docile, while the other celebrated individual fulfilment … (Alexander, 2002, p. 17).

In the 1960s educational developments were rapid and a distinctive primary
school practice began to emerge. Society was changing dramatically and, in the
context of the new liberalism, local authorities encouraged innovation in
schools. Primary schools found a freedom from constraints with the decline of
selective secondary schools and the consequent abolition of the 11-plus
examination in most LEAs, together with a decline in the role taken by their
inspectors.

The Plowden Report (CACE, 1967) was the most influential factor in the
emergence of a distinctive 'child-centred' primary school practice. The recommendations of Plowden included the establishment of educational priority
areas, the expansion of nursery education and more involvement of parents in
primary schools. However, the Plowden Report's influence on primary practice
came from its emphasis on placing the child 'at the heart of the education
process', non-streaming and a more humanist approach to teaching and learning. The philosophical position adopted by Plowden, and the freedom given to
primary headteachers to determine their own curriculum, combined to generate many of the characteristics of 'good primary practice' that until recently
were still the dominant orthodoxy in primary education: group work, topic-
based work and projects, integrated studies, display of pupils' work, discovery
learning, independent learning, differentiation and individual needs.

The current educational context

The Plowden Report was quickly followed by strong criticisms from right-
wing educationalists through a series of so-called 'Black Papers', the first of
which was published in 1969. The battle between progressives and traditional-
ists has continued ever since. Table 1.1 indicates some of the key words and
phrases that might characterize these contrasting approaches.

As these arguments continued between 1967 and 1988 there was no systematic monitoring or enforcement of the primary school curriculum.
Eventually, after a succession of discussion papers exploring the issues raised

Table 1.1 Contrasting progressive and traditional approaches to primary education

Progressive	Traditional
Child-centred	Subject-focused
Broad curriculum	Back to basics
Individual learning	Teacher-directed
Differentiation	Whole-class teaching
Choice	Prescription
Discovery learning	Direct teaching
Experience	Attainment
Informal assessment	Formal testing

in the debate, the government introduced the 1988 Education Reform Act. This was the most important Education Act since 1944 and the changes were profound. The main provision was the introduction of a National Curriculum. Teachers would no longer be free to be curriculum innovators. Instead they became, in effect, curriculum deliverers. Control of the curriculum was taken away from the schools and LEAs and passed to agencies accountable to central government. The National Curriculum Council (NCC) and the School Examination and Assessment Council (SEAC) were established to oversee respectively the content of the curriculum and the associated system of national testing. These were followed closely by the School Curriculum and Assessment Authority (SCAA), which combined these roles, and then in 1997 by the Qualifications and Curriculum Authority (QCA). The Office for Standards in Education (OFSTED) was set up to take over responsibility for inspecting schools, to ensure the implementation of the curriculum and to monitor standards.

In 1995 OFSTED commissioned research (Sammons, Hillman and Mortimore, 1995) to ascertain key characteristics of effective primary schools. The factors identified included:

- professional leadership;
- shared vision and goals;
- purposeful teaching;
- high expectations;
- positive reinforcement;
- monitoring progress; and
- home–school partnership.

'Good primary practice' had been replaced by 'effective primary teaching'. Schools had entered a new era where technique and performance were measured and monitored, where the school's standards were determined by pupils' achievements in national tests and the results published in league tables. Gone were the days where a primary headteacher could determine the curriculum and teachers could decide how to deliver it. Didactic formats, often at odds with teachers' perceptions of good primary practice, were introduced with the National Literacy Strategy (DfEE, 1998a) and later with the National Numeracy Strategy (DfEE, 1999a). At the turn of the millennium, dialogue about primary school practice had become characterized by language such as standards, levels, achievement, tests, targets, success, failure, improvement, effective teaching, management, leadership, development plans and, most of all, OFSTED inspections and reports. To consider the philosophical issues related in this shift of emphasis the reader is referred to Chapter 3.

The Diversity of Primary Schools

In England there is a bewildering variety of primary schools in both the state and independent sectors. Primary trainee teachers are often surprised by the diversity of schools in which they get placed. A trainee placed in a large and challenging inner-city junior school may complain that they have drawn the short straw when they compare their lot with the trainee placed in a small rural all-age primary school. Trainees have to come to terms with the huge diversity of primary schools and recognize that the experience of teaching in one school might be very different from another. Primary schools vary, for example, in terms of the age range of their pupils, the size of the school, their resources, the turnover of staff, their geographical and social setting and their religious affiliation, as well as having their distinctive curriculum expertise and extra-curricular opportunities. Cullingford (1997, p. 109) comments that 'it is simply not good enough to talk of primary education as though it is the same thing across the UK as a whole. It is not'.

One teacher described her experience as follows:

> My first teaching job was in a junior school in a small village with 37 children in a 1930s building. There were two classes, lower junior (13 pupils aged 7 to 9) and upper junior (24 pupils aged 9 to 11). The headteacher and I were the only full-time members of staff. We shared a tiny office. It was all very informal and friendly. My second job was in a town centre primary school with 570 children, aged 4 to 11, from a wide range of backgrounds and cultures. Everything had to be highly organized and tightly prescribed: 45-minute lessons, year group planning meetings, setting for maths and English, children lining up, desks in rows, endless staff meetings and policy reviews. It was like a different job altogether, requiring completely different skills. I'm now deputy head in an open-plan primary school where I'm part of a team of three teachers working with 80 children. I've had to start learning new skills all over again.
>
> (Primary school deputy headteacher)

Age ranges in primary schools

Schooling in England up to the age of 16 is now based on the following 'stages':

- Foundation Stage for children aged 3 to 5 years. The year in which pupils have their fifth birthday is called Year R (reception);
- Key Stage 1, for children aged 5 to 7 years (Years 1 and 2);
- Key Stage 2, for children aged 7 to 11 years (Years 3, 4, 5 and 6);
- Key Stage 3, for children aged 11 to 14 years (Years 7, 8 and 9); and
- Key Stage 4, for pupils aged 14 to 16 years (Years 10 and 11).

However, the ways in which pupils in these stages are organized into schools can vary enormously, depending on the local circumstances, demography and history. For example, within our own region we have maintained schools with primary-aged children that include:

- all-age primary schools taking children in Year R and Key Stages 1 and 2;
- infant schools for children in Year R and Key Stage 1;

- junior schools for children in Key Stage 2 (Years 3 to 6);
- first schools for children in Year R and Years 1 to 3;
- middle schools for children in Years 4 to 7;
- primary schools for children in Year R and Years 1 to 4;
- middle schools, for children in Years 5 to 8;
- first and middle schools, for children in Year R and Years 1 to 7;
- discrete nursery schools, for children in the Foundation Stage; and
- primary, infant and first schools with nursery classes.

The first three of these represent the most common patterns of primary schooling across the UK. A number of LEAs who have adopted the other models in the past are gradually reorganizing back to the primary and infant/junior structures to fit better with the Key Stages. There is also an increasing number of schools with nursery classes. This development is consistent with the government's intention to provide universal, free nursery provision for all 3-year-olds by the year 2004.

Categories of maintained primary schools

Maintained (state) schools are non-fee-paying, funded by taxes and mostly organized by LEAs. The headteacher and the school governors have control over the day-to-day organization and running of the school. The governing body of the school is overseen by the LEA, and a link adviser is allocated to each school by the LEA. Further discussion of the roles of governing bodies is provided in Chapter 6.

Primary state schools can be divided into four main types (Jacques and Hyland, 2003):

- Community schools (formally known as county schools), with no religious affiliation; the LEA is the employer.
- Voluntary controlled (VC) schools; these are usually Church of England, though there are some Methodist VC schools and some without religious affiliation. The LEA is the employer, but the governing body determines worship and may make some condition of appointment related to the school's religious ethos. The term 'controlled' means that the church has handed over the control of the school to the LEA, so the influence of the church is less significant than in a VA school.
- Voluntary aided (VA) schools, such as Roman Catholic, Church of England and Jewish and Muslim schools. The governing body is the employer; it determines religious instruction and will usually make some associated conditions of employment such as religious commitment. The term 'aided' refers to the fact that the LEA provides a large proportion of capital expenditure, as well as paying maintenance and teaching costs and salaries. The religious affiliation of a VA school is likely to have a higher profile than in a VC school.
- Foundation schools. There is a relatively small number of these, mainly former grant maintained schools. The governing body is the contractual employer. Most of the school's funding comes direct from central government, bypassing the LEA.

All state primary schools, other than special schools, should take children of all abilities. There is no selection at any level, although each school will have admissions criteria that have to be applied when the number of applicants exceeds the number of places available. Church schools, for example, may give priority to families who are church-goers.

Many children with special educational needs are provided for within mainstream primary schools. Sometimes this is through a special unit attached to the school, such as a unit for hearing-impaired children. However, for those children for whom a place in mainstream schooling is not appropriate, there is provision within special schools which cater for pupils with a range of moderate and severe special needs. These issues are discussed more fully in Chapters 9 and 10.

Alternative schools

Outside the state system, schools such as Steiner-Waldorf schools, Montessori schools and democratic schools provide education for primary-aged children based on alternative philosophies. Alternative schools are characterized by an emphasis on such principles as student-initiated learning, enquiry and discovery, shared problem-solving and decision-making. They tend to be fairly small schools, recognizing that it is difficult to foster positive relationships between pupils, parents, staff and the local community in larger schools. They claim to adopt a more holistic approach to learning than is possible in state schools. Steiner-Waldorf schools, for example, seek to cultivate feeling and will, as well as intelligence. Montessori schools emphasize young children's learning through activity and social development. Democratic schools give pupils a major role in decision-making about all aspects of school life and learning. The importance of dialogue is a key feature in alternative schools.

Alternative schools are free to experiment in a way that state schools bound by government orders are not. They are more concerned with the all-round development and achievement of pupils than performance measured by national tests and positions in league tables. At present, alternative schools receive no public funding at all. The government talks about diversity and parental choice, but within the state system this is limited to diversity within the centrally prescribed educational frameworks and legislation. However, a number of state primary schools are working to adopt principles applied in alternative education. For example, many primary schools now have school councils and a commitment to pupils participating in democratic discussion (see Chapters 8, 14 and 15).

The Primary Curriculum

The National Curriculum

The National Curriculum is a statutory entitlement for all children in state schools of the age of 5 and over. It was introduced to England (and Wales) in

1988. Since then it has undergone a number of revisions. At the time of writing, the version in use in primary schools was published in 1999 and became statutory in the year 2000 (DfEE/QCA, 1999).

The National Curriculum framework for Key Stages 1 and 2 provides teaching requirements for the three core subjects (English, mathematics and science) and the foundation subjects (design and technology, information and communications technology, history, geography, art and design, music and physical education). Non-statutory guidelines are also provided for teaching personal, social and health education, citizenship, modern foreign languages at Key Stage 2 and values in education. Schools are also required by law to teach religious education, but there is not a National Curriculum for this subject (see Chapter 16).

The four main purposes of the National Curriculum (DfEE/QCA, 1999) are:

- to establish the entitlement of pupils to a number of areas of learning, irrespective of their social background, culture, race, gender, difference in ability and disabilities;
- to establish standards by making expectations for learning and attainment explicit to pupils, parents, teachers, governors, and the public. The standards can be used to set targets for improvement, measure progress and monitor performance between individuals and schools;
- to promote continuity and coherence, facilitating transition between schools and phases of education and providing a foundation for learning; and
- to promote public understanding of the work of schools and in the learning achievements which are the products of compulsory education.

A central message from the government is that teachers have the power to decide how they teach the National Curriculum and the government supports them in this. However, in practice, many primary schools do not take advantage of this apparent freedom and opt for conformity to non-statutory guidance and what they perceive to be the expectations of OFSTED. For example, the QCA offers non-statutory guidance to implement the curriculum for the foundation subjects in the form of schemes of work. Many primary schools have adopted these QCA schemes as the basis for their planning. 'Teachers already have great freedoms to exercise their professional judgement about how they teach. But many teachers believe that either the Government, or OFSTED, or the QCA effectively restrict that freedom' (DfES, 2003a, p. 16).

The Foundation Stage curriculum

Non-statutory guidance is provided for teachers of children in the Foundation Stage (DfEE/QCA, 2000). The recommended curriculum for children aged 3 to 5 years covers the following areas of learning:

- personal, social and emotional development;
- communication, language and literacy;
- mathematical development;

- knowledge and understanding of the world;
- physical development; and
- creative development.

For each of these areas, the guidance provides 'early learning goals' which establish expectations for most children to reach by the end of the foundation stage. These 'are not a curriculum in themselves' but 'provide the basis for planning throughout the foundation stage, so laying secure foundations for future learning' (DfEE/QCA, 2000, p. 26).

The National Literacy Strategy

The two most significant and influential non-statutory documents affecting the primary school curriculum are the literacy and numeracy strategies. The National Literacy Strategy, introduced in 1998, is a non-statutory approach to teaching English within a highly structured framework. The history of the implementation of the NLS demonstrates very clearly the conflict between centrally generated policies that are seen as prescriptive and the primary teacher's own professional judgement.

In general, the majority of primary schools seem to have included the strategy as their preferred method of delivering the English curriculum across Key Stages 1 and 2. To begin with, the recommended structure of the 'literacy hour' (DfEE, 1998a) was a daily lesson consisting of approximately:

- 15 minutes of shared text work, when the teacher leads shared reading or writing with the whole class;
- 15 minutes of focused word- or sentence-level work;
- 20 minutes of independent reading, writing or word and sentence work while the teacher works with one or two ability-groups each day on guided text work; and
- 10 minutes when each class is brought back for a plenary so that what has been taught and learnt can be reviewed.

Although there was a perceived view that this was how it had to be done, many primary school teachers found it difficult to teach the English curriculum within this structure. Consequently, many teachers modified the structures of the literacy hour to suit their teaching style and the particular needs of the pupils in their classes. There is certainly now much more variation in literacy lessons and, with encouragement from the top, this is increasing. Over the course of a week children will spend time on each of the elements listed in the framework, but the time and emphasis may vary each day depending on the work the children are doing.

But the strategy goes further than just recommending a structure for the daily hour of literacy. It takes a particular view of how literacy is taught and learnt most effectively. Hancock and Mansfield comment, for example, on the NLS approach to teaching reading:

This is portrayed as learning about the smallest elements (e.g. the letter names and sounds) and then combining these to make words that enable the reading of phrases, sentences and texts. It is a beguilingly logical theory but it is probably more an account of how government would like learning to read to be, rather than how those children inside the process variously experience it.

(Hancock and Mansfield, 2001, p. 98)

The National Numeracy Strategy

The National Numeracy Strategy was set up by the government in 1999 to complement the National Literacy Strategy. Generally, primary schools have welcomed the structure and approaches of the NNS and it has been adopted widely as a means of delivering the mathematics curriculum. This may be associated with the fact that many primary school teachers are anxious about teaching mathematics and welcome the security of central guidance on what they should be doing and how to do it. Although the strategy refers to 'numeracy', its content covers all aspects of mathematics in the National Curriculum.

The NNS recommends that primary schools provide a daily numeracy lesson, increasing from 45 minutes for younger children to one hour for pupils in Key Stage 2. The lessons are designed so that everyone in the class works on mathematics at the same time and all the lessons follow a common format: an oral/mental starter, a main activity and a plenary. The distribution of time between these three elements can vary depending on the material. However, it is made very clear that all three elements should occur in every lesson and it is rare to see a numeracy lesson in a primary school nowadays that does not follow this structure. The NNS framework (DfEE, 1999a) provides an example of a programme of study for each year group, with the mathematical content suggested for each day of each week across the school year. The majority of primary schools seem to have adopted this example for their own long-term planning.

The NNS promotes a greater emphasis on mental calculations. Direct interactive teaching and questioning of either the whole class or groups of pupils are significant features of the strategy. There is a greater emphasis on whole-class teaching than had previously been the case in most primary school mathematics teaching. There is an expectation that for most of the time most of the children in the class will be working on the same mathematical topic. Differentiation should be limited to, at most, three groups working at different levels of challenge. In practice, teachers find that addressing issues of differentiation across the ability range is the major challenge that faces them in teaching this subject.

Extended problem-solving and mathematical investigations are not easily integrated into the prescribed format. This is a concern about the NNS voiced by many teachers, especially in relation to challenging the more able pupils. 'I let Jay and Ben work independently of the class. The numeracy strategy just doesn't meet their needs. It would be a waste of their time doing the mental starter with the others. At the moment they are working on a project which will probably take three lessons' (Year 6 class teacher).

The primary timetable

Over the course of a year, a primary school in England must be open for 190 days (38 weeks). These 38 weeks have conventionally been divided up into three terms of 12 or 13 weeks, with a long summer break. However, there is an increasing variety in this respect, with some LEAs moving to four-term and six-term models. The minimum recommended lengths of a full school week in England are 21 hours for pupils in Key Stage 1 and 23.5 hours for those in Key Stage 2.

There is no prescribed structure for the primary school day. Although there is considerable variety in this respect, a common pattern, particularly in Key Stage 2, would be two major teaching sessions of an hour or more in the morning, one for each of numeracy and literacy, with time also allocated to class registration and school assemblies. Schools are required to teach all the National Curriculum subjects to all pupils, but most schools find that science and the foundation subjects have to be squeezed into the afternoons and do not get the time that is needed to give the pupils the broad and balanced experience intended. Children in the Foundation Stage are more likely to experience a more integrated day, with smaller slots of teaching input at various times and opportunities for independent play activities.

Confident teachers, however, will always be ready and willing to respond to children's learning in a flexible way. Many would see such an approach as the essence of good primary teaching.

> When the National Literacy and Numeracy Strategy came in I thought, 'Give us a break!' Now I enjoy it. I'm slightly frazzled by the teaching hours per week but in a small school we can be flexible. Today I was outside with the children and there was a bucket of stagnant water with gnats' larvae, so we spent 20 minutes of the literacy hour talking about it. That wasn't in the plan. I'm happy to bend the curriculum.
> (Teaching primary school headteacher)

Grouping by ability

In larger primary schools, particularly in Key Stage 2, children from different classes are often put into sets for teaching on the basis of ability, particularly for numeracy and increasingly for literacy. In smaller schools setting is not a possibility, so teachers have to develop greater skills in differentiation; this will often involve identifying ability groups within the class and the provision of differentiated learning activities. At one extreme, primary teachers could find themselves working with, say, a high-ability set of children in one year group. At the other extreme, they could be teaching a class containing children from four different year groups across the whole ability range.

National testing

The National Curriculum (DfEE/QCA, 1999) provides level descriptions which enable children to be assigned a level of achievement. Levels 2 and 4 are the levels that are expected to be achieved by most pupils at the end of Key Stages 1 and 2 respectively.

Towards the end of Key Stage 1, children in Year 2 (the year in which they turn 7) are required to take national tests in English and mathematics, produced by the QCA. Towards the end of Key Stage 2 , children in Year 6 (the year in which they turn 11) are required to take national tests in English, mathematics and science. Scores on these tests are converted into National Curriculum levels, within the range 1–3 for Key Stage 1 and 1–5 for Key Stage 2. Teachers of Year 2 and Year 6 children are also required to make their own 'teacher assessments' of the pupils' levels of achievement in the subjects tested, based on evidence collected over the school year.

Schools send parents a report telling them what levels their children have reached in tests and in the teacher assessment. A summary of school results is published in the school prospectus and in the governors' annual report to parents. Primary schools are required to set targets for achievement in national tests, in line with government target-setting. For example, the government's target for 2002 was that 80 per cent of 11-year-olds would achieve level 4 in English and 75 per cent would achieve level 4 in mathematics. This target was not met.

The test results of primary schools with Year 6 pupils are published in league tables, designed to give parents information about standards. The major problem with these league tables is that raw results do not take into account the levels of achievement of the pupils on entry to the school. This has prompted consideration of ways of indicating the 'value added' to the pupil by the school. Each year schools receive an 'autumn package' from the standards unit at the DfES, containing their summary of Performance and Assessment data (PANDA). This shows the school how their pupils' achievements compare with those of other similar schools and gives them a basis for determining the value-added element of pupils' attainment levels in the national tests.

The QCA also provides optional tests for 8-, 9- and 10-year-olds that schools can use to check progress and to monitor levels of achievement. Many schools have taken to using these, so that children find themselves tested formally at the end of every year from Year 2 to Year 6. In addition, children are assessed throughout the Foundation Stage, by means of a profile which identifies their achievements in relation to the early learning goals.

Many comments made by teachers show a distrust of the whole system of national tests, league tables, target-setting and performance data: 'I am a Year 6 teacher and I am teaching to the test! It's ridiculous! We start drilling the children for the tests in February' (Primary teacher). Teachers are concerned that the tests focus too much attention on the narrow range of achievements that are most easily assessed in written test papers: 'I'm not sure what the tests mean. In science lessons John comes up with brilliant ideas, he can look at many possibilities, he has an enquiring mind and he knows a lot. But he has poor English skills so I know he won't do well in the science test' (Primary teacher).

Excellence and enjoyment in the primary curriculum

England's transition from a decentralized to a centralized education system was extremely quick. It was enforced in a determined fashion by the government through the process of school inspection. But, many primary teachers believed that the culture of national testing at ages 7 and 11 was detrimental to the ethos of primary education. They held firmly to the notion that teacher assessment of pupils' progress, achievement and problems on a daily, weekly and termly basis was a far more realistic measure of performance. By the year 2000 the pressure of national testing, the NLS and NNS, OFSTED inspections, league tables, naming and shaming of schools failing to achieve targets, and frequent press reports questioning teacher competence, had combined to undermine the morale of many dedicated teachers. Primary teachers would comment that the fun had gone out of the classroom, that the curriculum had been squeezed by the focus on tests in the core subjects and that creativity was being devalued.

The Department for Education and Skills (DfES) has responded to such concerns with the publication of *Excellence and Enjoyment: A Strategy for Primary Schools* (DfES, 2003a). This has formally recognized excellence in teaching and enjoyment in learning as key features of successful primary schools. The desire for all schools to develop individual strengths, to take ownership of the curriculum and to be creative and innovative is at the heart of this strategy. Not surprisingly, primary school teachers and headteachers welcome this move in thinking. There seems to be a perception that the wheel is turning again back towards the 'good primary practice' of former years, with more awareness of individual needs and greater flexibility.

> I am excited about the 'Excellence and enjoyment document' from the DfES. It takes us back to a more holistic approach. It's a welcome shift. OFSTED have changed their slant, not to be so concerned with teaching but to put the emphasis on the quality of learning. Yes, I'm very excited.
>
> (Primary school headteacher)

> At last I feel they are on our side! We have known for so long that we need to have flexibility if we are to respond to individuals. Teachers need control, they want to be creative. At last a document which recognizes this! I'm getting my staff to link areas of the curriculum next year. It feels good!
>
> (Primary school headteacher)

> I like to bring something into the classroom to interest and engage children in conversation and act as a springboard for learning. It helps them make connections. Two boys in this class went for a walk along a beach at the weekend and have now brought in some discarded egg cases from a baby skate and a dog fish. Children from other classes come in at lunchtime to have a look. The new document encourages this approach.
>
> (Year 2 teacher)

Focusing on the individual

In successful primary classes it is a joy to observe earnest concentration, to feel the energy of activity, to watch pupils co-operating in small and diverse groups, and to see them enjoying learning in a stimulating and interesting environment. There is a sense of order and respect, commitment to one another and a class identity. The classroom environment is bright and welcoming, examples of pupils' work are neatly presented. Effective primary schools place an emphasis on purposeful teaching methods to support learning, linking learning to the child's experience and valuing individual contributions.

Primary teachers know that children learn best when their individual needs and interests are taken into account. Their concern is that the present system, with its emphasis on prescriptive learning methods and large classes, has made this very difficult and that a 'one size fits all' approach is not appropriate for the needs of most children. Dedicated teachers want each child to succeed to the best of their ability. As a society we cannot afford to turn children off learning. Primary schools are communities. If we want a world in which children flourish and learn, then primary schools must operate as a microcosm of a society in which each individual counts and is valued.

Sadly not all schools achieve a sense of belonging for all their pupils. There are many reasons for this, such as lack of teacher continuity, high stress levels, lack of inspired leadership and teacher workload. It is certainly the case that primary teachers feel overburdened with administrative tasks, record-keeping, lesson preparation, planning and marking. But, in spite of this, primary school teachers' comments about their work suggest a real sense of involvement, an attitude of caring and a genuine desire to help each individual pupil to learn.

> Little things like Stanley finishing a piece of writing when he usually finds it hard to sit still, and the smile on his face when he shows it to me, make me feel that I have made something work.
>
> (Year 4 teacher)

> I have one boy in my class and he finds reading really hard. But he tries so hard and it seems so difficult for him. He is making progress, but it's so slow it's painful. Today he read a verse in his birthday card and a message written in it to the class without a mistake. He was so pleased and so was I. All the children clapped spontaneously! It was one of those moments.
>
> (Year 3 teacher)

> It's such a hard job. But when you see a child progress and begin to believe in themselves and feel pleased with what they have achieved, then you know why you do it.
>
> (Year 6 teacher)

So, in spite of the constant bombardment of ever-shifting government policy, the underlying joy of primary school teaching is still there for those who will embrace it. It lies, of course, in each small achievement of each individual child in the teacher's care.

Issues for Reflection

- How would you identify good primary practice?
- In what ways does the current culture of testing in primary schools have a detrimental or a positive effect on children's learning?
- Is the National Curriculum designed to meet the needs of the children or the needs of society?
- Why do so many primary school teachers opt to implement non-statutory guidance unquestioningly, rather than following their professional judgement in deciding what is best for the child?
- What would be the central principles that would guide your personal approach to teaching primary age children?

Summary of Key Points

- There is a continued tension in primary practice between a commitment to child-centred teaching and the demands of a centrally imposed subject-based curriculum.
- The current educational context is dominated by a national curriculum, national testing, levels of achievement, standards, target-setting and league tables.
- Primary schools are very diverse in nature and differ in terms of the age range of their pupils, the size of the school, their resources, their geographical and social setting, and their religious affiliation.
- Four categories of primary schools are community schools, voluntary controlled schools, voluntary aided schools and foundation schools.
- Alternative schools outside of the state system offer an education based on principles such as student-initiated learning, enquiry and discovery, shared problem-solving and decision-making.
- The most significant policies influencing primary practice at present are the National Curriculum, the Curriculum Guidance for the Foundation Stage, and the National Literacy and Numeracy Strategies.
- Primary teachers are concerned about the narrow focus of the curriculum caused by the emphasis on test results and the core subjects, particularly numeracy and literacy.
- There is a move back to an emphasis on excellence and enjoyment, recognizing the importance of flexibility and creativity.
- The most important aspect of primary teaching is the recognition of the needs and achievements of each individual child.

Suggestions for Further Reading

Books

Alexander, R. (2002) *Culture and Pedagogy*. Oxford: Blackwell. This book provides a comprehensive analysis of schools, school systems and classroom life in different cultures. It includes a detailed in-depth study of the English education system.

Burke, C. and Grosvenor, I. (2003) *The School I'd Like.* London: Routledge Falmer. Ideal schools are seen through the eyes of young people, indicating strong views and ideas for reform. The book is illustrated with children's poems, plans and pictures.

Carnie, F. (2003) *Alternative Approaches to Education, a Guide for Parents and Teachers.* London: Routledge Falmer. This book is designed to give parents and teachers information on the alternative education options available in the UK. The values, philosophies and methods of each alternative are described, taking account of the experiences of children, parents and teachers.

Cockburn, A.D. (ed.) (2001) *Teaching Children 3 to 11: A Student's Guide.* London: Paul Chapman Publishing. This comprehensive book about primary school teaching contains useful chapters on teaching English, numeracy and science in primary schools. It deals with all the practical issues of teaching that will confront a primary trainee teacher, as well as encouraging a reflective approach to practice.

Websites

Alternatives in Education website, www.AlternativesInEducation.co.uk This website provides guidance and information about alternative education provision in the UK.

DfES website, Standards Site, Primary section, www.standards.dfes.gov.uk/primary This site provides the latest government strategy for excellence and enjoyment in primary schools.

QCA website, Curriculum and Assessment section, www.qca.org.uk/ca All the information you need about the National Curriculum, curriculum guidelines and national testing is here, including recent changes to testing at Key Stage 2.

2
The School Environment

Helena Campion

The following topics and issues are covered in this chapter:

- how the school environment impacts on pedagogy;
- primary school buildings today;
- the way in which the organization of furniture, display and resources in a classroom facilitates or constrains different approaches to teaching and learning;
- the playground environment as an important factor in children's school experience; and
- the implications of virtual learning environments for schools of the future.

When walking into a school building as an adult, most of us do not take long to be reminded of our own school experience as children. The smells, sights, sounds, tastes and feelings of school are things which stay with us long after we have left. Yet for teachers, it may be that that there seems to be little time and resources put aside to develop the physical environment in which they work.

The development of education for children of primary school age in the UK has for more than a decade focused almost entirely on curriculum and pedagogical issues. This chapter, however, is about the school environment and how it impacts on the important issues of the pedagogy of teaching and learning and on the delivery of the school curriculum. The chapter draws together what researchers in the field have found. It seeks to raise some of the issues which relate to the school environment and to suggest ways in which teachers in a variety of settings can work towards creating a school environment where teaching and learning can be more effective.

Primary School Buildings Today

For well over a century considerable amounts of public money have been used to finance the building of schools. More recently the School Building Capital programme for England will have invested £8.5 billion in school buildings during the financial year 2003/04 (Teacher Net website). In addition, the Building Schools for the Future initiative begun in February 2003 promises 'to ensure that over the next 10 to 15 years all secondary pupils can learn in modern accommodation, fully suited to their needs and to the challenges of the 21st century' (DfES, 2003b; DfES, website). This government has already committed further substantial funding for innovative buildings for primary schools with a focus on considering ICT as an integral part of the school planning process, work pioneered by the Classrooms of the Future initiative (DfES, 2002a). This may be the future. But for a majority of schools the issues are more related to history than to the future, and to the legacy of school building projects of the past.

As educational fashions have come and gone with the passing of time, school buildings have changed enormously in their design. What has been put in these buildings in terms of furniture and decoration has also changed. The surroundings of a school may also have grown, shrunk or developed in a variety of ways. All these constitute the school environment. Yet they are not simply the setting within which the teaching and learning take place. They have a substantial impact on all of those who use the spaces and on the teaching and learning which takes place in them.

The diversity of primary school buildings

The legacy of school buildings is discussed by Clark (2002) who concludes that school infrastructure has been deteriorating for the past quarter of a century. Statistics gathered about the age of school buildings in 2002 show that most teachers in England are teaching in classrooms which are over 25 years old. In fact the statistics show that a substantial proportion of school buildings is even older than that:

- 9 per cent of school buildings in England are under 25 years old;
- 67 per cent, have been built between 1944 and 1976;
- 20 per cent were constructed before 1944; and
- 4 per cent are temporary buildings of one kind or another.

Although the fabric of the older buildings can be repaired and maintained, the buildings were designed around educational philosophies which are no longer current. For example, primary schools built before the 1950s would have been designed on the assumption of a didactic teaching style with minimal interaction between pupils, with most learning activities taking place at the children's individual desks controlled from the front by the teacher through chalk and talk, and with very little access to practical resources.

Generalizations may be made about what school buildings of various periods are like in terms of their structure and design. Victorian primary schools are characterized by high windows and ceilings, with regularly sized classrooms connected to the main school hall by corridors. Primary schools built in the second half of the twentieth century often contain a large amount of open space. Many of these schools were designed originally to support an open-plan teaching philosophy which broke down the traditional model of one teacher working all the time behind closed doors with one class. Twenty-first century schools reflect the need for flexibility of teaching modes with a variety of large and small spaces and non-rectilinear rooms. They use building materials which are sustainable and sympathetic to their surroundings and are likely to assume the availability in all teaching spaces of high levels of technology, such as interactive whiteboards and Internet access. The Classrooms of the Future initiative has commissioned a number of architects to brainstorm exemplar designs for new and improved buildings along these lines. However, the history of school architectural design is not the important issue here. The question is, what can teachers do with the space they are given in order to make it support the types of teaching and learning they believe are right for their pupils?

The way a school space is organized into teaching spaces for individual classes is clearly of crucial importance, although it is often the case that the choices in this respect that are available to a school's management team are very limited. However, whatever the age and design of the school building in which a teacher works, adjustments and developments to suit various styles of teaching and learning are possible where teachers work co-operatively to use the whole school space creatively. Teacher trainees on school placement or newly qualified teachers in their first post will quickly realize the importance of co-operating with colleagues over plans for pupils to access areas such as the computer suite, the school library, the playground, the school hall and shared rooms with specialist teaching resources, as well as spaces in corridors and additional small rooms that might be used for small-group activities.

Interestingly, Galton et al. (1999) note that, despite the development of more open spaces in primary schools over the past 25 years, little use has been made of these for the collaborative teaching and flexible learning styles for which they were designed. Galton et al. report that teaching spaces in primary schools of various ages and designs are in practice all used in very similar ways. It is rare indeed to go into a primary school and see anything other than a one-to-one matching of teachers and classes (or sets) to available teaching spaces. This could be because of shortage of time – with pressured teachers being unable to give the time needed to consider together how to use space more creatively – or it could be that teachers are just not open to the possibilities of more flexibility and collaboration. It is significant, for example, that in many of those schools that were originally designed as open-plan it is found that screens, partitions, walls and doors have gradually been introduced, suggesting that primary school teachers have learnt by experience that they and their pupils work most effectively within the security of their own defined and closed teaching space.

In general, then, most children of primary school age continue to spend the majority of their lesson time in one classroom (although they may move to different rooms for subjects in which classes across a year group are put into ability sets). This is in contrast to secondary school pupils who tend to learn in different classrooms designed and equipped for a particular subject. In primary schools, therefore, a teacher's classroom often has to be adapted throughout the week, and sometimes throughout the day, to suit the different demands in various curriculum areas, sometimes, for example, functioning as a science laboratory, or a music room, or a drama studio, or a changing room for physical education! However, teachers can develop the environment in which they teach in a number of simple ways. These are related to:

- how they use the available teaching space;
- how they use the available wall space; and
- how they use the available storage space.

Issues related to furniture, display and resources are directly related to the types of teaching and learning taking place in a classroom. The classroom furniture and the quality and quantity of resources and display materials are dependent on the school's levels of funding and budgeting for resources, over which the teacher may have little control. Teachers have to make the best of what they have inherited from previous teachers or own themselves. But, in spite of these constraints, imaginative and committed primary school teachers will use and organize what is available to support the children's learning activities and their own approaches to teaching. Those who come into their classrooms will pick up messages about the teacher's approaches to teaching and learning from what they see even if there are no teachers or children present.

Using the teaching space

The most basic question about the use of the classroom space that confronts the primary school teacher is how to arrange the furniture, particularly the children's seats and tables or desks. Some teachers, often those working with older pupils, will opt for a dominant teaching mode in which pupils will work independently or with a partner, and will therefore arrange the desks and chairs in pairs facing the front. Others will have a preference for pupils co-operating in small group activities or will make substantial use of ability groups within the class. They may, therefore, have the children seated in small groups facing each other around group tables. But the quality and style of furniture which is found in school spaces varies enormously, so a teacher's ideas of how to seat and group the pupils might be constrained by what is available. Unless the school is brand new, the furniture that a teacher will have in his or her classroom is likely to reflect the school's ability to purchase furniture gradually over a period of years, rather than a commitment to a consistent mode of teaching.

The issues surrounding how professionals organize the furniture in their classrooms are raised by Anderson et al. (1996). Their observations support what we have noted above, that in choosing the location of furniture in the class-room teachers will show how they intend teaching and learning to take place. For example, some of the typical classroom settings discussed by Anderson et al. reflect a commitment to the philosophy of an integrated curriculum in which the class will be working on different activities at any one time. Despite the fact that Anderson et al.'s study was completed well before the Foundation Stage (the curriculum for children aged 3 to 5 years) was introduced into British schools, some of the settings reflect the dominant pedagogy that is now found in nursery and reception classes. In these the furniture is arranged to allow specific areas of the classroom to be dedicated spaces for particular types of practical activi-ties; for example, there may be a wet-play area with a water tray, a painting area and a 'home corner' or role-play area. Because these areas are relatively small, children in an average-sized class of about 25 can be engaged in different tasks at the same time. However, the classroom layout must still accommodate the fact that at some times of the day the teacher will gather all the children together for a teaching activity or for a time to share.

Galton et al. (1999) consider further alternative layouts for classrooms. Each has advantages and disadvantages. For example, some layouts are better for a teacher-focused interactive teaching style and others are better for promoting co-operation and interaction between pupils. On the surface it would appear that the choice of layout reflects the dominant ways in which teaching and learn-ing might take place. However, a word of warning: although a teacher's com-mitment to a particular approach to pupil learning may influence the layout of furniture, the layout of the furniture does not of itself guarantee that the intended kind of pupil learning actually occurs. Galton notes, for example, that, although it is common in many primary schools to place children's tables in groups, the children generally work on their own for most of the time. He reports research evidence that when children do interact with the others at their table, their conversation is not usually related to the task in hand!

Current practice in many primary school classrooms is such that at differ-ent stages of the day pupils may, for example, find themselves:

- seated on a carpeted area around the teacher and a whiteboard;
- in their seats, facing the front, receiving instructions, responding to ques-tions, receiving input from the teacher;
- working on their own on a written or practical task;
- working with a partner on a written or practical task;
- working with a small group on a collaborative task;
- working within an ability group for a particular subject on differentiated tasks;
- engaging in structured or semi-structured play activities;
- engaging in free choice play activities;
- demonstrating or showing something to the rest of the class;
- watching a television programme or video recording or a data projection; or
- taking part in Circle Time (see Chapters 8, 14 and 15).

Clearly, no single arrangement of furniture or seating plan is going to be ideal for all these possibilities. Many primary school teachers, therefore, aim to have a flexible layout in which furniture and children are moved in order to allow for this variety of teaching and learning activities. The consequence is that the arrangement of the furniture and the seating of the pupils within the teaching space have to become major considerations in a teacher's planning and organization of lessons.

Filling the walls

The second question about the classroom environment that primary school teachers have to address is how to exploit the display areas on the classroom walls. They use these for three basic purposes:

- displaying material to which children can refer from time to time, such as class rules, number facts, key vocabulary;
- positioning visual aids, such as number lines, pictures, large-print texts and maps, where they can be seen by all the children and used for teaching purposes; and
- displaying children's work.

Often, particularly in classes in the Foundation Stage, the walls are not sufficient for the teacher's purposes, so they hang material from the ceiling or from washing lines strung across the room. And, of course, display of pupils' work is not limited to the classroom. It will often spread out into the corridors and into the school hall. Many schools pay particular attention to maintaining a high-quality display of pupils' work in the school foyer, to impress visitors and to communicate something of the school ethos and standards.

Hayes (1999) notes that the appearance of the classroom is one sign of a teacher's commitment to children. Hayes also notes that a teacher's time is increasingly pressured by other demands and suggests that it may be that displaying children's work is becoming less of a priority. However, he goes on to say that where display has a purpose in motivating children, where it can be a resource for further learning and where it stimulates pupils to think, then the time spent on display is justified. Many primary school teachers consider displaying children's work to be a crucial part of creating a learning environment. In reality, even though primary school teachers do feel pressurized by the different aspects of the job, a visit to any primary school will demonstrate that most primary school teachers still find time to put up some sort of displays. Drake (2001) discusses the theoretical and practical issues related to display. Although her ideas relate specifically to the Foundation Stage, the principles are applicable throughout the primary age range. She argues that display should be planned particularly where it integrates into the curriculum as part of a topic. She emphasizes the use of display as an interactive part of the curriculum offered in the classroom, and its uses in celebrating what children have achieved and in informing adults, children and parents.

To summarize, there are a number of reasons why teachers choose to give time to mounting and displaying the work produced by their pupils:

- to give the pupils a sense of ownership of their own class space;
- to give the learning tasks that pupils undertake an added layer of purpose-fulness, namely, to contribute to an attractive display;
- to motivate pupils to do their best work;
- to reward children who have made a really good effort, to celebrate pupils' achievements;
- to provide feedback to parents coming into the classroom about what their children are doing and achieving;
- to emphasize visual and aesthetic aspects of learning; and
- to provide examples to the children of the standard of work that is being aimed for.

Teachers' priorities vary. Some view display of pupils' work as an essential part of their teaching, creating a positive environment for learning in their classrooms; others view it as an optional extra to be fitted in if time allows. Display is nevertheless a crucial element in the creation of the classroom and school environment.

Filling the cupboards

The third issue confronting a primary school teacher related to the creation of a productive classroom environment is the provision and organization of resources. What resources there are and how they are organized and accessed affect substantially the nature of the teaching and learning that take place in a classroom. Some teachers exercise very strong control over pupils' access to their resources, so that a child may not even sharpen their pencil without per-mission. Many other primary school teachers believe that children should be responsible for the resources as much as possible, as part of their commitment to the pupils' personal and social development. Emma Cotton, for example, believes that independent access to resources is crucial if children are to develop their independent learning skills. In her setting, 'all the resources are visible and accessible to the children at all times' (Anderson et al., 1996, p. 32). This kind of freedom to use resources is dependent on the children and the teacher having a shared understanding of rules related to health and safety. Taking a different emphasis, Hayes (1999) stresses that the use of consumables needs to be monitored by the teacher in order to minimize waste, and implies that teachers have to have a more positive oversight of access to resources to ensure that children employ the correct tools for the job in hand.

So, a primary school teacher has to consider how to balance these different perspectives when planning the organization of resources in the classroom. The systems in place for pupils to access these resources – as for display and furniture organization – will impinge directly on the type of teaching and learning that takes place in that classroom. Where teachers adopt a teaching style in which the pupils have more responsibility to choose tasks and activi-ties independently then clearly more independent access by pupils to resources is necessary than would be in a more prescriptive approach. Finally, in their planning of the use of resources, teachers have to remember the importance of building in time and establishing procedures for getting them back to where they belong when the children have finished using them!

The School Grounds

School grounds vary as much as school buildings do. These variations are a result of the setting of the school, whether rural, suburban or urban, the time in which the school was built and the priority which has been placed on developing the school grounds. Most school grounds contain to a greater or lesser extent some of the following: tarmac, grassed areas, trees, bushes, fencing or hedging, play equipment and floral displays. In some schools a considerable amount of time and financial resources are spent on developing and improving the spaces in the school grounds. The organization Learning Through Landscapes has pioneered much of this work.

Meanings in the school grounds

Titman's (1994) research into the semiotics of the playground – published by Learning Through Landscapes – is revealing both in terms of what children make of the spaces around them and in terms of what schools can do to enhance provision in their grounds. Simply put, the theory of semiotics puts forward a case that each thing (known variously as a signifier, denotion or token) has a meaning which is connected to it by an individual or a group (this meaning is known as the signified, designation or type). The meaning is constructed by the relationship between the thing and the individual or group. This complex philosophical theory is applied practically and simply to elements of the school playground in Titman's research report. The relationship between the 'signifiers' in the playground and what they 'signified' to the children was explored through collages of trees, grass, tarmac and other elements of the school environment.

One element which Titman found to be a negative signifier was tarmac. Children perceived this to be both a dangerous surface and a reflection of cheap provision. In fact, tarmac is the predominant 'all weather' surface in school playgrounds. Most school grounds also contain what are generally regarded by adults as positive signifiers, such as grass, bushes, trees and flowers. However, the fact that these are often, sometimes permanently, out of bounds for the children can turn them into negative signifiers. Specific problems are caused by bushes, which Titman found to be mainly seen by children as dens. Bushes provide a secret place for children which they enjoy, but their behaviour there can be difficult to monitor and health and safety issues are raised when children are out of sight of the adults who are supervising them. Another possible positive signifier is trees, which Titman discovered children associate with climbing. However, the trees in most playgrounds are considered strictly out of bounds on safety grounds, and climbing or swinging on them is certainly not allowed. It is also common to provide other elements which are positive signifiers such as grass and flowers, symbolic of environmental issues and considered to be of aesthetic value by the children. However, the limited access allowed and the small area given over to these features reduces their positive impact on the playground environment.

Many schools now also provide seating and play equipment. Titman reveals that the children regard such provision as a recognition of their needs. However, children do not always make use of such provision in the ways that teachers might consider safe and appropriate.

Why school grounds are important

Teachers who aim to improve the quality of the environment will examine the amount of space given to these different elements of the playground. They will give some consideration to how they might make better use of elements regarded as positive signifiers while maintaining a focus on health and safety regulations. It should not be assumed, however, that improving the school grounds is simply a matter of aesthetics and making playtime fun for children. Research into children's play and playtimes pioneered by the Opies in the 1950s and 1960s (Opie and Opie, 1969), continued more recently by Sluckin (1981) and Blatchford (1989; 1994), has shown that playtime is extremely important to children throughout the primary age range. In most schools children spend at least as long in the playground as they do in literacy lessons, yet there is very little government-generated advice and support on creating positive environments in the school grounds, when compared with that generated, for example, in relation to the teaching of literacy. Where focus is given by the government and LEAs to issues relating to playtime, it is almost exclusively with a focus on bullying and how to tackle it. Titman asserts that the outdoor school environment and the messages it sends have a significant effect on the way children behave in that environment: 'Our research, and that of many others, provides strong support for the need to recognize that amongst a range of possible causes for such [inappropriate] behaviour, the physical design and nature of the environment have significant influence' (Titman, 1994, p. 102).

The school's grounds also provide many opportunities for teaching and learning. There are many obvious ones related to environmental science, the study of places and their uses in geography, and using the space for games and physical education. However, there are also opportunities for children to use the spaces of the playground and school grounds right across the curriculum, from practical mathematics to inspiration for creative writing. Many primary school teachers find that the children work productively in this environment, especially when the weather is pleasant. Even when the grounds are covered in snow, creative primary school teachers will see the potential learning opportunities in experience of the outdoor school environment.

In summary, the creation of a positive outdoor school environment has to be regarded as being as important as that created indoors. The pioneering work of Titman (1994) reflects how important it is for a school to consider the school grounds. Her work suggests that all the users of the grounds – teachers, children, supervisors, caretakers, cleaners – need to be involved in the process of developing provision outdoors. For practical suggestions and help, the organization Learning Through Landscapes provides low-cost materials and advice which teachers can use to get their own projects started.

The Future for School Environments

In the twenty-first century it is certain that the majority of schools will have to continue to make the best of buildings designed and built over the previous 150 years. I have described how this can impact on teaching and learning above. However, there is a new 'environment' under development in school, and its impact on teaching and learning in the future can only at the moment be guessed at. This is the 'virtual learning environment' (VLE).

The Internet in schools

In 1969 the US military developed a system of communication which meant that even when some phone lines were out of action, essential command systems could still communicate with one another. In 1992 the physics laboratory at CERN, the European Organization for Nuclear Research, in Switzerland began to publish information on something they called the 'world wide web' (Grey, 2001). Shortly after, Netscape launched their browser software, Navigator, in 1994 to help people – at that stage mainly scientists – to find information on the web. Bill Gates, the head of Microsoft, began to take notice of these developments and the following year his company began to sell the Windows 95 operating system with the browser Internet Explorer embedded. This began Microsoft's contentious domination of the personal computer and Internet browser market. It is striking that in the nine years between the inception of Internet Explorer, which has made the Internet truly popular and accessible to all, and the publication of this book, the Internet has become a crucial communication tool in our society.

The rapid progress of technology was reflected in the educational world by the UK government's National Grid for Learning initiative, begun in 1998, which promised to connect all schools to the Internet by 2002, and to train all teachers to use it as a tool in teaching and learning. By the year 2000, 92 per cent of schools were already connected (National Statistics Online website) and the number switching to broadband fast-access connections was steadily increasing. It is a matter of debate whether Bill Gates foresaw this opportunity back in 1995. I doubt if many teachers could have guessed then how important the Internet would become as an educational issue.

The future

The only certain thing about the future of virtual learning environments in schools is that we cannot predict the future. Technology advances at an amazing rate, often faster than education can develop to make use of it. Virtual learning environments of various kinds are now available to schools throughout the UK through companies and local education authorities. Some LEAs such as Norfolk and East Riding have invested significant resources in developing their own VLEs (Norfolk Esinet for Learning website; East Riding Intranet for Learning website). The purpose of these is for schools to share news and ideas and to display work. They are also intended as doorways – what in e-learning-speak are called 'portals' – for teachers and pupils to make the best use of other Internet resources, with opportunities for teachers to recommend websites. With the allocation of £100-million worth of 'e-learning credits' by the DfES in 2003 (DfES website) schools may also access web-based learning resources via the learning environments provided on line by the LEA. These environments and learning resources have been designed to allow pupils to rehearse, develop and research what they are learning about. Crucially, they also allow teachers and pupils to communicate with others, using email and discussion boards. Teachers and learners in the twenty-first century can significantly benefit from making the most of what is on offer in these VLEs. They will be able to communicate both locally and internationally with other teachers and learners. They will be able to publish and share what they are doing quickly and easily. They will be able to include others who are distant in their teaching and learning experience. They will be able to use the technology for a range of purposes which we cannot conceive of at the moment. Flag-carriers for ICT and the Internet firmly believe in this future for web-based learning.

To these ends the government has invested significant amounts of funding in providing computers, connectivity and training for teachers and pupils. In reality, however, the impact of ICT in primary schools to date has been very mixed. This may reflect the fact that technology is constantly developing and changing, and it moves on too quickly for many school and LEA budgets, and for many teachers. It is also recognized that computers linked to the Internet are in many classrooms but that in many schools they are an infrequently used resource. Sometimes this is for simple practical reasons, such as the computers being sited in a computer suite too far from the classroom – another example of how choices in the layout of the school environment can impinge on learning – or there being insufficient computers to be used effectively in the types of whole-class teaching strategies which currently predominate in primary schools. As a consequence, there are missed opportunities for teachers and learners to use VLEs. Until computers with fast and reliable Internet connections are firmly embedded in the design of each classroom, linked to interactive whiteboards and in a way which is easily accessible to all, these opportunities will continue to be underutilized.

Optimists and flag-carriers hope that the solution for technology lies in the Classrooms of the Future initiative. David Milliband, in his capacity as DfES Ministerial Design Champion, set out the vision for this initiative:

> We need to try out new ideas now. We need to look at ways of designing inspiring buildings that can adapt to educational and technological change. ICT can give schools the option of teaching children as individuals, in small groups and in large

groups, and can provide electronic links to other schools and facilities in this country and abroad. That will not happen if we do not design spaces in schools that are flexible and will facilitate various patterns of group working. Flexibility is key, because whatever visions of education we design our buildings around, we can be sure that they will need to perform in a very different way in a few years' time.

(DfES, 2002a, p. 1)

The initiative involves 12 LEAs in designing and building classrooms with this vision in mind. They are described in the publication as 'adventures in design' and the aim is to pilot ideas for schools which will be built in the future. The classrooms are also designed with many current educational issues in mind, not just the role of ICT in the curriculum, but also issues such as flexibility in grouping pupils for learning activities, inclusion of pupils with special educational needs and disabilities (see Chapter 9), and community use of school buildings. The projects are also designed with sustainability of building development and construction in mind. Exciting and innovative as these projects are, however, the vast majority of teachers will continue to work in classrooms that are over 25 years old. How the Classrooms of the Future will help influence the vast majority of 'ordinary' classrooms in schools built in the nineteenth and twentieth centuries is currently unclear. However, what is clear is that, in order to make the best of the opportunities afforded by virtual learning environments and to offer equality of opportunity across the school system, the next 20 years should see all classrooms become connected to the Internet, enabling all pupils to access web-based learning across the curriculum.

A Final Reality Check

This chapter invites all teachers and trainee teachers to examine the learning environment in their school and classroom. It suggests ways in which furniture, displays and resources can be used to facilitate different kinds of teaching and learning. It raises issues of provision for playtimes in the school grounds and, finally, it calls for the integrating of virtual learning environments into every classroom. This is clearly a tall order for even the most dedicated and ambitious teacher. However, it is to be hoped that in raising these issues and investigating the history and future of school learning environments, I will have prompted teachers to do what they can on a daily basis to develop the aspects of the school environment for which they are responsible. One thing which all the researchers and commentators mentioned in this chapter agree on is that the school environment is a crucial factor in successful teaching and learning.

Issues for Reflection

- Examine an actual teaching room, and look at the spaces in which the teacher teaches from different angles and levels, and observe the way in which all the users of the room use the space. How would you adapt things to make it easier to teach in the ways you would find best?

- Visit a number of classrooms in order to get ideas about different ways of organizing furniture, display spaces and resources. How do various teachers make the best use of these?
- Think about the other people who share a primary school teacher's work-space, such as children, parents, teaching assistants, cleaners, teacher trainees and their supervisors. Reflect on the arrangement of the classroom space from their point of view. How might a teacher make the classroom space suit this variety of users?
- Even small changes made to an environment can have an important impact on the way the space is used for teaching and learning, so desirable changes do not all have to be achieved at once. Identify examples of some small changes which in your experience have had a significant impact on teaching and learning.
- Teachers should consider the outdoor environment of their school to be as important as the indoor one. In your experience, what do children enjoy doing on the playground? In what kinds of areas are there likely to be prob-lems? How can a school modify this environment to help children to behave positively at playtime?
- To make ICT as accessible as possible, in what ways should classroom furni-ture be positioned and used. In which lessons and in what ways might primary school teachers want to use ICT as an integral teaching and learning tool?

Summary of Key Points

- School buildings are diverse. Many are over 25 years old. Few buildings cur-rently in use were built with current practice in teaching and learning in mind.
- The way in which furniture, displays and resources are organized can facil-itate or constrain different approaches to teaching and learning.
- The playground environment is as important as the school environment, and children perceive it in many ways. The way in which playgrounds are organized and resourced affect the way children behave in the space.
- Virtual learning environments will provide opportunities to learn in new ways in the future.

Suggestions for Further Reading

Blatchford, P. (1994) *Break Time and the School: Understanding and Changing Playground Behaviour*. London: Routledge. This is a book which enriches understanding of playground behaviour and gives practical suggestions about tackling problems.

DfES (2002) *Classrooms of the Future*. London: DfES. This document can be ordered in hard copy or downloaded as a PDF file from the DfES website. It contains some information about the project and plans for the classrooms.

Galton, M., Hargreaves, L. Comber, C. and Wall, D., with Pell, A. (1999) *Inside the Primary Classroom 20 years on.* London: Routlege. This study revisits issues tackled in an earlier publication and considers the changes which have taken place in primary education over 20 years.

Sluckin, A. (1981) *Growing up in the Playground.* London: Routledge and Kegan Paul. This case study of playground behaviour was undertaken in the late 1970s, but many of the issues raised are still relevant.

Titman, W. (1994) *Special Places, Special People: The Hidden Curriculum of the School Grounds.* London: Learning Through Landscapes. This is a fascinating research project into the playground environment with some suggestions about how it could be developed. More information can be obtained from: Learning Through Landscapes, 3rd Floor, Southside Offices, The Law Courts, Winchester, Hampshire, SO23 9DL. Tel. 01962 846258.

3

Teachers' Values and Professional Practice in Primary Schools

Sue Cox

The following topics and issues are covered in this chapter:

- the central place of values in educational practice and policy
- the concern of reflective teachers – teachers as professionals – to engage with values;
- the relationship between values and social and cultural contexts;
- the ethical and educational implications of teachers' decisions and actions, and the influence of values on both content and process in education;
- a conception of education as valuing learning for its own sake and learning to think and to reason;
- the entitlement of all to education in a socially just society;
- conceptions of education inherent in recent educational policy; and
- the GTCE's acknowledgement of the values base of education.

Why do people become teachers? The profession continues to attract dedicated people, despite the heavy workload and high public expectations associated with it. People are unlikely to be dedicated to something which they do not think is worthwhile. It is because they value children's education that they are prepared to disregard or overcome the apparent disincentives. Teachers' motivation is maintained by those aspects of their work which are central to their sense of vocation – working with children and making a difference to their lives (Scott and Cox, 1999). This underlying commitment of teachers demonstrates that values are inherent in education. Teachers believe that, by educating children, they are not only making a difference, but making a difference for the better; that children will benefit from what they do. This is, arguably, part of the concept of education.

31

This much may sound self-evident and uncontentious, but it raises questions which are penetrating and difficult to answer. Why and how do teachers, and society as a whole, value education? In what ways do we consider it to be worthwhile? What sort of difference do educators want to make; what are we trying to achieve and why? More specifically, given that becoming educated entails learning, what should children be learning?

My intention in this chapter is to show why these questions are important and to discuss some ways of thinking about them, from a philosophical perspective. They are the kinds of questions that have occupied educationalists, philosophers and thinkers since at least as far back as Plato. Yet, interestingly, over the past two decades – a period of time that has seen a plethora of initiatives emerging from governments and policy-makers – there has been a notable lack of discussion about the point or purpose of education, of what education is for (see, for example, Blake et al., 2000).

Values in Educational Policy and Practice

Values and policy

This lack of discussion about what education is for does not mean that education is no longer underpinned by values, only that values may remain implicit rather than explicit; unexamined and unchallenged. Many educational initiatives rest on the assumption that what they promote is worthwhile and justified. It is taken for granted that there is a consensus about what we should try to achieve. In some cases, there is possibly even a lack of awareness, on the part of those who are responsible for these initiatives, that such assumptions are being made; a lack of awareness that there is matter for debate at all.

To illustrate this point, we can take the targets that were set for schools by the UK's Labour government. In 1997 it was stipulated that 80 per cent of 11-year-olds in English, and 75 per cent in mathematics, were to achieve level 4 in the end-of-Key-Stage national tests in 2002. These targets rested on several value-laden assumptions. First, that these are the subject areas on which we should focus – for, inevitably, if specific standards are to be reached only in these subjects, then these are the areas that are considered worthy of most attention; second, that these are desirable levels for 11-year-olds to achieve in those areas; and, third, that testing children through these tests is an acceptable way of identifying standards. We could also question whether the tests are an effective measure of children's ability, or whether children of this age can reasonably be expected to achieve these levels. These are matters that can only be settled by empirical research. But the assumptions I have mentioned are concerned with what is desirable, acceptable and what we ought to do. They are all issues of value. I am not commenting on whether these assumptions are defensible or not – I am only pointing out that they are made. Justifying or challenging the assumptions are matters for further discussion.

When there is failure to address the kind of assumptions that underlie educational policy and practice, then it follows that what teachers do in the classroom may, or may not, be desirable, acceptable or worthwhile. These are essential areas for debate if we want to ensure that children receive the best education. It is probably fair to say that in the particular example mentioned above, this kind of discussion did not take place.

There are often further implications. For example, the extent to which the targets above were achieved had an impact on the positions of schools in league tables and the results achieved in OFSTED inspections. This in turn led to a narrowing of the curriculum, as teachers attempted to reach the targets. It resulted in a tendency to spend much of Year 6 in primary school coaching pupils for the tests or 'teaching to the tests' (Earl, 2001; OFSTED, 2002; *TES*, 2001). These outcomes, again, may or may not be desirable. They are not, in themselves, necessarily a good or a bad thing. This will depend on how we view them and, once again, this is related to our educational values. The fundamental issue is that values are inescapable in education.

Values, teachers and professional practice

'Values are not my concern'
A response to what I have said above may well be that the discussion about underlying values and priorities is too far removed from the classroom and the everyday demands of teaching to be of concern to practising teachers. It might be argued that the kinds of decisions that rest on values are best left to those with designated responsibility, such as policy-makers. In the example above, the argument might go, it is the job of teachers to meet the demands of achieving the given targets however they can, rather than to question their existence in the first place. The wider debate should be engaged in by politicians, academics or by the public at large, perhaps, but need not be the concern of teachers. There are two sorts of reason why this might be seen as a reasonable response, one practical and one ethical.

First, there are practical reasons for not taking on this responsibility. To take the case of student teachers, it might be considered expedient to leave these matters in the hands of others, especially at a time when they are under extreme pressure to meet the demands of their teaching practice. They may feel that they have little time for such abstractions and that their priority is to be told what they have to do in the classroom and to be given guidance and ideas on how to do it. They may be happy to accept that if this material is gained from a reliable source it will be relevant to what children ought to be doing in school; that in the UK, as long as it is appropriate to the prescribed National Curriculum then it is best to leave decisions to others.

Second, there might be the perception that teachers do not have a right to concern themselves with these issues of value, at least not to the extent that they should influence what happens to children. As an individual, accountable to other 'stakeholders' (to use a term currently in vogue), such as parents, employers and society at large, a teacher may feel it would be an abuse of their position to have any say in decisions about what children should learn, or what kind of standards children should be expected to reach, or what assessment procedures should be used. This is an ethical reason for leaving decisions to others.

'Ought' implies values

There are counter-arguments to both these positions. With regard to the first, it might seem that it is the practical nature of the activity of teaching which suggests that such abstract and theoretical issues as values are irrelevant to it. On the contrary, it is because teaching is a practical activity that it is bound up with values. Whenever a teacher, or anyone else, takes a particular course of action, judgements are necessarily involved. A teacher may make a judgement, for example, that a particular child, Tamsin, needs more of their attention because she is having difficulty in a particular area or because she is grasping concepts fairly readily and could be challenged further. Such judgements are based on the teacher's appraisal of Tamsin and her situation. All the relevant factors will be considered, such as what she has already learned, what she might be capable of learning and how she might need to be challenged. Some of this information – such as what she is able to achieve – might appear to be factually based, although even in this respect the teacher's values and beliefs will inevitably influence how she makes this assessment. Other aspects are clearly evaluative – what Tamsin needs, for instance. The judgement that she needs attention in a particular area is based on the assumption that Tamsin *should* be given it and that whatever specific difficulties or successes Tamsin is experiencing are worth attending to. Deciding on how she needs to be challenged depends on making choices about what is appropriate to her as an individual and to the subject matter she is learning. In terms of the action a teacher takes, their decision is made on the basis of what they think they ought to do. Whenever *ought* is involved, then values are implicit. There is a logical connection between values and teachers' decisions about what to do.

Values embedded in social and cultural frameworks

This may seem to suggest that teachers must consciously reflect on their actions. In reality, this is not necessarily the case. For instance, an experienced teacher may follow a routine that has been set up for responding to a particular situation, or they might seem to know intuitively what to do. Likewise, student teachers may watch closely what other teachers do and follow their example. Then again, they may respond to what they have been told to do by someone more experienced or by someone in authority over them.

In any case, it would be misleading to assume that actions necessarily require some prior, specifiable, intention or justification. This is a logical point. We live our lives in the context of the collective values of the various communities and social groups of which we are a part and carry out our actions in the light of these. All of us acquire *know-how* about what to do and how to do it from being part of these cultural groups, without necessarily being aware of what gives our actions meaning and point. This does not imply that our actions are devoid of value. On the contrary, these cultural groups sustain the frameworks of values in which our actions have meaning and point. These collective values and meanings are implicit in what we do. Thus, if an experienced teacher working with Tamsin responds to her in a routine way, it is because they are familiar with this sort of situation and with what children like Tamsin need, and they know what to do. Or, they have acquired a disposition to respond in a certain way, because they are part of a caring community so they will notice that Tamsin needs attention and will act accordingly. But their actions are not arbitrary. The way they respond to Tamsin is dependent on what is valued within the social and cultural frameworks to which they relate. However, whilst a teacher or student teacher may or may not consciously justify their own action, if it is to benefit Tamsin it must be justifiable. And if a teacher was called upon to justify what they did, or if they wanted to reassure themselves that they were doing the right thing, they would necessarily refer to a set of values to do so. So, whilst it may seem irrelevant to teachers to concern themselves with issues of value, this cannot be because values are irrelevant to their actions.

Reflective teachers

Since values are implicit in whatever they do, it could be argued that it is crucially important for teachers to *reflect* on what they do and to gain some insight into what these values are. It is theoretically possible that everything a teacher might do in the classroom could fall into an unreflective category: maintaining routines, acting intuitively or following the example of others. But this would mean that their role would be like that of a technician – someone who has acquired, through a process of training, or apprenticeship, a range of technical skills to apply to a given situation. This *technicist* view of practice is often contrasted with a *reflective* approach (Schon, 1983). In reality, much of what teachers do will undoubtedly be unreflective, but teachers are unlikely to behave like technicians all the time, as they see themselves as more than this. Teaching reflectively may well be one of the defining criteria of what it is to be a professional.

Shared understandings

To return to the second reason for leaving certain decisions to others – the ethical one, that teachers do not have the right to concern themselves with issues of value – similar counter-arguments apply. The reality of classroom life and teaching is of teachers constantly interacting with children. Each of these interactions reflects an implicit judgement or decision about what to do and how to do it. Given that none of these actions are value-free, for the reasons discussed above, teachers are inevitably bringing values to bear on what they do, and professional teachers would need to be aware of what they are.

However, whilst this might mean that teachers appear to be taking things into their own hands rather than deferring to the needs and priorities of the various stakeholders in education, it is misleading to assume that they must, therefore, be imposing their own values on the situation; as if, in some way, they were acting completely autonomously. This would presume that one can think independently of others. There is little sense in this interpretation of autonomy or, indeed, of values. As I have already pointed out, what we believe and value is inevitably shared, to some extent, with a wider group or groups of people as, on any level, our understanding of the world develops in a social context. On the other hand, this does not mean that the values held by an individual teacher are necessarily consistent with those of other stakeholders in education. Beliefs and values depend on the specific social and cultural contexts which give them meaning and these can intersect and overlap in varying ways, so there will, undoubtedly, be differing ideas. What it does mean is that there is some potential, at least, to develop shared understandings of what kind of education we want for our children. Given the varying interests and the power relations between different social groups and contexts, and the inevitable limits to full communication, these understandings will be multifarious and multifaceted, but in our culturally diverse and democratic society this diversity of view is, in any case, desirable. The public debate is essential and teachers can, and should, be part of it.

Content and process

When teachers question what they are trying to do, they ask about what they are teaching – the content – and how they are teaching it – the process.

What we teach

It is not difficult to see why teachers may feel that they have no part in the discussion about what they should teach. In the UK, for Key Stages 1 and 2, this is prescribed in great detail by the DfES through the National Curriculum (which is statutory) and through the NLS and NNS (which are non-statutory, but schools have been strongly encouraged to implement them by the DfES). The QCA has produced detailed schemes of work for the other subjects in the curriculum, which are again non-statutory but which are widely followed in schools. There are prescribed Early Learning Goals for the Foundation Stage (3–5-year-olds). The content of the curriculum is thus centrally defined. It is generally acknowledged that teachers currently work in a climate of 'top-down' control of what they teach (see the discussion of centralized control in Chapter 1).

The potential for teachers' professional values to influence the content of their teaching, then, seems limited at the policy level in the current context. But, if teacher professionalism is to be maintained, then teachers do need to retain the ability and need to be given the opportunity to bring critically reflective capacities to bear on such matters. This issue of centralized control and its implications have been widely discussed by some of the most influential writers on primary education (see, for example, Richards, 2001).

At the classroom level, there may be more opportunity for teachers to bring their judgement to bear on the content of children's educational experience, since teachers inevitably transform the curriculum when they put policy into practice. Children are individuals and the local circumstances of each school and classroom differ too, so the curriculum will inevitably be adapted in practice. Moreover, for the reasons indicated in the previous section, classroom teachers will interpret curriculum content differently and they will have varying levels of commitment to its many facets, bringing their value positions into play.

Intrinsic and extrinsic value

One way in which this transformation occurs is related to *how* teachers value the content of the curriculum. This is, perhaps, best explained through an example of something we might want children to learn. Say, for example, we want children to learn how to structure a piece of fiction. How does the teacher value this? Do they value it in terms of what lies beyond it? For instance, is the ability to structure a story valued because it fulfils the requirements of the National Literacy Strategy or because it will enable the child to gain a level 4 in the English test? In both of these cases the teacher is valuing the learning for an extrinsic reason. In a climate of central control, in which compliance and performance are valued, no other justification need be given. But if, as I have argued, teachers should adopt a more reflective and professional approach, then there are alternative possibilities to consider. Might being able to structure a piece of writing be valued because in itself it is a worthwhile thing to learn? Might it have intrinsic value rather than extrinsic value – in other words, might the reason for learning it be that it is worth learning for its own sake? The teacher who values learning intrinsically, in this way, might well enable the children to gain level 4 in the English test, though this would not be their primary reason for teaching it. Instead, their main aim would be to help the child to understand and know how to write well.

How the teacher values what he or she teaches children can also influence what the children learn. In this case, this way of valuing story-writing – intrinsically – may well be part of what the children themselves learn from the teacher. As well as understanding how to write a story, they come to appreciate it as a worthwhile thing to do. Rather than learning that story-writing is worth doing only for the extrinsic rewards it brings, such as a good test result, the child learns to appreciate its intrinsic rewards. The teacher's values have the potential to influence the content of the child's learning, without this having been stipulated in the curriculum.

How we teach

This brings us to the processes of teaching. If the children learn that structuring their stories well carries its own rewards, then this may well be a result of the way the teacher conveys this to the children. The teacher's own enthusiasm, the attention they give to the children's own writing, and the way they respond to it, will all help to show the children that it is worth doing well for its own sake. What is more, a teacher's commitment to certain qualities in writing will be expressed in their concern to ensure that the children understand what these qualities are. This will influence how they go about their teaching. Legally, teachers still have control over the ways they teach, although it has to be acknowledged that both the approaches to the structure and organization of the curriculum in schools and the teaching methods that teachers use have undoubtedly changed in response to official recommendations in recent years. Some teachers would seem to have experienced a loss of the creativity that they have associated with their job in the past. Despite this, on the grounds discussed earlier, teachers are in a position to retain ownership of the minute-by-minute judgements about how they teach in the classroom, and professional teachers will ensure that these are guided by well-considered principles.

It might be objected that when the content of the curriculum is predetermined, then how it is taught is not at issue. All that is required is for teachers to ensure that children learn it by whatever method is the most effective. In other words, teachers have only to find out what works. This, however, begs many questions. There are both ethical and educational questions to raise about methods or processes themselves. To return to Tamsin, for example, it was suggested that the teacher might make the judgement that Tamsin should be given more attention. Such judgements would be made with regard to how the teacher sees both Tamsin's right to attention and their own responsibility to give it. These are ethical matters. It is unlikely that a teacher would give attention to Tamsin at the expense of other children without taking into account issues of fairness and equality of opportunity. A principled teacher would have in mind the need to ensure that Tamsin, along with all the other children in the class, is given the opportunity to learn, without prejudice of any kind. It is clear, then, that the teacher's decisions about how to go about teaching involve ethical considerations. Again, in their quest to do their best by Tamsin, educationally, they would teach using methods and processes that were appropriate both to her and to what she was being taught – ensuring that she learned to think, to reason and to understand. Educational considerations thus come into the teacher's thinking about the way they teach.

Behaviour management

To further explain the link between the processes of teaching and values, I will take as an example an area which is of major concern to student teachers: the issue of behaviour management. Most teachers would agree that for learning to take place, some degree of order in the classroom is required. If there is no sense of co-operation or collaboration in the classroom, if children cannot hear the teacher or each other, if some children distract others from educational activities, then worthwhile learning cannot take place.

One response may be that the behaviour of the children must be *controlled* (my choice of word here is significant) in order for other things to proceed. All kinds of strategies might be adopted, commonly involving rewards of some kind to encourage the children to behave in the way the teacher prefers. Rewards may be used rather than punishments on the grounds that it is unethical to punish children, so values have already come into the decisions about strategies. Whilst punishments may work in getting children to behave, rewards are deemed more acceptable. However, there are more complex issues here. There are values inherent in the reward/punishment approach to behaviour management which in themselves are open to challenge. It could be argued that a teacher who gives a reward for good behaviour is implicitly showing disrespect for the child, because the strategy is ultimately manipulative. Rather than making the behaviour itself the focus for the child's learning, the teacher has used the child's desire for the reward as the means of obtaining the behaviour they require in a morally questionable way.

As before, the values which inform the teacher's strategies have an impact on *what* the children learn. As in the story-writing example above, the teacher is implicitly teaching the child that good behaviour is valued for extrinsic, rather than intrinsic reasons. The message is that good behaviour is only worth entering into because it brings extrinsic rewards of some kind. The child learns to value the rewards, not the good behaviour. The child has not learned about why they should co-operate. They are not gaining an understanding that there are reasons for behaving well which are implicit in a group of people being able to work together, such as respecting each other and being fair. These are reasons which show that behaving well is intrinsically worthwhile. Instead, they are learning to value the team points, the treat, or the teacher's praise which good behaviour brings. Whilst it might be expedient to use such strategies to train children – and, of course there are many situations where teachers need to do so – if this is all we do, then we may be falling short as educators.

What my analysis of this example illustrates is the general principle that the way teachers act (*how* they do things; the strategies or processes they use) and the values these actions reveal, may have moral implications and also educational ones. I have begun to justify the content of teaching and the processes of teaching in terms of particular sorts of ethical and educational beliefs and principles.

Wider Frameworks of Values

The context of policy and practice

In the first part of this chapter, I talked about how the frameworks of values in the wider social and cultural contexts in which teachers work necessarily impact on teachers' values and their actions. To give this more meaning, in this section I discuss the frameworks of values in which we might locate some of the ideas I have introduced.

Market-led education
Earlier I discussed the sort of 'top-down' climate of decision-making in which teachers have worked for some time. There has been much discussion in recent years about the value frameworks that gave rise to the centralized control of education that teachers have experienced. A prevailing view is that the current conception of education has been shaped by a marketplace ideology, and this in turn has influenced policy. 'Choice and the market' were the watchwords under the Conservative government which was in power in the UK in the 1980s and 1990s. The premise is that standards are driven up where competition exists between schools. For this to take effect, there need to be ways of comparing schools' performance and this is where national testing and league tables come into the picture. A centralized National Curriculum, where children across the nation are taught the same material, makes such comparisons possible. When there are objective ways of measuring a school's success, then there are criteria by which parents can make their choice of schools for their children and there are benchmarks to which failing schools can aspire.

This market-led model, creates a hierarchy of schools. This state of affairs might seem to sit rather uneasily with the comprehensive ideal of equitable educational provision for all, which we might associate with a Labour government. Since1997, when Labour came to power, there have been strategies to ensure that as many children as possible achieve the highest standards, suggesting a more egalitarian approach – the literacy and numeracy targets for 2001 might be seen as an expression of this. However, the market-led agenda has survived. Whilst the targets may indicate that children's achievement is a priority, at the same time they maintain the emphasis on performance and outcomes as a means of judging and ranking children, teachers and schools.

Ownership of the curriculum?

At the time of writing it is yet to be seen whether this market model will continue. In May 2003 the DfES launched the Primary Strategy (DfES, 2003a). In this there are indications of a move to redress the emphasis on centralized control. Primary schools are to be given some measure of ownership of the curriculum. The strategy document claims that the government wants all schools to 'take ownership of the curriculum, shaping it and making it their own' (ibid., p. 3). The document acknowledges teachers' sense that government strategies have imposed constraints on teachers' freedom to use their judgement. However, it asserts that 'teachers have much more freedom than they often realize to design the timetable and decide what and how they teach' (ibid., p. 3) and that the 'central message … is that teachers have the power to decide how they teach, and that the Government supports that' (ibid., p. 16). Schools are to be encouraged to 'be creative and innovative in how they teach' (ibid., p. 3), to focus on the needs and abilities of the individual child and to promote creativity and enjoyment of learning in children. This may amount to official acknowledgement and endorsement of the fact that teachers can, and do, transform the content of the prescribed curriculum, and retain control of teaching processes, in the ways I have already discussed. Alternatively, it may be intended to go further, implying that the centralized curriculum should be open to more fundamental modification. However, these messages are set in the context of the new target of 85 per cent of 11-year-olds achieving level 4 in literacy and numeracy, with the Primary Strategy document claiming that this is not incompatible with its encouragement to exercise curricular freedom. The testing regime is set to continue.

Economic rationalism

Whilst the extent to which this kind of initiative will mark a significant shift in the government's approach to education is questionable, the market system that has prevailed in recent years has a range of implications. Within it, parents are consumers and education is a commodity. It has an exchange value. It is valued not so much in terms of the difference it makes to individuals' ways of thinking, or to the development of children's minds, as in terms of a product that is acquired, which can be traded in for further advantages. This utilitarian view of education is apparent in the emphasis which is given to the role of education in securing employment and economic prosperity in the future – reflecting an ideology of *economic rationalism*. From this point of view, education is the means of achieving further valued rewards. Its value is derived from these extrinsic ends rather than from its intrinsic worth.

Towards a conception of education

I have shown in the discussion of classroom examples in the previous section that this conception of educational value is limited, and I suggested that the content of teaching and the processes of teaching might be justified in terms of alternative ethical and educational beliefs and principles. The justification rests on a rather different view of education than the one that is extant in current educational policy. Rather than representing education as a commodity, available in the educational marketplace, it is conceptualized as an entitlement. Rather than being a product to add to a basket of items which can be exchanged for other valued goods, it is a process to which every child has a right and which focuses on each of them becoming educated. I have suggested that such processes should be ethical as well as educational and I have suggested that becoming educated entails seeing the intrinsic meaning and point of what is learned. This is rather different to acquiring an education for extrinsic purposes.

To see the meaning and point of what they are learning, of course, implies that children must understand it. This rules out any teaching that focuses only on being able to perform, to produce right answers, to achieve the level the teacher requires or to absorb and regurgitate curriculum content, all of which can be achieved without any understanding. There are many teachers who are currently concerned that by focusing on achieving test results they are failing to develop children's ability to think deeply and to reason well. On the other hand, a focus on outcomes is quite consistent with a *commodity* conception of education where the demonstrable product is all that is required to show that an education has been acquired. Ironically, this may be short-changing children.

The sorts of ethical and educational principles that are implicit in my analysis should now be more apparent. I have argued for a conception of education that does justice to teachers' professionalism and that is guided by principles of social justice. Within this conception we would aim for children to learn to think, reason, understand and to gain appreciation and understanding of the value of what they learn.

Professional values and practice

One of the wider groups to which all teachers belong is the teaching profession itself. This has recently received recognition in England and Wales through the formation of General Teaching Councils (GTCs), following the precedent set by Scotland. These bodies have established professional codes. This is a recent development and it is an encouraging one, in that it explicitly acknowledges teaching as a profession and the values base of education. The General Teaching Council for England (GTCE) code, which is 'intended to be an evolving document' (GTCE website), was produced following wide consultation with teachers. 'Through the code, the council can affirm the fundamental beliefs, values and attitudes that underpin all that teachers do' (ibid.).

In order to achieve qualified teacher status (QTS), student teachers in England are now required to demonstrate that they understand and uphold the code of the GTCE by fulfilling the following specified criteria:

1. They have high expectations of all pupils; respect their social, cultural, linguistic, religious and ethnic backgrounds; and are committed to raising their educational achievement.
2. They treat pupils consistently, with respect and consideration, and are concerned for their development as learners.
3. They demonstrate and promote the positive values, attitudes and behaviour that they expect from their pupils.
4. They can communicate sensitively and effectively with parents and carers, recognizing their roles in pupils' learning, and their rights, responsibilities and interests in this.
5. They can contribute to and share responsibly in, the corporate life of schools.
6. They understand the contribution that support staff and other professionals make to teaching and learning.
7. They are able to improve their own teaching, by evaluating it, learning from the effective practice of others and from evidence. They are motivated and able to take increasing responsibility for their own professional development.
8. They are aware of, and work within, the statutory frameworks relating to teachers' responsibilities (DfES/TTA, 2002).

Points 1 to 7 above reflect ethical principles that are consistent with the conception of education and teaching that I have discussed in this chapter. Point 7 makes specific reference to the reflective approach to teaching which, I have suggested, underpins professionalism. The last point is, of course, a legal, rather than an ethical matter.

This chapter has raised some issues about values in education and teaching that should encourage teachers to adopt a professional approach to their practice and to engage with the values which inform their teaching. This kind of reflection and analysis helps to develop a principled and coherent approach to education and teaching, through which they can justify what they do and can help to ensure that practice in schools really does benefit children. It should help teachers in England to interpret and, perhaps, develop the professional code of the GTCE in a way that is educationally rich and professionally and personally meaningful.

Issues for Reflection

- What do you consider to be your most important aims in your teaching?
- Describe some examples of your own practice as a teacher or of your observations of other teachers' practice. Reflecting on these, what underlying values might they reveal? How would you justify some of these examples?
- Explore any inconsistencies between your own educational aims and values

and what you do in the classroom.

- Thinking about a school with which you are familiar, what do you see to be its priorities for the children? Discuss some of the implications, in the light of different ways of valuing education and different conceptions of education.

Summary of Key Points

- Although it may seem irrelevant to teachers and student teachers to concern themselves with issues of value, values will, nevertheless, be central to what they do.
- A reflective approach to practice, whereby teachers become aware of the way values are inherent in the judgements and decisions they make as part of their everyday work, could be seen as essential to being professional.
- Teachers' judgement, and, therefore, values, can influence both the content of their teaching and the processes. What, and how, teachers teach have both ethical and educational implications.
- A conception of education which prioritizes extrinsic values has both ethical and educational implications which are open to challenge.
- Market-led frameworks of values have informed current policy and practice and have created a conception of education as a commodity.
- An alternative entitlement view implies that all are entitled to become educated and this means coming to see the intrinsic meaning and value of what is learned.
- There is now a professional code laid down by the GTCE with criteria for professional values and practice which student teachers must fulfil in order to gain QTS.

Suggestions for Further Reading

Cole, M. (ed.) (2002) *Professional Values and Practice for Teachers and Student Teachers.* 2nd edn. London: David Fulton. Each of the eight requirements for professional values and practice that are needed to meet the 2002 Standards for the Award of QTS are discussed in this book.

Fielding, M. (ed.) (2001) *Taking Education Really Seriously – Four Years' Hard Labour.* London: Routledge Falmer. This book provides critical insight into recent educational policies and issues and the surrounding debates, from a variety of perspectives. It includes chapters written by some prominent educationalists.

Journal of Philosophy of Education: The Journal of the Philosophy of Education Society of Great Britain. Oxford: Blackwell. This academic journal is published four times a year and contains articles by international authors on all aspects of the philosophy of education.

4
Teaching as a Profession

Ralph Manning

The following topics and issues are covered in this chapter:

- what makes teaching a profession;
- the establishment of the General Teaching Councils;
- the contribution of the GTCE to the teaching profession;
- developing the professional aspects of the teacher's role;
- teachers' professional autonomy;
- the implications of teachers' contracts; and
- issues of teacher workload and the roles of other adults supporting teachers in schools.

Many people in different forms of employment lay claim to being members of a profession. But what actually constitutes a profession, and are teachers right to use this title in respect of their work? This chapter examines the place of teaching as a true profession. The most significant development in recent years for the profession has been the establishment of the General Teaching Council in England and similar GTCs in Wales and Scotland. The focus of this chapter is on some of the expectations, rights, responsibilities and opportunities for teachers that are changing as a result of the GTCs' formation.

Can We Recognize Teaching as a Profession?

Teaching is often described as a profession, but what does that mean for teachers and those who use their services? The reader is referred to Ozga and Lawn (1981), among others, for an in-depth discussion of the issue. Here we shall concern ourselves, in a simple form, with the most commonly agreed characteristics which identify a form of work as a profession:

1. It has a prestigious role that performs an essential service for its clients.

2. Admission is controlled by qualification requiring extensive training in skills and knowledge.
3. It has a high degree of autonomy.
4. It regulates the work of its own members to safeguard standards in the public interest.
5. It maintains and continues to develop an established body of special expertise and systems.

These characteristics can all be applied to a number of recognized professions: law, medicine, architecture and accountancy are all good examples. It is fairly easy to argue that the first two criteria have also applied to teaching for many years. Although teachers may disagree with the assertion that they are generally seen as a prestigious group within society (The *Guardian* website, GTCE/Guardian/MORI 2003 Teacher Survey), many parents still hold their own children's individual teachers in high esteem and public expectations of teachers have clearly increased over the years. It is on the last three points that, until recently, following the formation of the GTCs, the nature of teaching as a true profession has been disputed.

Autonomy?

In particular, teachers have complained that in their work they now have little autonomy, and that their professional judgement is undervalued. How much has the body of expertise been established, maintained and developed by those who work in teaching, and how much has been dictated by others outside the profession with other vested interests? Education in England and Wales has been highly politicized as evidenced by the significant number of additions and changes to legislation over the past 15 years. As has been argued in Chapter 1 of this book, since the introduction of the National Curriculum in 1988, much of the perceived body of special expertise – the skills and knowledge of the teacher – has been increasingly prescribed by central government, at times with apparently little regard to the voices of actual practitioners. The introduction of the National Literacy and Numeracy Strategies presumed to cover not just the content of the curriculum, but also the structure of the lessons and the teaching styles to be used.

Safeguarding standards?

In terms of regulation, teachers have become increasingly accountable to multiple external agencies. These include the DfES's prescribed curricula and initiatives, monitored by school inspection carried out by OFSTED. Other agencies of accountability are the LEA conducting its own monitoring and intervention, reports to parents and governors, the publication and comparison of national test results, and specialist intervention from social and health bodies, to name the major players. However, many of these agencies make

of practising teachers in exercising judgements about teaching and

self-reflection has been emphasized in initial teacher training
he past 20 years (Pollard, 1996). Many teachers' personal dedication
ork and the care of their pupils has made them constructively critical in evaluating their own performance and that of others. Teachers are
awarded QTS following a process of initial teacher training. This usually
involves some measure of professional judgement being made by qualified
practitioners in schools where trainees serve their teaching practices. Yet,
until recently, practising teachers have had no formal role in regulating standards of teaching after the award of QTS. Having attained QTS, teachers
were registered with the DfES, but there was little formal recourse for
dealing with conduct and competence issues beyond the school's governing
body and the LEA/employer.

Maintaining and developing expertise?

In the area of maintaining and developing expertise, there have been no agreed
expectations of continuing professional development. Opportunities for training and further development have varied from school to school and between
LEAs. Until recently, classroom practitioners have had no formal role in developing and maintaining expertise and systems. However, LEAs are now making
more use of, for example, advanced skills teachers (ASTs), leading mathematics
teachers and others with specialist expertise to work alongside colleagues in
other schools to improve the quality of teaching and learning.

The General Teaching Councils

The formation of the GTCs

On 1 September 2000, the nature of teaching as a profession in England and
Wales changed considerably with the introduction of the GTCs in England
(GTCE) and Wales (GTCW). Scotland had had its own General Teaching
Council (GTCS) to regulate and advise on the profession since 1966. The
history of the GTCs actually began around the same time as the establishment
of other professional councils (the General Medical Council was founded in
1858). Over a period of nearly 150 years, there were several attempts to set up
a professional council for teachers in England, including failed parliamentary
bills at the end of the nineteenth century. However, it was not until 1998 that
legislation was finally passed to establish the GTCs for England and for Wales.

The establishment of the GTCs meant the creation of statutory professional
bodies, independent of government, to regulate and to develop the profession.
The role of the GTCs is comparable to that which the General Medical
Council (GMC) has in regulating the work of medical practitioners. Each
respective GTC now has responsibility for the registration of all teachers prac-

tising in maintained schools, and those in the independent sector who choose to join. In order to practise as a qualified teacher in a maintained school in England and Wales, it is now a requirement for an individual to be registered with the appropriate GTC. The GTCs now have a pivotal role in maintaining high professional standards, in two key aspects:

- the maintenance of high professional standards through regulation of the profession by members of the profession; and
- the provision of evidence-led advice in order to maintain and develop expertise and systems within teaching.

Suspicions and objections

At the GTCE's inception many teachers were suspicious of the new organization. Some were initially confused about its role. Although the movement to establish GTCs was actively supported by the main teacher unions and associations, the GTCE initially faced some hostility from two of the largest associations – the National Union of Teachers (NUT) and the National Association of Schoolteachers Union of Women Teachers (NASUWT), who feared there would be an encroachment on their own roles of defending members' interests, particularly in conditions of employment.

Other teachers objected to the imposition of another apparently new authority which they feared would *dictate* rather than *listen* to them, and would compound the insult by levying a new professional fee upon them in order to fund its work. The fact that the GTCE was instituted by government legislation and launched with start-up funding from the DfES until it could become self-supporting, also led to charges that it would not be truly independent of government.

Thus, the early years of the GTCE have been marked by a struggle to communicate its remit and *raison d'être* to serving teachers and clearly to differentiate the parameters of its work from other agencies and associations in education. For the interested reader the long and sometimes turbulent struggle to establish the GTCs is described comprehensively in Sayer (2000). However, for our purposes here we will concentrate on the role and impact of the GTCE.

The composition of the GTCE

The GTCE comprises 64 voluntary members. All are unpaid, except for the Chair and Vice-Chair who undertake part-time secondments to the council to fulfil their council duties. A total of 25 of the council members are practising teachers elected by registered teachers. There are nine members who are teachers nominated by the teacher unions and associations. A further 17 are nominees from other national bodies with interests in education; examples of these are the Association of Chief Education Officers, the Universities'

Council for the Education of Teachers, the National Governors' Council and the Equal Opportunities Commission. The 13 remaining members are appointed by the Secretary of State, but they are not accountable to that office and bring their own independent views to the work of the council. Their appointments are intended to ensure that the council has a balanced membership including expertise from different phases of education, contrasting school situations and parents' representatives. In fact, in order to ensure the GTCE's independence, the government has no representation within the council at all.

The GTCW, though smaller, has a similar structure, comprising 25 members, of whom 12 are elected, nine are nominees from unions and stakeholder organizations, and four are appointed by the National Assembly for Wales.

In all, over two-thirds of the GTCE's council membership are practising teachers. The inclusion of 'lay' members on the GTCs is comparable to moves within the GMC to widen its membership in the public interest. The lay members represent other stakeholders in education. They ensure that the views and decisions of the council do not simply reflect teachers' self-interest, but culminate in a measured, well-informed view of what sustains high standards in teaching and learning. In this key respect, the GTCE's composition contributes to its remit in a way that is fundamentally different from the teacher unions and associations, whose prime concern is, rightly, the protection of their own members' interests. Advice or negotiation on matters of pay and conditions in particular are strictly beyond the remit and interest of the GTCE.

However, it is natural that at times the interests of the GTC, and those of the teacher unions and associations coincide, especially since matters of principle concerning high professional standards in teaching and learning are often of practical benefit and self-interest for teachers too. An obvious example would be a common desire to reduce class sizes, which could be interpreted both as an issue about the quality of teaching and learning and as an issue concerning conditions of work.

Towards Greater Professional Autonomy

Will the GTCs satisfy teachers' desire for greater professional autonomy? This remains to be seen. The legislation establishing the GTCs in England and Wales passed on limited powers from the DfES.

Dealing with conduct and competence issues

One clear example of greater autonomy is in the area of the GTCE's regulatory work. The GTCE has a clear mandate to investigate, judge and issue disciplinary orders on cases of unacceptable professional conduct and serious professional incompetence. These are new roles for which no other agency had responsibility prior to the GTCE starting its casework in 2001. Prior to this, most issues of incompetence and misconduct (put together under the legal title of 'capability procedures') were at an end once a teacher had been dismissed from his or her post (DfEE, 2000a). There were two problems with this: a teacher sacked from one LEA could still be employed in another, even where their action(s) may have rendered them unsuitable to continue teaching; conversely, a teacher who may have been dismissed, but whose situation could be mitigated, may have found themselves effectively barred from teaching by harsh references provided by the dismissing employer. Only in extreme cases – those involving child protection issues – would the DfES intervene effectively to bar a dismissed teacher from obtaining employment in another school. This used a record of prohibited teachers known as 'List 99'. Child protection cases are the one area which the DfES has retained the power to investigate, instead of the GTCE.

Entry to the profession

Regarding the control of entry to the profession following the successful conclusion of ITT, the GTCE now awards QTS on behalf on the Secretary of State for Education. However, the standards which must be satisfied to attain QTS are set out in separate legislation (DfES/TTA, 2002) developed and maintained by the Teacher Training Agency (TTA), although these now also reflect the GTCE's Code of Professional Values and Practice for Teachers (GTCE website). This code was agreed by the GTCE in February 2002, as a set of positive statements defining the high professional expectations that teachers have of themselves. It is also used as an underpinning set of principles upon which all of the GTCE's work is founded. The importance of this code in relation to teachers' professional values is discussed in Chapter 3.

Induction and beyond

The GTCE also has a remit to hear appeals from newly qualified teachers who have failed to complete their induction period successfully. This is a process which had been initiated under the DfES's own appeals procedure and was passed on to the GTCE in 2001. See Chapter 17 for further information about induction.

Beyond induction into the profession, the assessment and accreditation of higher forms of practice – passing the Performance Threshold or becoming an AST – are made at the discretion of employers using external agencies. This is a further activity within the profession carried out without recourse to practising teachers or to any standards of practice yet to be set by the GTCs. In time, it may be that the GTCE and GTCW could become involved in accreditation of a higher standard of registration, such as the Chartered Teacher status being developed in Scotland (Scottish Executive Education Department, 2001), which will be accredited and registered by the GTCS. However, this is not being advocated at the present time in England or Wales.

of the curriculum

control of the school curriculum is concerned, the present National
m (DfEE/QCA, 1999), is prescribed in legislation developed and
d by the Qualifications and Curriculum Authority, but the GTCE
has asserted teachers' expectations that practitioners should have more public
trust and greater freedom. It argues that teachers must exercise their own professional judgement to shape the curriculum within their schools to fit the
needs of their pupils (GTCE, 2001a; 2001b).

Making the GTCs' voice heard

However, on the basis that respect is earned rather than granted, the GTCs
will most likely establish their authority to speak through using the evidence
accumulated from careful analysis of education research and through the data
accumulated from their regulatory role. Through its statutory role in teacher
registration, the GTCE is also compiling a significant database of the teacher
population. Charged with providing advice on issues of recruitment and retention in the profession, the GTCE will find this database to be extremely useful
in providing information about the profile of the teaching profession and in
the prediction and alleviation of potential problems in recruitment and retention. It is these streams of evidence that are likely to provide the GTCE with
a unique and authoritative voice in shaping future education policy.

The statutory audiences for advice from the GTCs are the Secretary of State
for Education (for the GTCE), or the National Assembly for Wales (in the case
of the GTCW), as the respective governments seek to develop their education
policies. Those governments can choose to listen, act on or ignore this advice.
But they must remember that it has been developed not from teachers' self-
interest but from a wide range of expertise and evidence vested in maintaining
high standards in education. The longer the quality of this advice is proved to be
sound, well-researched and balanced, the greater the argument will become for
the profession's right to direct more of its own practice in the future. The
Department of Health (DoH) is wary of dictating clinical procedure to medical
practitioners. It is anyone's guess how long it will be before the DfES decides
that the curriculum and strategies to maintain the highest quality of teaching
and learning are also best determined by the practitioners themselves.

Promoting autonomy

However, greater autonomy is not always granted from outside; *sometimes it
needs to be seized from within.* It is as much for the teaching profession itself,
as well as other stakeholders in education, that the GTCE has a role as a collective advisory body. Hence the GTCE also advocates that teachers should
begin to assert greater autonomy for themselves, communicating useful classroom experience and best practice in teaching and learning between members

of the profession, independently of the intervention of the DfES and other agencies. It has also emphasized that teachers learn from one another by seeking collaborative opportunities, and that these should be planned as a very legitimate and highly constructive form of continuing professional development (GTCE, 2003a). These could be through formal mechanisms, such as Networked Learning Communities, or informally between schools or teachers with common interests.

Action research

Another way in which the GTCE is keen to promote continuing professional development is through action research. This is best defined by Elliott (1991) as the teacher researching through their own classroom practice, rather than others, usually non-practitioners, carrying out research and providing results and conclusions to research-passive practitioners. Action research recognizes the contribution of teachers' own classroom experiences and their children's learning in generating evidence that can shape practice. Again, this can be through formal channels such as higher degrees or funded research projects, or simply through the teacher informally recording and learning from their self-evaluation and the analysis of the process and outcomes of their children's learning.

Public trust

In the area of public trust and accountability, the GTCE has confirmed that teachers are well aware, and indeed accept, that a public service of great importance to the nation and charged with wisely investing public funds must be held accountable for that privilege (GTCE, 2001c). However, it is also arguing that public trust in teachers' professional judgement must increase for teachers to have the flexibility to plan teaching and learning effectively for their classes. There have been recent moves at the end-of-Key-Stage assessment to raise the value of teacher assessment alongside the written national tests. It is yet to be seen if this actually raises respect for teachers' judgements.

OFSTED inspection

Regarding the role of OFSTED in the accountability mechanism, the GTCE has been very forthright, arguing – in its advice to improve recruitment, and particularly retention – that the inspection process needs radical transformation. For example, from a paper entitled 'School self evaluation and peer review', the GTCE states:

> OfSTED inspections have mostly been seen by the profession as a punitive, expensive and time-consuming system of 'policing' schools, resulting in snapshot views of school performance at a particular time, high stakes judgements and the 'naming

and shaming' culture. ... [schools] could have a greater role in steering and shaping their own improvement, charged as they are with providing high quality education, raising standards and developing teacher professionalism.

(GTCE website)

Expectations of Teachers

The job description and expectations of teachers in England and Wales are usually set out in broad terms in a contract from the employer. In the case of maintained schools this is usually an LEA. The contract will then make reference to a further document: the *School Teachers' Pay and Conditions Document* (DfES, 2002b). This document, supplemented by a manual referred to as the 'Burgundy Book', is updated periodically to reflect the government's reassessment of teachers' pay scales and conditions. Such updates usually occur annually, after the School Teachers' Review Body (STRB), an independent panel, has met and made its recommendations on changes to teachers' pay and working conditions to the government.

The document sets out the fine detail of salary scales, contractual obligations and entitlements for teachers in England and Wales. For the most part, this is a fairly straightforward if somewhat lengthy contract, aimed at making the legal expectations of the teacher reasonably clear.

Towards the end of the document it turns to statements of a teacher's professional duties (DfES, 2002b, ss 64–6). Much of this is general and easily understood in the context of a teacher's working life and the GTCE's *Code of Professional Values and Practice for Teachers* (GTCE, 2003b).

Professional working time

Up to the time of writing the controversial section of the *School Teachers' Pay and Conditions Document* (DfES, 2002b) has been the section describing the teacher's working time. In this section, there is a statement about 'directed time': a full-time teacher must be available for teaching and other duties on 195 days (190 of these for teaching) specified by the employer. This is further qualified by the clause:

> Such a teacher shall be available to perform such duties at such times and such places as may be specified by the head teacher ... for 1265 hours in any school year, those hours to be allocated reasonably throughout those days in the school year on which he [*sic*] is required to be available for work.

(DfES, 2002b, cl. 67.3)

If that were all that was said many would consider this to be generous to the teacher, typically representing approximately 32.5 hours per week over a 39-week school year. This clause would help fuel the common public misconception that teachers work short days and have long holidays. However, this section also contains a very significant caveat:

Such a teacher shall ... *work such additional hours as may be needed* to enable him [*sic*] to discharge effectively his [*sic*] professional duties, including, in particular, the marking of pupils' work, the writing of reports on pupils and the preparation of lessons, teaching material and teaching programmes.

(DfES, 2002b, cl. 67.7, emphasis added)

This effectively wrote into all teachers' contracts that they needed to work for as long it takes to do as much as there is! Not surprisingly, as public expectations increased and demands upon teachers have grown over the years, this last clause has become notorious in negotiations concerning teachers' pay and conditions.

Review of teacher workload

Matters came to a head in 2001, following the McCrone Report into teachers' pay, conditions and career structure in Scotland and the subsequent acceptance of the majority of its recommendations (Scottish Executive Education Department, 2001). When the English teacher unions and associations launched joint action against increasing workload, the then Secretary of State, David Blunkett, agreed to set up the Teacher Workload Study, an independent review of teachers' workload carried out by the management consultants, PriceWaterhouseCoopers. This review was directed by a steering group comprising the heads of the main teaching and public sector unions/ associations, the Local Government Association, the STRB, and some representatives from large public companies. The steering group did include the DfES, which also chaired the group, but ultimately, DfES representation was a minority within the group.

In its *Interim Report*, the Teacher Workload Study noted that:

- teachers' working weeks are more intensive than most other occupations, with 50–60 hours being the norm (PriceWaterhouseCoopers, 2001a, p. 1).
- teachers carried out between 9–11 percent of their work at weekends and 15–18 percent before the formal school day starts or after 6pm on weekdays, with evening and weekend work accounting for around 25 percent of total working time (ibid., p. 14).
- additional administrative time is 'real' because it must be purchased and is rarely offset by reduced teacher salary costs; but additional teacher time is *free* (ibid., p. 19, emphasis added).

This last point was a significant finding, pointing to the way in which the Working Time section in teachers' contracts implicitly enabled more tasks to be added to the teacher without apparent cost to the school. This contrasted sharply with the extra payments that schools needed to make whenever they chose to draft in more hourly-paid administrative staff. It is notable that at the time of writing, draft amendments to the *School Teachers' Pay and Conditions Document* have not yet included removing or revising the open-ended clause regarding working time (DfES, 2002b, cl 67.7).

The true picture of teacher workload which emerged showed the woeful lack of funding and support within the maintained education system, and the *Final Report* made several further key points:

- Teachers in many schools perceive a lack of control and ownership over their work, undertaking tasks – particularly documentation – which they do not believe are necessary to support learning, or which could be done by support staff rather than by teachers or more efficiently using Information and Communications Technology (ICT) (PriceWaterhouseCoopers, 2001b, p. 1).
- [teachers] felt that the pace and manner of change was working against achieving high standards, that they were insufficiently supported to meet these changes, and not accorded the professional trust that they merited (ibid., p. 1).
- Within the context of DfES's national programme to transform the school work-force and secondary education, we therefore believe an essential strand will be to reduce teacher workload, foster increased teacher ownership, and create the capacity for managing change in a sustainable way … (ibid., p. 2).
- Headteachers and teachers were overwhelmingly in favour of guaranteed time for planning and preparation within the working week. They felt this measure had potential to raise quality … reduce overall hours worked and reduce stress (ibid., p. 4).

In its contribution to the process, the GTCE prominently argued that in the interests of high-quality teaching and learning, *all* of a teacher's professional duties must be formally recognized as needing appropriate time, not simply those which occur during contact time or during a teacher's classroom per-formance. In its advice to the next Secretary of State, Estelle Morris, the GTCE asserted the necessity of allocating 'professional time' for all aspects of the teacher's professional role (GTCE, 2001b, p. 1–2). Tasks such as planning, preparation, pupil assessment and record-keeping, meeting with parents and other agencies, were not spare-time activities but must all be carefully consid-ered as complementary parts of a teacher's core professional role. In doing so, the GTCE enabled the Secretary of State to change the language of the dis-cussion from one of 'workload' to 'professional time' and in particular the nature of 'planning, preparation and assessment (PPA) time'. Importantly, this helped elevate the debate at government level from one about teachers' con-ditions of work to one about sustaining and improving the quality of teaching and learning for pupils in schools.

Working with Other Adults in Schools

Are the results of the Teacher Workload Study likely to have any tangible effect on the profession? At the time of writing, the jury is still out. It is clear that to make the kind of investment in additional teachers required to meet the desire of the profession for guaranteed PPA time, as expressed in the Teacher Workload Study, would require a significant step-change in education funding. Not surprisingly, so far the government has been unwilling to pursue that approach.

Instead, in November 2002, the Secretary of State announced plans to pursue transformation of teachers' working time, by remodelling the school workforce to make more effective use of support staff and systems within schools (DfES, 2002c). At the same time the DfES launched a series of Pathfinder projects in schools, experimenting with funding and identifying alternative ways of reducing teacher workload. At the time of writing, these findings have yet to be made public.

Higher-level teaching assistants

This new agenda, under the title of School Workforce Remodelling, culminated in an unprecedented agreement in January 2003, between the DfES and several of the teaching and appropriate public sector unions/associations (available on the Teacher Net website). There was broad agreement to increase the use of teaching assistants (TAs) and to reshape their roles and responsibilities to provide support for teachers to undertake the multiple demands on their professional time. This would include the development of a new role of higher-level teaching assistant, with different areas of responsibility, such as behaviour management, pastoral care and learning support.

However, the detail behind the agreement had very mixed reactions. The largest teaching union, the NUT, refused to sign. It feared that the government's agenda was to replace difficult-to-recruit teachers with less costly TAs who would directly teach classes, while qualified teachers would increasingly take on the role of managing the overall teaching and learning process for larger numbers of pupils. Some advocates of this approach cited the use of triage in hospitals, arguing that scarce resources such as teachers would need to take on a role more akin to a hospital consultant, whilst higher-level teaching assistants took on the front-line nursing role. Not surprisingly, many teachers objected to this view, seeing it as putting further distance between the teacher and the pupil, when for many teachers their love of teaching is in the day-to-day direct, interactive teaching of their pupils.

Other teacher associations, such as the NASUWT and the Association of Teachers and Lecturers (ATL), saw potential in the agreement to provide much needed relief to their hard-pressed members. They also argued that the reality on the ground was that in many schools, TAs and other non-QTS staff were already actively engaged in class supervision and teaching. This is particularly evident in the Foundation Stage where a QTS teacher may lead a team of staff including nursery nurses and TAs. Staff in special schools also pointed to their multidisciplinary approaches in the classroom, where to the casual observer it may not be apparent who has QTS and who does not.

The GTCE's response

The GTCE's response to proposals for the introduction of higher-level teaching assistants and the roles of other adults in the classroom was cautious. Charged with maintaining high standards of teaching and learning, the GTCE welcomed the increased use of support staff but *only* where this would *add value* to the teaching carried out by qualified teachers. It argued that an interactive relationship between the teacher and pupil is central to teaching and learning, and that all pupils should have guaranteed access to teaching from teachers with QTS. The council further emphasized teachers' views of the importance of the teacher being empowered to make their own flexible decisions about how best to use other adults – either to support the learning of individual pupils or groups, or to undertake administrative or clerical tasks on behalf of the teacher – according to needs identified by the teacher. The GTCE rejected proposals for additional new management and teaching structures to be imposed upon schools, and asserted that appropriate structures should be decided by headteachers with respect to their own local school context (GTCE, 2003c).

Issues for Reflection

- In what ways can teachers assert their own professional autonomy to a greater extent than at present?
- How can teachers use evidence from a typical classroom situation to contribute to their own and other teachers' professional development?
- In your experience, what proportions of the teacher's time are spent on different types of non-teaching activities? Which of these are essential or helpful for teachers to carry out in order to promote high-quality teaching? Which activities are possible to delegate to support staff?
- In what constructive ways can the teacher make use of higher-level teaching assistants without reducing the pupils' opportunity to learn from a qualified teacher?

Summary of Key Points

- In 2000, teaching in England and Wales was at last formally established as a profession with the creation of the GTCs. These bodies have a statutory-appointed measure of self-regulation. They also have the remit to gather and pass on evidence-led advice from the profession to both policy-makers and teachers themselves in the interests of maintaining high standards of teaching and learning.
- With the establishment of the GTCE the present time is arguably a watershed not just for the development of teaching as profession, but also for the future of school education, its funding and structures for the first half of the twenty-first century.

- There are many differing views and possibilities for change within education, depending on the perspectives of the different stakeholders. The GTCE has given teachers and key stakeholders, distinct from the government, a unique and authoritative voice in the debate that can be listened to, not as promoting teachers' self-interest, but with legitimate concerns to safeguard the best interests of pupils.
- Teachers should seize the initiative in establishing greater professional autonomy. Practitioners are encouraged to make more use of their own professional judgement. The GTCE advocates that teachers should be involved in all forms of professional development, including action research, as well as having a bigger role in the systems of public accountability and improvement.
- Teachers' professional working time must include proper allocation for planning, preparation and assessment, along with the other professional duties that are necessary to complement the teacher's role in the classroom.
- Teachers need to decide for themselves how they can make flexible use of support staff, both in supporting their pupils' learning and in providing some relief of their workload through the delegation of administrative and clerical tasks.

Suggestions for Further Reading

Booklet

GTCE (2003) *Commitment: The Teachers' Professional Learning Framework*. London: GTCE. The Teachers' Professional Learning Framework (TPLF) document provides a map of professional development experiences for all teachers, as well as for those who support, advise and facilitate teachers' learning and development.

Websites

GTCE website, www.gtce.org.uk The information page of this website has links to many items of interest discussed in this chapter. The TPLF document above can be accessed here (www.gtce.org.uk/TPLF) as well as many other key GTCE documents on professional practice.

The Guardian website, GTCE/Guardian/MORI 2003 Teacher Survey, education.guardian.co.uk/microsite/gtc This is the home page of the MORI survey commissioned jointly by the GTCE and *The Guardian* newspaper. It is the most comprehensive survey of teachers' motivations and concerns for teaching ever undertaken in the profession.

5

Primary School Teachers and the Law

Peter Gibley

The following topics and issues are covered in this chapter:

- the duty of care that is legally expected of a primary school teacher;
- the distinction between accident and negligence;
- the principles of *in loco parentis* and 'behaving like a reasonable teacher';
- school rules in the context of general policy-making and the Human Rights Act 1998;
- the responsibilities of teachers towards Family Law, including gathering evidence and report-writing, stemming from the Children Act 1989;
- the need for a protective climate for adults to share sensitive information within the school for effective child protection;
- parental responsibility and the implications for schools; and
- the implications for teachers of the Data Protection Act 1998.

In this chapter I explore some of the effects that legislation has on the duty of care that is expected of a primary school teacher working in the British education system. The chapter provides the legal context for the teacher's pastoral-care role that is discussed in Chapter 8. The establishment of a protective climate for adults to share sensitive information within the school is seen as crucial for effective child protection.

The Duty of Care

Accident or negligence?

In a large class of 9- and 10-year-olds one child accidentally poked another in the eye with the pair of scissors he was using. The parents sued the LEA, alleging negligence on the part of their employee, the teacher. They lost the case: it was found to be an accident (*Butt* v *Cambridgeshire and Ely County Council*, 1970). Thirteen years later a court awarded £31,000 in damages against an LEA when a child aged 7 was stabbed in the eye by a pair of sharp pointed scissors he was using in an art class. In *Black* v *Kent County Council* (1983), Sir John Donaldson, Master of the Rolls, said that it was *reasonably foreseeable* that the use of sharp pointed scissors involved quite a degree of risk where children of this age were concerned. The staff should have avoided such risks.

As so much legislation crowds in on teachers in daily contact with pupils, anxiety underlies the thinking and practice of many of them: I hope I can get through, day by day, without a crisis. Can I care for the children in my class with the necessary discipline, yet without confrontation? Most importantly, if I am challenged over my handling, will the system support me or might my whole career be thrown into jeopardy over one distorted incident? Grasping the difference between the two cases of the scissors, however, should provide a good teacher with considerable comfort. The key lies in the court's recognition that a genuine accident cannot reasonably have been foreseen. Where a teacher can be shown initially to have assessed the risks thoroughly and to have set up appropriate activities or equipment, a successful defence may be mounted.

Nowhere, perhaps, does a teacher feel more vulnerable than in physical activities. Young children are often encouraged to explore apparatus freely in lessons and in the playground. In 1955, adjudicating in the case of a 5-year-old boy who fell from a climbing frame in the school playground, the judge said that children as a rule at this age 'will not go further than they can manage' and he found that the parents had failed to establish negligence on the part of the supervising teacher (*Berridge* v *Isle of Wight CC*, 1955). Higher-risk activities must be subject to thorough assessments of those risks and particularly in their different contexts: it is common sense that different ages, experiences and abilities change the assessment of the same risks. The risks of a riverside picnic for a class of 4-year-olds differ from those faced by 10-year-olds who may safely sit closer to the flowing water and move around more freely.

When an accident has occurred and the question of professional negligence has arisen, courts have shown a real understanding of the burden placed upon teachers. When something has gone wrong, in spite of the reasonable forethought and conduct of a teacher, courts have consistently found in the teacher's favour. Nevertheless media interest is high when any public servant is alleged to have fallen short of a required standard, and the exposure, even at local level, can be brutal and unrelenting. When allegations against children are made, the adults under the spotlight are often suspended or forced to take sick leave whilst an investigation in which they may play no part, drags on interminably.

Vicarious liability

You might have noticed from the cases cited above that actions for negligence are often brought against employers rather than individual teachers. Under the principle of 'vicarious liability' an employer is held to be liable for the

actions of his employees while they are acting in the course of their employment. It follows that LEAs will issue such guidance as they think necessary to
ensure that their employees act responsibly and to keep them out of the
courts! Schools that supplement LEA guidance with sound support and well-
drawn policies, assisted by their governors, do most to ensure that their staff
can undertake the full curriculum with genuine security. The role of the
governing body in relation to school policies is explored in Chapter 6.

In loco parentis

Many teachers understand themselves to be *in loco parentis*, literally trans-
lated as 'in the place of a parent'. They are expected, it is commonly thought,
to behave in their classrooms just as a reasonable parent would behave at
home. In 1893, Mr Justice Cave in *Williams* v *Eady* (*The Times*, 1893), said that
the 'duty of a schoolmaster is to take such care of his boys as a careful father
would take care of his boys'. The perception of how Mr Average would behave
would be the test, providing a clear link to the public that teachers serve. Mr
Average became famously defined as 'the man upstairs on the Clapham
omnibus'!

The courts struggled from those early days of public education to reconcile
the equation of home and school. For many judges, schools and public places
were seen as extensions of the home and their judgments reflected that
perception. But as long ago as 1938, Mr Justice Hilbery said,

> You have to consider whether or not you would expect a headmaster to exercise
> such a degree of care that boys could never get into mischief. Has any reasonable
> parent yet succeeded in exercising such care as to prevent a boy getting into mis-
> chief, and if he did, what sort of boys would we produce?
>
> (Barrell and Partington, 1985, p. 439)

By 1962 courts were separating home and school to the extent that a teacher
should have 'to take such care as a careful father applying his mind to school
life' where there is 'more skylarking and a bit of rough play' (*Lyes* v
Middlesex County Council, Croner, 2001, s. 3, p. 757). In spite of, or perhaps
because of, their own robust boarding-school experiences, judges were
making important easements in the heavy burden of the original concept of
in loco parentis. By 1968 girls get a mention in legal pronouncements! Mr
Justice Geoffrey Lane, (*Beaumont* v *Surrey County Council*, Croner, 2001, s.
3, p. 757) said: 'It is a headmaster's duty, bearing in mind the known propen-
sities of boys and indeed girls between the ages of 11 and 17 or 18, to take all
reasonable and proper steps to prevent any of the pupils under his care from
suffering injury.' Common sense, that great ally of human decision-making,
was in the legal frame by 1990 when Mr Justice Simon Brown said that 'a
balance must be struck that did not stifle initiative and independence, which
should be encouraged' (*Porter* v *Barking and Dagenham LB and Another*,
The Times, 1990).

Behaving like a reasonable teacher

So where does all this leave teachers exercising that essential duty of care within the peculiar social difficulties of contemporary society? It should be genuinely comforting to acknowledge that modern-day legal judgments consistently reflect the nature of modern-day society. Indeed, it is difficult to find a case where the reasonable behaviour of a teacher has not been supported in the courts.

In 1962, in the case of *Lyes* v *Middlesex County Council* Mr Justice Edmund Davies acknowledged that 'school life happily differs from home life'. Thus saying, he separated the parent from the teacher and allowed society to expect that a teacher should behave as a reasonable teacher should behave. No longer could direct comparisons be drawn between the actions and responsibilities of a prudent parent and those of a caring and careful teacher. For a teacher to test the rightness of a proposed action by considering what a parent might do – for example, about a punishment – would be quite unreliable. A parent might reasonably send a very young child to her room for a cooling-off period, but a responsible infant teacher would not leave an upset 6-year-old to calm down alone, tempting as it might be to get away from the commotion.

However, it is right that there is a proper state of awareness, although not of anxiety, expected of every teacher for the safety and care of every child although, in pastoral terms, the teacher's care will rightly decrease and change as pupils get older. A parent might reasonably expect that her 4-year-old is never left to work on her own. Within the same school, 9-year-olds routinely make complicated decisions about their own welfare, staying in at playtime or wandering safely over the school site without an adult beside them. In the high school, students may leave the school at lunchtime to make purchases in local shops and nobody would expect the school staff to know exactly where they are. The essential common element is that the responsible adults are aware at all times of the framework of rules within which those children in their care are operating and, crucially, that the children understand them, too.

The Rule Book

Individual freedoms are most properly developed within structures. These require rules. Rules can seem restrictive and provocative, too often leading to confrontation and punishment. Yet, whilst rules may be anathema for young people, they are essential for schools, as indeed they are for every other formal or informal institution. Teachers are rightly in the vanguard of those who promote individual freedoms whilst understanding that even the most rudimentary grouping must have order based upon accepted rules. Many teachers have been influenced by William Golding's novel *Lord of the Flies* (Golding, 1954), in which a group of boys, alone on an island, struggle to set up a social structure that will save them from destroying themselves. In many institutions, school councils (see Chapter 8) ensure ownership and understanding of school rules, whilst teachers develop those necessary rules with the children in their own classes and display them prominently.

The legal authority for school rules

The legal authority for school rules in the present day stems from the Education Act 1996 (DfEE, 1996b) when Articles of Government made it a duty for headteachers to promote self-discipline with proper regard for authority. They had to secure acceptable standards of behaviour to regulate the conduct of their pupils. The Act gave school governors the power to advise and to oversee. As school rules arise from legal Articles of Government, they have the force of law, provided they are properly drawn up and made known. Courts have regularly upheld the reasonable enforcement of proper school rules, and teachers should have confidence when working within a framework of well-drawn local rules. School uniform, the wearing of jewellery and make-up, and attendance and participation in activities are common battlegrounds and the legal ground for schools in these respects is firmer than is generally perceived to be the case.

School uniform

The Education Act (DfEE, 1996b) empowers school governors to decide whether uniform should be worn or not. They would be wise to consult the school staff and everyone should act reasonably regarding style, cost, ethnic difficulties and sanctions. Specific requirements for activities such as physical education (PE) or swimming are permissible, indeed essential on the grounds of health and safety. Thus, limitations on the wearing of jewellery including ear studs, the length of hair and the style of shoes and their heels, may often be prescribed.

Common sense and reasonableness

If the argument for the creation or enforcement of a particular rule is infused with large doses of reasonableness and common sense, the way forward is probably clearer – and likely to be safer too. Concern for safety is at the heart of the majority of school rules; and rightly so, as the legal threshold for schools to cross is higher for safety issues, for it remains set against the standard of a reasonable parent. When parents leave their children in the care of a school they must have an unqualified expectation that their children will be returned to them safely. The only way that an institution can accept that huge responsibility is by devising codes of conduct and of behaviour that will ensure the health and safety of the children in all the varied situations and activities they are going to meet. It is in the light of that supportive framework that those everyday crises, nearly all of which will never get near a court of law, should be regarded. Considerable comfort should be drawn from the presence of common sense and reasonable rules.

The Teacher's Role

The influence of external agencies

Several agencies empower and constrain schools. However, the situation has become more confusing since the move to devolve power to individual schools. This has brought about a serious increase in the school's responsibility and a shift of accountability from the LEA to the school. It is, perhaps, inevitable that the relationships between national government, the LEA and the headteacher have become blurred. National government directs through Acts of Parliament as well as sending instructions straight to schools and separately to governing bodies. These may have considerable sums of direct funding attached. The LEA can and does make requirements of its schools. Whilst being forced to delegate increasing sums of money to its schools, it retains some specific but limited powers, for example over special educational needs (SEN) provision, school transport and admission policy.

Guidance arrives from various quarters: the QCA for curriculum matters, the DfES itself, the LEA and a multitude of private and specialist bodies. Professional associations regularly provide excellent guidance and background papers for their members: the heads' associations are particularly helpful. However, to implement all this effectively, little of this forest of paper will leave the headteacher's desk in unmodified form. Teachers need and deserve clarity and brevity in the documentation which underpins their roles and responsibilities. Most schools have an effective diffusion and dilution system for information. This essential process, managed by the headteacher and governors, should ensure that teachers stay on the right side of directives and advice, and can be confident that they are operating on secure legal grounds.

The importance of local policy-making

The making of policies and their adoption is essential for every school and for every teacher. But, although it may be that a policy is researched and written from scratch, it most commonly involves the adaptation and personalization of external documents to ensure there is a close fit with the needs of an individual school. Initial readings and discussions may lead to the formation of working groups to come up with a draft policy. The draft is scrutinized by at least the senior management and, unless it is seriously amended by them, it is submitted to the governors for ratification. Finally, it is confirmed as the school's current policy and, therefore, as the expected practice, and it passes into the review timetable. At this point the policy should be shared with everyone who should be following it, for this forms the real working constraint upon every teacher. All staff should only have to refer to the school's own policy on an issue to determine the legality of their own actions.

To achieve this working awareness amongst all relevant parties, schools usually provide each teacher with a staff handbook and keep it updated. It may not matter very much whether a child is admonished for walking on the wrong side of the corridor, but the detention of a child without reference to the school's policy could have serious consequences for a teacher.

Let us suppose that a conscientious teacher keeps back an 11-year-old for half an hour after the end of school to help the child to finish an important piece of work. The child lives close to the school and walks home alone every day. Some 20 minutes later the headteacher and the mother arrive in the class-room and the parent angrily demands the child. The headteacher is not too pleased either. When they are alone the headteacher asks the teacher to refer to the school's policy on detention. Assuming this is a sound document that takes into account the requirements of the Education Act 1996 (DfEE, 1996b, s. 550b), what key element has the teacher overlooked? The policy states that the parents are entitled to 24-hours' notice. This may have been the teacher's only failing in this case, but it is sufficient to render the 'detention' unlawful, however well-intentioned it might have been.

It follows therefore that if teachers must have regard for the policies of their schools, there must, indeed, be policies and everyone should not only be aware of their existence but understand the words within them and their implications. The responsibility for the existence of the full range of localized policies rests with the governing body. In practice this is usually delegated to the headteacher, with the governors keeping a watching brief.

Once the fundamental importance of effective policies is recognized, a com-fortingly large range of pitfalls and stumbling blocks is avoided for the teacher. For example, the consequences of a well-intentioned but incorrect administration of medicine will be avoided, the correct form of restraint will be used for the right reasons, or the appropriate amount of homework will be given. Variations from recommended practice will be judged by outcomes and by the external inspection system, but rarely by the courts.

The right to exclude a child is enshrined in the School Standards and Framework Act (DfEE, 1998c) and that is all a class teacher in a primary school needs to know! The headteacher and governors will liaise with the LEA to ensure that they tread carefully through the minefield of legislation which rightly surrounds the removal of a child's right to a place in a school.

The Human Rights Act 1998

Matters of detention and discipline, even of school uniform if some would have their way, may be called into question under the provisions of the Human Rights Act (HRA) (DfEE, 2000g). It took a generation or two for the UK to sign up to the HRA even after it had itself been a major player in the formation of the European Convention on Human Rights. That delay only served to increase the fears that adoption of the HRA by the UK would lead to unwar-ranted interference in our daily lives and would cause particular difficulties for schools. In fact, although the maintained sector of education is subject to the Act as a 'public authority', there have been few difficulties and no major challenges in the courts over educational matters.

At the time of the Act coming into force the DfEE (2000g, p. 2) said: 'A well-run school, which follows DfEE guidance on admissions, exclusions and special educational needs, will have nothing to fear.' The fact that fairness, lack of discrimination and freedoms are no longer just desirable but rights and entitlements, does mean that here also there must be appropriate policies in place and they must be adhered to. Inside a sound framework, young people can still be disciplined and restrained, made subject to a school dress code and, even, excluded when all else has failed.

The teacher's actions must be proportionate to the offences and fair, factors which present little difficulty for most teachers in their day-to-day dealings with pupils. Exclusion might well be seen as the logical outcome of a dispute over the wearing of school uniform, for example, but the timing of the imposition of that ultimate penalty would be a major factor in determining the proportionality of the school's disciplinary actions. Nonetheless, that children's rights are now positively enshrined in the HRA and that schools are under this particular scrutiny should be seen as sensible and in close harmony with the ideals of an ethically sound community and the promotion of good citizenship skills.

The Teacher and Family Law

Children, teachers and carers in a turbulent society

Many schools and classrooms are oases of calm for children living difficult lives. Many teachers offer themselves as supportive counsellors to those in their care. It is important to understand that such sensitivity and kindness, though often and freely given, is enshrined in legal obligation. That is not to devalue such manifestly good humanity but rather to underpin it and make it consistent and universal.

It should be clear to everyone why schools, and particularly teachers, have such a vital role to play. School staff may be the closest adults to children in need. In the early years particularly, close bonds often exist between vulnerable and abused children and their adult carers and teachers. All reliable analyses of social trends show an unrelenting increase in family breakdown and rearrangement: turbulence and instability permeate the home environment from which so many children come to school to be educated and in which teachers meet their needs. The HRA and much anti-discriminatory and inclusive legislation seek to ensure that each individual is equally valued, but it is the Children Act (DoH, 1989) that has been uniquely far-reaching in its comprehensive reform of children's protection and welfare.

The Children Act 1989

The overriding aim of the Act is to promote and safeguard the welfare of children. It places a duty on all agencies to work together for the benefit of the child. It is aimed particularly at the local authority, most obviously at Social

Services, but emphatically at all those who have a responsible interest in the welfare and safety of children. Those agencies gathering the necessary background information for the court may lean heavily on the school for help. Apart from the obvious factual information, the school may be asked for their assessment of the capability of the parents to meet the child's needs and for another set of views newly enshrined in the Children Act, those of the child. In the aftermath of the Act, school records now need to show new information for teachers, not only to furnish evidence but to take account of directions of the courts as the legal process develops and concludes. Such information includes:

- who has rights over the child;
- where the child must live as defined by any Residence Order in place;
- who else may have access to the child as determined in any Contact Order;
- what action may not be taken by a named individual in a Prohibited Steps Order; and
- what particular action must be taken, consistent with the exercise of parental responsibility, which might form the basis of a Specific Issue Order.

A dispute about religious activity in school might be resolved by a Prohibited Steps Order. A Specific Issue Order might determine a child's next school. Of course, courts are only asked to make these orders when those adults around the child cannot or will not agree. Even then the Act orders the court to try to make no order, because even at the last minute agreement is likely to be in the best interests of the child.

Teachers might find themselves assisting in the working of another of the Act's new orders: the Education Supervision Order (ESO). When an ESO is in place the local authority may be granted control of a child's attendance for up to a year initially, with extensions possible of up to a maximum of three years. The child's attendance at school would be closely monitored by the Pupil Attendance Service, and the school's register of attendance would become a key document.

The welfare checklist

The Act places children at the centre of their own affairs, no longer allowing them to be perceived as possessions of their parents. To ensure that this happened, a welfare checklist was devised and imposed on all assessments. It is here that 'the ascertainable wishes of the child' are called for and teachers are often able to give great assistance in obtaining them most reliably. It is helpful to place the child's wishes in context by recording here all the aspects of the child's life which a court has to take into account, through the welfare checklist:

- the ascertainable wishes and feelings of the child concerned, considered in the light of the child's age and understanding;
- the child's physical, emotional and educational needs;

- the likely effect on the child of any change in circumstances;
- the child's age, sex, background and any characteristics which the court considers relevant;
- any harm which the child has suffered or is at risk of suffering;
- how capable each parent, and any other person in relation to whom the court considers the question to be relevant, is of meeting the child's needs; and
- the range of powers available to the court.

It will readily be seen that those who framed this list sought to allow judges the maximum discretion so that they could take almost anything into account to achieve the best outcome for the future care of the child.

Reports and records

From time to time a teacher may be asked to make a written or oral report to the Social Services or to the court, covering several areas of the welfare checklist. It may be impossible to get a balanced view of the issues around a family when only one natural parent may be in regular contact with the school. Files and records may contain a wealth of material, some factual and some anecdotal. There may be notes of conversations and telephone calls, and the teacher will have work records and perhaps an incident log. There is also the attendance record. Although there may be a great deal of source material, it is absolutely essential that the verbal or written report that leaves the school has integrity. It must be clear and without bias or prejudice. If judgements or recommendations contained within the school's reports are substantiated by facts, they will be useful and in the best interests of the child: a recipe for some peace of mind, even when the evidence that the teacher provides may have far-reaching consequences for the child.

Information-sharing in a protective climate

Every school is required to have a designated teacher for child protection who may take the lead in information-gathering and dissemination. Often in a primary school this is the headteacher. It is vital that schools provide an effective protective climate within which all staff can freely voice concerns and feelings. Teachers need to be able to share seemingly trivial concerns and observations in an atmosphere of respect and complete confidentiality. All staff should understand that the free flow of such information, in an atmosphere of respect and trust, is an essential weapon in the constant battle to break open the secrecy which surrounds the abuse of children and young people. Some minor concerns may amount to a serious case of neglect or abuse which might not otherwise be recognized. Investigating tribunals and courts have more than once severely criticized schools and teachers for the absence of such a protective climate.

Parental responsibility

Significantly for schools, the Children Act (DoH, 1989) introduced the concept of 'parental responsibility' (PR), revising the definition of parents. Suddenly a wider range of people could exercise parental rights. Not only could an unmarried father acquire PR more easily but other family members, those who cohabit and foster parents could do so too, if it could be shown to be in the best interests of the child. Parental responsibility can only be removed on the making of an Adoption Order. In this case the child ceases to be the legal offspring of the original parents. Decisions about who gets a copy of newsletters and the annual school report, who should be consulted about major decisions over educational matters or who has the right to a teacher consultation may now involve a much wider range of people but they are a lot easier to make when the school's own records are up to date and available to teachers.

The two most common issues for teachers around PR are the request for a change of name, and collection from school and access to children during the day.

The request for a change of name
The request for a change of family name seems most irresistible in the case of the child who may be living solely with the mother and her new partner, who are themselves planning to marry and unite their children, under one family name. The request has to be refused, however, at least until the mother can satisfy the school that the child's natural father has given his consent. He retains PR if they were formerly married or he may have acquired it since their separation. If he is out of contact it would be for a family court to decide whether adequate steps have been taken to consult him and, if so, whether a change of name could be made without his consent.

Collection from school and access to children during the day
It is not unusual for a parent who has care of a child under a Residence Order to ask the teacher not to allow collection or contact by the other parent. If the estranged parent has PR and there is no order in existence preventing collection or access, the school has no right to intervene and discriminate between the two parents. The school should not be used as a contact centre for a parent to spend time with a child, but the school might justifiably make an exception when it was felt that to do so would be in the best interests of the child.

The Data Protection Act, 1998

There is a huge array of administration around the Data Protection Act (HMG, 1998), yet for teachers who handle information with discretion and common sense, whether on paper or computer, there should be few problems. The Act does, of course, impose rights and obligations, the key obligation for teachers probably being in relation to disclosure. In the same way that a finance house must show us the information they hold to decide our creditworthiness, so must a school disclose the information it holds to any person who can show an entitlement to that information.

The technicalities of registration and the storing and use of data should not need to be the concern of the teacher. The school will have a policy and it must be followed. However, one aspect of information-gathering must be emphasized to avoid real difficulties. All written records and notes must be fair and free from unsubstantiated judgements. Common sense helps us in determining whether a statement can be written and read by others, and most particularly by the subject, without embarrassment. For example, a teacher should not be taken aback by Mr Jones's angry response when he reads in his son Jimmy's record that 'Mrs Jones has shown herself to be a difficult woman!' The teacher might, more safely, have written, 'Mrs Jones and I had some difficulty in agreeing about the causes of Jimmy's behaviour'. Although Mr Jones might not like to read that either, it is nevertheless a statement of fact that can be substantiated. Schools have, by law, to keep a continuous record of each child under a *unique pupil number* and to pass the main file on to the next school. Records that are free from unwarranted or personal judgements will help to ensure that past crises in the family, or between home and school, do not tarnish the new institution's views of children before they have arrived.

Issues for Reflection

- A teacher's conduct must be 'reasonable'. Is that a fair and adequate threshold?
- A child runs across a classroom, slips near the sand tray and stabs another child with the scissors she is holding out in front of her. What do you think are the legal implications of this incident for the teacher?
- Mum arrives late and fails to find her 7-year-old daughter, who is apt to wander off. The teacher does not know where she is. The routine has always been clear to the child. The teacher, with 32 children in the class, has done all that can reasonably be expected. How would the material in this chapter relate to this incident?
- Should a teacher give an estranged parent a separate interview if it is requested when they know that it is vigorously opposed by the caring parent?
- What might teachers put in a report for a child's legal representative in a disputed care case? Assume that teachers are aware that one parent cares for the child better than the other: should they tell the court how they feel about the parenting?

Summary of Key Points

- The standard of care expected of a teacher has become that of a reasonable teacher. The duty of care is discharged by a process of risk assessment within an effective framework of rules.

- School policies are seen as the practical determinant of the legality of teachers' actions.
- The teacher's role in Family Law is of great importance and the Children Act 1989 made the welfare of the child paramount. Teachers may assist, particularly, in clarifying the ascertainable wishes of young children. Sharing sensitive observations, in a safe and confidential climate, protects vulnerable children most effectively at school.
- The Human Rights Act 1998 has some bearing on schools but best practices have had to change little to accommodate the demands of the Act.
- Teachers need to be aware of the Data Protection Act 1998 when handling information

Suggestions for Further Reading

Books

Suschitzky, W. and Chapman, J. (1998) *Valued Children, Informed Teaching.* Oxford: Oxford University Press. The relationship between the teacher and the pupil, the climate for learning and the influence of the home and community are thoughtfully explored in this book.

Croner Legal Guides (available separately for teachers, headteachers and governors, from Croner Publications Ltd, Croner House, 173 Kingston Road, New Malden, Surrey KT3 3SS). The guides are very comprehensive but expensive for individual teachers. Many schools and institutions make them available for their staff. An update service is available. Loose sheets are sent to replace those in the guide as new Acts of Parliament, statutory instruments and case law make changes to the guide necessary.

Websites

Croner CCH Edinfo-Centre website, www.edinfo-centre.net This site offers up-to-date case law and news, and a free emailed newsletter.

Optimus Publishing website, www.optimuspub.co.uk A monthly 12-page *Education Law Update* is available to subscribers. A free sample issue can be obtained.

Acknowledgement

I would like to acknowledge the help I received from Miss Pam Cary, Assistant County Solicitor, County Hall, Norwich when I was writing this chapter.

6
School Governors

Tony Blake

The following topics and issues are covered in this chapter:

- the role of the governing body in the strategic management of schools;
- the difficulties in recruiting governors, ensuring that they are effective and ways of developing their expertise;
- the contribution that governors can make to school improvement;
- the ways in which governors can oversee the curriculum and the responsibilities that governors have in relation to the curriculum;
- the governors' responsibilities in relation to school buildings;
- the responsibilities that governors have in overseeing the finances of the school and in ensuring that money is spent wisely;
- the ways in which governors contribute to and monitor decisions that are made about staffing and staff development; and
- the role that governors have in drawing up and agreeing the school improvement plan.

Governors are in a strange position. Many have little or no expertise, at least initially, in the areas in which they are asked to work in schools, but successive governments have given them significant responsibilities and power. As a group of 'non-experts' exercising their powers over highly qualified, dedicated and hardworking staff this situation has the potential for conflict. How are we to manage this potential minefield to ensure that governors and school staff work together to create a learning school, continuously improving its teaching provision and the learning of its pupils?

The aim of this chapter is to help teachers understand the role of the governing body in maintained schools in England. In it I suggest that the only way to ensure maximum impact by governors on a school's performance is by a mutual understanding of their role as a *critical friend* by governors and staff. I will explore the manner in which this might be achieved.

Schools have often felt very vulnerable in recent times. Constant new initiatives, pressure from government and LEAs to achieve ever higher targets and the burgeoning amount of paperwork have caused anxiety and stress amongst headteachers and their staff. Governors have to tread a very fine line in fulfilling their legal role and in giving their school strategic direction for improvement without adding to the burden of the staff through whom these improvements are delivered. To challenge, to support and to move the school forward at a pace which engages and energizes staff, that is the daunting task of the school governor in today's schools. In this chapter I consider various ways in which the balance might be maintained and how governors can participate in taking the school forward.

The Role of the Governing Body

The role of school governors is complex and multifaceted. This group of people may, in various combinations, contain parent governors, teacher and staff governors, foundation, co-opted, ex officio and appointed governors. The number of governors may vary according to the size and type of the school. The conduct or overall management of the school is under the direction of the governors who have power and responsibility over:

- admissions;
- children's attendance and behaviour;
- the curriculum;
- SEN provision;
- the length of the school day and the school year;
- premises;
- staffing;
- finance;
- links with parents;
- complaints;
- inspection; and
- performance management.

Recruitment

There is a government initiative to try to encourage more people to become school governors, but the huge number of responsibilities that they now have proves daunting to many well-meaning, community-spirited people who do not feel they have the knowledge and expertise to enter fully into the roles expected of them. A recent edition of *Governors* (DfES, 2003c) cited managing the headteacher as a function of the governing body that some were finding problematic. Being asked to ensure the degree of challenge and rigour needed for effective appraisal can be a major concern for a non-specialist. How many of us would feel able to be involved in similar systems for doctors and lawyers based on the premise that we occasionally use their services?

Expertise and training

The way that most governing bodies go about the business of ensuring that all the areas for which they are responsible are addressed is by creating committees so that members with particular expertise or interest may focus on specific areas. These groups then report back to the full governing body on work carried out and decisions taken. If they are wise, they seek help and advice in discharging their duties. This might come from training supplied by Governor Support Services or from a sharing of expertise by school staff. People may be co-opted to the governing body to provide advice in an area such as the recent Public Finance Initiative. Headteachers have recently been asked (DfES, 2003c) to consider becoming advisers to school governing bodies. The DfES would like to see more serving headteachers take on this role, sharing their management and performance appraisal expertise with governors.

Most governors have their own responsibilities at work and at home, and can find it difficult to devote sufficient time to gaining the expertise that their role demands. Jane Phillips, Chair of the National Association of Governors and Managers, stated recently that 'a lot of governors are very time-restricted and they use this as an excuse not to go to training' (DfES, 2003c, p. 7). The DfES is therefore looking at methods to deliver training through ICT and websites, and in ways which will make it easier for governors to develop their understanding of their role.

Adopting a strategic role

The introduction to *The Governor's Handbook* (Reeves, 2002, p. 4) states that 'being a governor is an enormously important, responsible and rewarding task. It is also one that can be very time-consuming and bewildering'. In order to tackle the conflicting demands on the governor, to minimize the bewilderment and time commitment, and to maximize the positive effect governors can have on the performance of a school, they need to focus on school strategy. Governors are at their most effective when working at a strategic level, focusing on the big idea, vision and values of the school rather than getting bogged down with the details of day-to-day management which is the responsibility of the headteacher. Working in this way allows governors to more easily establish a relationship with a school and its staff which enables them to be both critic and friend.

Governors and School Improvement

Guidance on the law for governors provided by the DfES (GovernorNet website, Information for School Governors) says that the main purpose of the governing body is 'to conduct the school with a view to promoting high standards of educational achievement'. To be effective, the governors' contribution to school improvement, has to be carried out in conjunction with school staff and parents. Attempting to influence the performance of a school without sufficient training and knowledge of the many factors which con-tribute to school effectiveness may cause resentment and resistance among the staff. This would be counter-productive as they are the people who will carry out the improvement agenda. At the other end of the scale, governors who fail to act because they feel that they have inadequate knowledge, or who lack confidence in dealing with difficult issues, also fail to contribute effectively to school improvement. How, then, can governors challenge schools to improve standards without being charged with interfering?

Finding out about standards

First, and fundamentally, governors need to know how well the school is per-forming. There are many ways in which they can gather data to form a picture of present performance. The government supplies a great deal of data to schools and governors about the academic performance of pupils as measured by the end-of-Key-Stage national tests and by the statutory teacher assess-ment. Governors need to understand what this data does or does not say about their school. They need to know about the particular cohort that these results refer to, their attainment when they entered the school and the value-added element that the school has achieved for each child. Bald figures may provide only limited information about how children are achieving.

Government figures show how the school is comparing with similar schools and knowing this gives the governors a wider framework for comparison. However, this may need interrogating further and many governors may need help with this. Performance data and results are important sources of infor-mation for governors but they need to be set in a context if they are to provide a basis for action. For example, if 'similar schools' are indicated only by numbers of parents claiming free school meals for their children this could be misleading. Parents in some areas might prefer to provide their children with a packed lunch rather than claim a free meal (as, in my experience, is often the case in rural areas). A school where this happens might not be comparable with other schools identified as 'similar'. Similarly, a straight comparison of performance between the end-of-Key-Stage-1 assessment (at age 7) and end-of-Key-Stage-2 assessment (at age 11) may also be problematic. It is not easy to compare the performance of a very young child on tests that are taken over a period of time and marked by the teacher with the results of a time-limited, externally marked examination at 11. Far more indication of progress is pro-vided by both ongoing teacher assessment and the QCA tests that many schools use at the end of Years 3, 4 and 5 (when children are aged 8, 9 and 10).

All the learning opportunities provided by the school

In addition to examining data about pupil performance, governors should look at how the school is developing other kinds of skills. These are seen by many in education as of equal importance in preparing pupils for a full life.

Are the children learning to play a musical instrument and what variety of instruments do they have the opportunity to play? Are the children given the opportunity to try different sporting activities, not just football, netball and rounders but canoeing, sailing, squash, tennis, orienteering, skiing and others? How many after-school or lunchtime clubs such as chess, ICT, music and languages does the school provide? Do the children have the opportunity to develop their social skills as well as their academic and general knowledge during day and residential school visits? Are the children provided with the chance to take part in drama, dance, a choir, perhaps an end-of-term play or musical? In order to have this kind of knowledge about their school, governors need to attend as many school events as possible. This can provide them with a picture of the varied opportunities for learning that the school offers and may increase their awareness of what else could be offered. Involvement with all the activities of the school makes the twin role of critic and friend more achievable. Staff are more motivated to act to effect school improvement with governors who they know appreciate them as professionals and are aware of all aspects of the work that they do.

Sources of information

The headteacher's termly report to the governing body, government data, teacher assessments, SEN reports, attendance figures, exclusion data and performance reviews are all available to governors and supply vital information about the school's performance. Performance data alone might reveal very little but being aware of it helps governors to ask appropriate questions. Governors should ask parents what they think of the school. A broad awareness of how parents feel about the provision for their children's education can be gained from a simple questionnaire. Parents can raise issues with governors at the statutory Annual Meeting for Parents or they can contact individual governors, particularly parent governors. Items raised by parents should always be followed up by governors.

Governors and the Curriculum

The National Curriculum

A central function of schools is to provide a wide-ranging curriculum so that children can learn well. The governors have to make sure that this is happening and to do this they need to know about the curriculum. The National Curriculum (DfEE/QCA, 1999) tells schools broadly what children should be taught, but the detail and how it should be delivered is up to each school. Schools must provide teaching in all the statutory subjects and children must be given access to religious education and collective worship. Schools have to promote the spiritual, moral, cultural, intellectual and physical development of children as well as addressing their personal, social and health needs. Most primary schools now deliver sex and drugs education and all are encouraged to follow the non-statutory guidelines on the delivery of personal, social and health education (PSHE) and citizenship across the curriculum. The governing body has a particular responsibility for sex education. They have to establish a sex education policy and ensure that this is available to parents.

Curriculum governors

It is useful if governors have a specific link to an area of the curriculum and report on progress in this area at full governors' meetings. Individual governors often take on responsibility for one or two curriculum areas, so that all curriculum areas are covered by the governing body. This enables individual governors to develop their understanding of a small number of subjects and how they are taught in the school. Having responsibility for subjects enables governors to build relationships with subject leaders. They may discuss the development plan for that subject and report the funding and resource needs of the subject to the full governing body. By working with the subject leader, the link governor is able to gain an understanding of the improvement agenda for the subject for which they are responsible.

Observing teaching and learning

Schools and governors need to draw up an agreed protocol for governor visits to schools and observations of teaching. When governors observe lessons they and the teacher need to be clear about what they are looking for. Are they setting out to find out about teaching methods? Are they trying to gauge if the children are learning and making progress? Lesson observations can be of benefit to both governors and teachers when teachers share the learning objectives of the lesson with the governor prior to the observation and then are able to answer questions after the lesson. It is imperative that a visit to a school by a governor is not seen as an additional pressure by school staff. It should be a two-way interaction with an exchange of information on both sides.

Governors and the community

Another important role that governors have is to take account of the social and economic context of the school and the particular circumstances and needs of the children. As local people they are in an ideal position to make judgements about this. They can use this knowledge when they are looking at the appropriateness of the curriculum, and evaluating policies such as those for teaching and learning, homework and marking. The critical element of the governors' role lies in asking the right questions and to do this they should have a full knowledge of all a school provides, its ethos, aims, objectives and learning provision. Only then can they plan for improvement.

The strategic role of the governors

It would be impossible for governors to have a detailed knowledge of all the content of the curriculum, although their individual links with subject leaders and their reading and approval of school policies helps. However, the governors' role is a strategic rather than a practical one. To fulfil their strategic role they should first ensure that all aspects of the curriculum are actually taught in their school. Second, they should collect evidence that it is being taught well and that the children are learning and making progress. They can receive evidence from inspections, local advisers, comparative data and through reports from the headteacher and subject leaders. If individual governors are observing and monitoring and representing the needs of various subjects to the governing body as a whole, then all governors will be appraised of changes and progress in all areas of the curriculum.

It is important that governors understand the difference between governance and management. Governors set the aims and principles of the curriculum, oversee the school's provision and make sure that the school is working within all relevant laws. They should make sure that a school's plans, polices and practice support the provision of a broad, balanced and differentiated curriculum that allows all children to learn and achieve. The headteacher manages the organization and delivery of the curriculum on a day-to-day basis within the framework set by governors. Thorough knowledge of what goes on within this framework is beneficial to governors and the critical element of their role, as it helps them to ask the right questions.

Governors and School Premises

Buildings

School improvement includes managing and improving the environment for teaching and learning. An interest in this area shows staff and children that the conditions in which they work are important to the governors. Some governing bodies may have someone among them with expertise in building matters, but some may not. A premises committee is usually seen as the best way effectively to manage the school's building needs. People with particular interest or expertise are usually members of this group, but they may also co-opt people with the necessary skills and buy in advice from the LEA or outside bodies if necessary.

The governing body has to control the use of school premises both during and outside the school day, and to decide on the charges to levy on external users of the premises. Most schools actively encourage the use of their buildings by suitable external groups. This can bring valuable income into the school budget and can also place the school firmly at the centre of community activity. Governors are usually enthusiastic about developing the school's role in the community but they need to make sure, via the headteacher and staff, that this does not result in damage to classrooms and equipment. Teething problems in after-school use can usually be rectified in a positive way by goodwill and effective liaison between the parties concerned. The headteacher normally takes day-to-day charge of who can enter school premises and advises the governing body where appropriate.

Health and safety

Health and safety is a very important factor in the use of school premises, both during the day, by staff and children, and in after-school activities. In most schools, representatives of the premises committee carry out regular checks on the condition of the buildings. It is the responsibility of the governing body to ensure that the school has a health and safety policy and that risk assessments are carried out. In Foundation and VA schools the governors are legally responsible for health and safety. In Community and VC schools the LEA has the ultimate responsibility. It is the headteacher's duty to comply with LEA and governing body directions. The premises committee, working with the headteacher, is responsible for seeing that the school has adequate insurance, making sure that there is a strategy for budgeting for repairs and building improvements and ensuring that health and safety issues are met. An agreed school premises plan plays an integral part in the school improvement plan.

Finances

Best value

Throughout the decision-making process on how money is spent in the school the governors and staff have to make sure that they follow a best-value policy. This ensures that funds are not wasted and that the staff are enabled to go about their teaching duties with the best resources available, within normal budgetary constraints. The premises committee then have to take note of the best-value policy in making recommendations about building needs. All committees need to take note of the tenets of the policy, but it is the finance committee that has an essential role in formulating the policy.

The generally accepted principles of best value are indicated by the 4 Cs. These are:

- challenge;
- consult;
- compete; and
- compare.

In challenging, the governing body is asking why something is done. Asking 'why?' shows that the governing body has high expectation of everyone and this contributes to their role in setting ambitious targets for school improvement. Challenging questions can open up the possibilities of change and prevent stagnation.

Through consultation, the governing body shows that it requires clear information about the school, it consults on major changes, actively seeks a wide variety of opinions and keeps people informed of the results of its consultation.

The competing aspect ensures that governors employ robust financial procedures to get the best service at the best price, that financial decisions are made in the best interests of children and parents, that satisfaction with services is monitored and that alternative sources of supplies and services are regularly investigated.

Finally, in comparing, governors use a wide range of data to compare the performance of their school with others on many different levels and ensure that decisions about school spending are made with a view to cost-effectiveness. If the 4-Cs approach is carried out with efficiency it can greatly enhance the performance of governors in their roles and can effectively include both the critical and friend elements.

Overseeing the budget

The decisions of the finance committee have a great effect on the efficient running of the school. In law, the governing body as a corporate body is responsible for all the money received by the school. This includes the core budget, funding from the DfES, grants, bursaries, gifts and donations made by parents, community members or companies. The governors may be able to generate additional funding themselves. This includes income from letting the school premises, charging for school activities, grants from government or other sources, bursaries, donations, sponsorship from local businesses and fund-raising in the school community. All the money that the school has is the core from which staff are paid, services purchased and resources provided. It is held on trust by the governing body and must be managed wisely in order to raise standards for the children in the school. Decisions about spending affect the education provision at the school and therefore the teaching and learning that take place there.

Governors have major decisions to make on the priorities for the use of the school budget. These priorities, in addition to ensuring that there are enough teachers, teaching assistants, caretakers, cleaners, road crossing patrols, books, computers and so on, is formulated and detailed in the school improvement plan. Funding must be provided for staff training and for cover to enable staff to attend courses during school time. The training is linked to either school priorities or individual development priorities linked to appraisal and performance management. The action plan following an OFSTED inspection also has financial implications for training and resources that have to be addressed. Budget plans have to show spending plans for the current and future years, usually up to three years ahead.

In addition to the spending necessary to keep the school functioning at a high level, the finance committee has to have a plan for covering the school against contingencies or emergencies in the short term. They can only save money which is surplus to requirements as the budget should be spent to benefit the children in the school at that time. Money should not be saved unless there is a good, planned reason for doing so.

The day-to-day handling of the budget falls to the headteacher, but it should be monitored regularly by the finance committee, who report back to the full governing body. Additional monitoring takes place by the LEA finance department and auditors. Financial management is also an important focus for OFSTED inspections. A monthly budget control report is generated to indicate patterns of expenditure and the pattern of spending against the plan for the year. Having checked that actual spending follows the agreed plan, governors also have to ensure that the spending has given value for money. Careful spending by the governing body to ensure that teachers have the right tools for the job and that they are well supported by teaching assistants and relevant training can contribute to a positive working atmosphere in the school, which in turn can help to raise staff morale.

When governors visit schools they become aware of the additional resources that teachers and children need. This awareness can help them to make the budget relevant to improving teaching and learning. The governors' vigilance about how the school budget is spent is shown to parents through a financial statement in the governors' annual report to parents. This is a public expression of their accountability.

Staffing

Governors are responsible for the staffing of the school. As the school staff are the people who make things happen they need to be treated with professional respect and given the right resources and trust to do the job. Without the commitment and goodwill of a dedicated, skilled and well-motivated group of staff, the vision of the headteacher and governors will not be realized. Staff are far more likely to respond to the challenge if they know they are appreciated and that their goals are shared and understood by the governing body. Governors will want to get to know members of staff, support them in what they are doing and understand their work with children. They need to know what is happening in the school and how people are getting on in order to make better informed decisions about the school and the staff. However, managing and leading the staff is the job of the headteacher, and governors do not take up specific personal issues on behalf of members of staff.

Appointments

The governing body has several important strategic responsibilities for the staffing of the school. It is likely that a personnel committee will carry out many of these responsibilities. As staffing inevitably uses up the majority of a school's budget, some schools have effectively combined personnel and finance issues by establishing a single committee covering both of these concerns. The governors' role in deciding how many people should work in a school and what kind of staff they should be is a fundamental one, particularly in a primary school. All curriculum areas require expertise, and governors should be alert to the need to recruit teachers who will give the school a vital balance in terms of curriculum skills. Schools also need well-trained teaching assistants who can work with children to develop their numeracy, literacy and other subject skills. Governors need to take advice from the headteacher and staff on where support is needed to enable teachers to teach most effectively and, budget permitting, to ensure that teachers and children have the classroom support they need to maximize learning. Perhaps the most fundamental role that the governors have is to appoint a headteacher for the school, as the quality of the headteacher is a significant factor in raising school achievement.

Performance management

In addition to ensuring that the school is staffed with skilled teachers with a variety of curriculum strengths, it is the governors' duty to ensure that the school has a suitable performance management policy, which is effective in understanding teachers' needs, recognizing achievement and setting challenging targets for improvement. This duty does not involve governors in the actual appraisal of individual teachers; this is the headteacher's responsibility. However, they are directly involved in appraising the performance of the headteacher and setting targets for next year. They may enlist the help of an outside adviser to appraise the headteacher. Governors must ensure, via the headteacher, that money is available to fund training needs identified as part of the performance management cycle. Failure to do this lowers morale and lowers the status of the entire appraisal process. Governors do not have access to the final appraisal statements of staff, which are confidential to the appraiser and appraisee, but they must support the staff in trying to achieve their targets.

Staff pay

Decisions about staff pay also have to be made by the governing body. Working with the headteacher, it is important that they explore issues of fairness and parity, and establish a pay policy and structure that enables staff to progress up their professional ladder. Teachers' pay structures are governed by the legally binding *School Teachers' Pay and Conditions* document published annually by the DfES. Governors must work within the provisions of this document, although they have some flexibility. They have to consider a salary range for each member of the leadership group, usually the headteacher and any deputy or assistant headteachers. This salary range is usually based on the size of the school. The salaries of the leadership group are reviewed each year with the governors taking account of the performance review of the headteacher and, for deputy and assistant headteachers, the advice of the headteacher.

Currently, the progress of teachers up the basic pay spine is virtually auto-matic, but this still needs to be ratified by governors on the headteacher's advice. Teachers who reach the top of the basic pay spine may apply to the headteacher to cross the threshold. This involves an assessment of their work against several criteria which is ratified by an external assessor. Once on this upper pay spine, teachers may continue to progress up the spine at two-yearly intervals on the recommendation of the headteacher. Only a proportion of the threshold pay-ments are paid into the school's budget and this is therefore an addition to overall staff costs. Additional allowances may also be given for management responsibilities, recruitment and retention, and for working with children with SEN. The flexibility that governors have when making decisions about pay brings with it a requirement to formulate a framework that is equitable and that can be funded. Decisions to be made about which roles deserve management allowances, which responsibilities within the school warrant recruitment and retention points, and whether the budget can afford to subsidize threshold pay-ments for deserving teachers can be problematic. If a previous year's threshold payments have been allowed it could be seen as very unfair to withhold pay-ments from teachers the following year because of budgetary pressures.

There will always be teachers who feel they are not being treated correctly with regard to payments above the basic pay scale, but if the governors have an open, fair and transparent policy which is scrupulously followed and if deci-sions are backed with good evidence, then staff are more likely to feel appre-ciated and have a sense of being fairly treated.

Other staff issues

Governors also have a role to play in times of industrial action, redundancy and redeployment, and in dealing with complaints about staff conduct and capability. National, LEA and school policies exist, giving advice on the han-dling of all these matters. If governors adhere steadfastly to these stated poli-cies and follow recommended procedures with the help of their LEA, then they are seen to carry out what is often a difficult role with equity.

The School Improvement Plan

The school improvement plan is a very important document. It sets out what the school wants to achieve in the next three to five years. It contains targets for improvement in the areas that the school has prioritized and shows how the school will work towards these targets. All the information that governors collect through their, committee work, observations and involvement with the school can be used when governors contribute to and approve the school improvement plan.

Throughout this chapter I have mentioned ways in which governors might ensure that they have a full knowledge of the school's performance in the widest possible sense. This is necessary if governors are to contribute to school improvement and agree realistic and challenging targets. After full consultation with staff, with input from all subject leaders via governor links and possibly a meeting with the school management team, a joint group of governors and staff should begin to draw up the school improvement plan. Although it is a long-term plan, it is evaluated and updated every year, which gives continuity with previous years but flexibility to include both new government initiatives and emerging priorities for the school.

The plan may include a number of elements based on school priorities. The setting of these priorities is a whole-school task and a wise governing body includes all interested parties in discussion before formulating them. The resulting document represents challenging objectives, aspirations and targets shared by the whole-school community. In this, the involvement of the governing body can be as both critic and friend in that they can ensure that the targets set for academic achievement are realistic yet rigorous, but that they work to give staff and students the maximum opportunity to achieve these targets by the provision of a good working environment, suitable class sizes and high-quality resources.

The role of the governor is a complex one. To get the balance right in all areas of their responsibility is a major task but one which is worth striving for. Governors can ensure that they are fulfilling the strategic element of their work by participating in training and in gaining as much knowledge as they can about the school, its staff, children and parents, its needs as regards resources, finance, buildings and staffing. They can join with the headteacher and staff in planning for improvement and raising standards. A thorough and sympathetic knowledge of all aspects of the school and the staff's day-to-day involvement with children reinforces the perception of governors as friends of the school and makes the critical element of their role more acceptable and therefore more effective.

Issues for Reflection

- Schools often have difficulty in recruiting school governors. Why do you think this is? Why should people become school governors? What might they get out of this work?
- What does the term 'critical friend' mean? Is it possible for governors to be both critics and friends?
- Can governors make a positive difference to the performance of a school? How?
- Is it possible to have non-professionals effectively involved in a professional situation? What difficulties might arise and what are the benefits of involving outsiders in the management of schools?

Summary of Key Points

- Governors play a part in helping schools to move forward. To do this the governing body acts as a critical friend to the headteacher and to the school.

- As critical friends governors offer support and constructive advice, act as a sounding board for ideas and proposals, and provide help when it is needed. Critical friends can also challenge, ask questions, seek information, improve proposals and so seek to arrive at the best solution.
- The governing body needs to have oversight of all aspects of the school including the curriculum, buildings, finances and staffing.
- The role of the governing body is a strategic one. This includes setting up a strategic framework for the school, setting its aims, setting policies and targets, reviewing progress and reviewing the strategic framework in the light of progress.
- To do their job well governors need to become involved in the life of the school and undertake training.
- All the information about the school that governors have can contribute to the school improvement plan. This is drawn up in partnership with the headteacher and school staff and then approved and monitored by the governing body. The school improvement plan provides the strategic framework for the school and is used to guide the future development of the school and the education it provides.

Suggestions for Further Reading

Books and booklets

DfEE (2000) *Roles of Governing Bodies and Head Teachers*. London: DfEE. This is a concise and very clear overview of the duties of governing bodies. It provides a useful starting point for those wanting to find out about what governing bodies do.

DfES (2001) *A Guide to the Law for School Governors*. London: DfES. This publication contains all the regulations that apply to governors. It is updated regularly. It is available as hard copy and on the Governornet website (see below).

DfEE (1999) *The National Numeracy Strategy: Information for Governors*. London: DfEE. National Literacy Trust (1998) *A Literacy Guide for School Governors*. London: National Literacy Trust. These two booklets contain very useful information for all governors but especially for those with responsibility for literacy or numeracy. They suggest ways in which governors can learn about the curriculum that is offered in schools.

Website

Governornet website, Information for School Governors, www.governornet.co.uk The governors' website contains useful up-to-date information for school governors on all aspects of school governance and has links to other useful sites.

7
Parents and Teachers Working Together

Ann Browne

The following topics and issues are covered in this chapter:

- the history of parental involvement in schools;
- current requirements and expectations for parental involvement in schools;
- reasons for parents and teachers to work together;
- parents' and teachers' perspectives on home–school partnership;
- some barriers to parental involvement;
- how to form positive partnerships;
- parents' and teachers' expectations of each other;
- initial contact between schools and parents;
- different forms of written communication with parents;
- advice on writing for parents;
- involving parents in school during the school day;
- involving parents for whom daytime help is difficult;
- the school in the community;
- involving parents at home through homework, games and home–school note-books;
- meetings between parents and teachers; and
- helping parents to understand the education system.

This chapter is about teachers and parents working together. Parents are a child's first and enduring educators. Teachers are professionals with a knowledge of education including knowing what children need to learn and be able to do in order to succeed at school. When parents and teachers share their knowledge about children and education there are benefits both to children's attitudes to school and to their learning.

The History of Parental Involvement

The 1970s

The benefits of parental involvement in education are now readily accepted by parents and educators. There is a large body of literature that provides evidence of the gains in pupil achievement that can accrue when parents actively support their children's learning at home and in school. Before 1970 few parents were actively encouraged by schools to become involved in their children's education and most parents had little contact with teachers. School and home, parents and teachers, were quite separate. The starting point for the change that began to take place in the 1970s was the Plowden Report, *Children and their Primary Schools* (CACE, 1967, p. 43; see also Chapter 1), in which it was suggested that 'by involving the parents, the children may be helped'. The report contained a number of radical suggestions for involving parents more fully in the life of the schools including:

- parent–teacher associations (PTAs);
- freedom for parents to choose schools;
- home visits by teachers;
- community schools;
- pre-school contact with parents;
- meetings between parents and teachers;
- school open days;
- provision of information about the school; and
- provision of reports for parents.

The momentum of the 1980s

Progress towards the Plowden recommendations was slow and patchy. Even by the beginning of the 1980s parents' contacts with teachers and the formal aspects of children's schooling in many schools were often limited to parents' evenings, end-of-term concerts, sports days and fund-raising events. Few parents were involved in classroom activities and most had little understanding of the curriculum or teaching methods. During the 1980s a number of research reports again drew attention to the benefits of primary schools involving parents more fully in the education of their children. These reports were particularly about parental involvement in reading. The most significant were the Haringey Project (Tizard et al., 1982), the Belfield Reading Project (Hannon and Jackson, 1987), Hackney Parents, Children and Teachers (Griffiths and Hamilton, 1984) and the Kirklees Paired Reading Initiative (Bushell, Miller and Robson, 1982). There were a number of similar initiatives throughout the 1980s and their cumulative effect changed the climate for parental involvement. They convinced teachers that parents could make a significant contribution to children's learning and they widened the focus of parental involvement to include the home as well as the school.

More recent developments

During the 1990s parental involvement became almost routine and, today, both parents and teachers expect that parents will be involved in primary children's learning at home or at school (Bastiani and Wolfendale, 1996). The growth of parental involvement in children's education received continuous government and official support throughout the 1990s, beginning with the Education Reform Act 1988 (DfE, 1988).

In this Act it was stated that children's learning must be formally assessed and parents must be informed of the results. As a result parents were, and continue to be, notified of their own child's results in end-of-Key-Stage national tests. Each school's results are published widely in the form of league tables for Year 6 pupils and in school prospectuses and governors' annual reports to parents for Year 2 and Year 6 pupils. This information helps parents to see how well their child is doing in relation to other pupils of the same age and has encouraged parents to find out about what their child is learning and how well they are being taught.

The Children Act (DoH, 1989) gave official recognition to the important role of parents in their child's education. In 1998 guidance on home–school agreements and homework (DfEE, 1998d; 1998e) sought further to increase parents' commitment to their child's education and their school and to involve them more fully in children's formal learning at home. The *Curriculum Guidance for the Foundation Stage* (DfEE/QCA, 2000, p. 9) includes as one of its key principles the importance of partnership between parents and teachers in order to bring about 'a positive impact on children's development and learning'.

In 2001 the SEN Code of Practice (DfES, 2001a) emphasized that partnership with parents is essential if children's needs are to be assessed thoroughly. The document stresses the need to promote effective levels of collaboration and communication between parents and schools. Alongside this raft of legislation the present government is promoting a number of high-profile educational initiatives, including in 1997 Education Action Zones (EAZs) (DfEE, 1997), followed later by Excellence in Cities (DfEE, 2000b). These are regeneration programmes that are intended to boost educational achievement by underperforming pupils by involving families who are at risk of being marginalized from mainstream education. Sure Start is another recent multimillion pound government initiative with an emphasis on partnership between parents, education and health services.

Research, legislation and policy over the past 20 or so years have all contributed to the present situation where teachers and parents alike appreciate the benefits of communication and collaboration in order to foster children's learning. However, despite this recognition, sustained contact and involvement is not always easy to establish and maintain. Schools may be constrained by resources. Levels of expectation of both partners need to be realistic and schools have to treat all pupils and parents as individuals with different priorities, ambitions and needs. No one system will meet the needs of all teachers, parents and children, and so schools need to develop their own detailed parental involvement strategies (DfES, 2003a).

Why Parents and Teachers Should Work Together

Schools have to work with and consult parents because the legislation contained within the Education Reform Act (DfE, 1988), the Children Act (DoH, 1989) and the SEN Code of Practice (DfES, 2001a) has made it a legal requirement. But what are the specific and demonstrable benefits to children, parents and teachers? These are summarized below:

- Research into parental involvement, summarized by Dyson and Robson (1999), provides evidence that involving parents in children's learning is likely to enhance the attainment of children and improve their attitudes to learning.
- If parents become involved in children's early education they are more likely to maintain this involvement.
- Parents know and understand their children very well. If they can share their knowledge, teachers can build upon children's previous experiences and interests when planning the curriculum.
- Children are more likely to feel secure and to accept school norms if they know that their parents and their teachers communicate, have good relationships and share educational values.
- When teachers and parents share information there is the opportunity to find solutions to problems that are acceptable to both parties and that can be reinforced at school and at home.
- Parents have a wealth of expertise and they may be able to draw on this to contribute to, and enrich, the experience of all children.
- Parents are likely to have positive attitudes towards teachers and school which can result in more positive pupil attitudes and behaviours and higher school attendance.
- Parents may develop higher expectations for their children and, in the long term, this may result in a greater likelihood of children completing school and attending college.
- Parents may grow in self-confidence and decide to continue their own education.
- Teachers have the opportunity to learn more about children's experiences and their parents' values, and the more they know about pupils the better they can provide for their learning.

The Parents' Perspective

Who is a parent?

The legal answer to this question is given in Chapter 5. Given that starting point, it is easy for teachers, who have a clear, professional focus on pupil learning and educational initiatives, to forget that parents are people too. Parents may work, have domestic chores to do, have responsibilities to members of their immediate and extended family, and have their own leisure interests and hobbies. They could be renovating a house, caring for an elderly relative or studying for a degree. While the well-being of their children is of central importance to parents and they will want their children to learn and succeed at school, their child's educational development is not the only thing that they have to think about. While subscribing wholeheartedly to the idea of parental involvement, there can be impediments. Think of a family breakfast time, where in the midst of the bustle of cereal, milk and orange juice, making packed lunches and the fastening of outdoor clothing, the child produces her reading book. Time to learn that list of spellings or collect information about coffee production has run out. There is only just so much time in the day.

Teachers and parents

Listening to children read and helping them with their mathematics home-work are important, but these are not the only ways in which parents con-tribute to children's success at school. Perhaps the most important way in which parents influence children's learning is through the transmission of atti-tudes to education and school. Parents who value education and learning are likely to make a significant contribution to children's attainment because their children will have positive attitudes to school and school work as well as edu-cational aspirations. Parents also provide a home curriculum that is independ-ent of the school curriculum. They provide children with conversations, activities and opportunities for learning about the world.

Teachers can sometimes forget about the significant contribution that parents make to children's learning before and beyond formal schooling. They can become overly concerned with tests and targets and lose their broader vision of what education and learning are for. Home and school both con-tribute to children's education in different and in complementary ways. The difference enables the child to have a rich learning experience. The overlap, where parents become involved in school tasks and where teachers take note of information from parents and children about interests and achievements out of school, makes it even richer.

Barriers to parental involvement

There are a number of barriers to parental involvement. Most parents are interested in their children's education but many do not know what schools expect from them, or how they can contribute to their child's schooling. They may not know how best to help their child, even if they wish to because they do not have sufficient knowledge or understanding of how different areas of the curriculum are taught. Increasingly, children live with parents who both work or with a single parent. In either case it may be difficult for these parents to be involved during the school day. In some cultures there is no tradition of parental involvement in school (see also Chapter 13) and some styles of school management do not encourage collaboration between parents and teachers. A clear school policy and thoughtfully considered procedures for working with parents are central to effective parental involvement. Schools where parents are actively welcomed as part of the school working community are likely to have good teacher–parent relations. However, encouraging and supporting parents' involvement in their children's learning demands time and energy, so commitment is crucial. This may especially be the case in areas of social deprivation where there may be little history of parental involvement and where some parents may have negative memories of school and authority. Finally, teachers must feel positive about working with parents.

Negative feelings about parents and their contribution to their children's education make it difficult for teachers to form effective partnerships with parents and can breed resentment, anxiety and frustration amongst them. Negative assumptions about parents' attitudes and understandings can make communication difficult. Sometimes teachers make assumptions about the parents' role in contributing to a child's difficulties, or assume that parents are unwilling to recognize the reality of the child's situation. It can be difficult when parents challenge decisions made by the teacher or by the school, but it is not helpful to regard parents as adversaries. While teachers may be the experts on education, parents know their children better than a teacher who works with 30 or more children for a limited time each day and for less than two-thirds of the year, so it is always worth listening to what they have to say.

Positive partnerships

In order to work effectively with parents, teachers need attitudes that will help them to develop positive partnerships. Hornby (2000) suggests that genuineness and respect for parents' opinions, even when they run counter to their own, are the key to good relationships. They should try to develop empathy with parents and attempt to see the child's situation from the point of view of the parents. Most parents appreciate teachers who are able to be open and honest about their children, who are able to communicate with sensitivity and who are able to be realistic and constructive in their response to children. Good interpersonal skills, including listening and assertiveness skills all help.

Parents' and teachers' expectations

Hornby (2000) asked parents and teachers what they want from each other. Although there are some differences between the responses from each group there are also many similarities and complementary expectations.

The main things parents want is for teachers to:

- consult them more and listen to their point of view;
- be open and approachable;
- be willing to admit it if they do not know something;
- treat all children with respect;

- make allowances for individual differences between children;
- identify and attempt to remediate learning difficulties;
- discuss their children's progress at informative and well-run parent–teacher conferences;
- correct classwork and homework regularly;
- provide regular detailed reports on their children's progress;
- be involved with PTAs; and
- make more use of parents as a resource for teaching and for their own child's learning.

The main things teachers want is for parents to:

- be open with them about children's special needs or health problems;
- tell them about any home circumstances which could affect pupils;
- co-operate in reinforcing school discipline at home;
- help reinforce the school programme at home through such things as supervising homework or listening to children read;
- have realistic expectations of what their children are capable of doing;
- attend meetings with teachers to discuss children's progress;
- read and acknowledge reports and letters sent home; and
- volunteer to help out in various ways in school.

Hornby summarizes the optimum relationship between parents and teachers as one in which 'teachers are viewed as experts on education and parents are viewed as experts on their children. The relationship between teachers and parents can then be a partnership which involves the sharing of expertise and control in order to provide optimum education for all children' (Hornby, 2000, p. 20). The four key elements of such a partnership are two-way communication, mutual support, joint decision-making and the enhancement of learning at school and at home.

Establishing and Maintaining Contact between School and Home

Initial contact

The first contact that many parents have with their child's school occurs when they visit the school to confirm that they want a place or they place their child's name on the waiting list. During these visits headteachers usually show the parents around the school and will take them into classes and show them what the school can offer. Parents can ask questions and examine resources. In some schools parents may be shown around by children. The first thing that parents see when they visit schools is the internal and external environment. They will notice whether the grounds and the school are well cared for and whether they are child and parent friendly. Apart from the welcome they receive from the headteacher and other staff, they will notice whether there are other signs that parents are valued by the school. In the entrance hall there may be a parent noticeboard, displays that explain the curriculum and the work that the children are doing, and invitations to parents to contribute to school work. They may see evidence of their own culture and language in displays. They may observe parents working with children in the classes that they visit.

Schools usually arrange a pre-admission meeting for the parents of children who are new to the school. These meetings are an opportunity for teachers to explain the curriculum, the routines, the ethos and the philosophy to parents. The meetings should also be an opportunity for parents to talk about their expectations and their children, and to ask questions.

Some schools are able to release Nursery and Reception staff to visit parents and new entrants at home. This can be an excellent opportunity for teachers to learn about children's interests and experiences, and to begin to establish a relationship with children and their parents. Often teachers will take photographs and school-made booklets showing school activities. These are a good starting point for a discussion about the curriculum and styles of teaching. They may ask parents and children to begin to make a booklet at home which contains pictures of the child, the family, favourite toys and books, interests and likes and dislikes. This enables parents to tell teachers about their child and teachers can learn a great deal from these booklets that are brought in when the child begins school.

Written communication

After these early meetings most parents may have little direct or sustained contact with school staff apart from parents' meetings or open days and, so, communication will take place largely through writing. Parents will have been given a copy of the school prospectus when they made their first visit to the school. As well as containing useful information about routines, the curriculum and the way teaching is organized, these are often lively booklets with pictures and comments contributed by the pupils. There may also be a section about partnership, with some suggestions about how parents can become involved in children's learning at home and at school. Another early and important written communication that parents receive from the school is the home–school agreement. This is a statement explaining the school's responsibilities towards its pupils and the parents' responsibilities from the school's perspective. Parents and children are asked to agree to a number of requirements that support learning. They and the child's teacher or headteacher all sign the document. Schools and governors, who have responsibility for ensuring that there is a home–school agreement, usually take great care to ensure that this document is written in a way that appreciates the contribution that parents make to their child's education. Figure 7.1 is an example of such an agreement used by a local first school.

Other regular written communication includes school newsletters and school reports. Newsletters give parents essential administrative information about dates of terms and meetings and can contain reminders about school concerns such as punctuality. They should also contain information about the

HOME–SCHOOL AGREEMENT

The School

The school shall do its best to:

- Encourage a love of learning
- Provide a broad balanced curriculum and quality education
- Meet the needs of your child as far as possible within an environment where all have the opportunity to succeed
- Be open and welcoming and offer you opportunities to become involved in the life of the school
- Keep you informed about school matters and your child's progress
- Care for your child's safety and happiness.

Signed (Headteacher) (Chair of Governors)

Parents/Carers

I/We shall do my/our best to:

- Support my child in learning at school and home
- Support the school policies and guidelines for behaviour
- See that my child attends school regularly, on time and properly equipped
- Attend school events and open evenings and to discuss my child's progress
- Let the school know about any concerns or problems that might affect my child's work or behaviour
- Value my child's achievements.

Signed (Parent/Carer)

Child

I shall do my best to:

- Learn
- Take part in school life
- Accept responsibility for my actions
- Respect children, adults and property in school
- Be helpful and co-operative
- Help others feel happy.

Signed (Pupil)

Figure 7.1.   Example of a home–school agreement

work that the children are doing and suggestions for home activities related to the work. Copies of songs or rhymes that the children are learning may also be sent home in the newsletter, as well as suggestions about weekend or holiday activities. They can be a means of disseminating information about new resources or current initiatives. Many schools like to celebrate children's achievements in the newsletter. Newsletters are an important way of giving all parents information about the daily life of the school and about what their children are doing and learning.

All parents receive an annual report on their child's progress, usually towards the end of the summer term. They can vary greatly in style, organization and content. They may contain brief comments about the work the child has done and the progress that has been made in each area of the curriculum, but they can go beyond this. They can give specific examples of the child's achievements and strengths and show how the child has met individual learning targets. They may also specify what the child will need to work at during the next school year and suggest new learning targets. Most reports contain a space for parents to respond to what has been written and so they can be an opportunity for dialogue about learning and about individual children.

Parents also receive letters from teachers about school visits and special events to which parents are invited, such as sports day or end-of-term productions. In some schools the children write some of these letters and this is a good way of encouraging parents to read them. Occasionally, teachers may need to write to parents about a child's problems with learning or behaviour. These letters need to be written with care and sensitivity. Teachers might also write to parents about significant achievements. Doing this prevents parents from opening all personal letters from school with dread. Less personal but nevertheless informative and significant are the annual report on the school that governors send to parents and the summary of OFSTED inspections which parents receive about once every four years. The governors' report may serve as a reminder to parents that, through the elected parent-governor, parents have a representative who will make sure that any parent concerns will be discussed, responded to and, if appropriate, be attended to by the governors and staff (see Chapter 6).

Writing for parents

Written communications between school and home are important. They give parents the opportunity to reflect on important information about their child or school matters. They also make sure that all parents receive the same, rather than second-hand, information and they are easy to refer to when there is time or information is needed. In order for parents to get the most out of letters, newsletters and reports written communication needs to be simple, short and human (McConkey, 1985). The following guidelines might help.

- Keep sentences short.
- Avoid jargon and technical terms.
- Avoid using unnecessary words and phrases such as 'at the present time' instead of 'now'.
- Avoid confusion by being direct – say what you mean.
- Use positive statements even when expressing a negative; saying, 'Jane's absences have affected her progress' is better than 'Jane's poor attendance means that she has not made progress'.

- Use precise and common words such as 'trying' rather than 'endeavouring'.
- Avoid telling parents what they already know, as in 'Tom has a bubbly personality'.

Diagrams, cartoons, children's drawings and photographs can enliven a written text and can help to get the message across. It may be necessary to think about translating some written communication into the children's home languages. The LEA may be able to help with this. For parents who have reading difficulties it may be possible to produce a tape-recording of the prospectus, newsletters and reports. Increasing numbers of parents now have access to the Internet and, so, schools are beginning to make written material available on their websites. Having the school prospectus on the computer may help to solve the common problem of mislaid pieces of paper.

Involving Parents in School

During the school day

Some parents like to offer to help in school during the school day. They can be a valuable asset to teachers, especially if they are given support and the tasks they are given match their skills and experience. Many parents find great pleasure in working in school and discover renewed confidence in themselves or new skills that can lead them to further their own education. A significant number of parent helpers are inspired by the experience in school to become TAs or teachers themselves.

Some schools have established parent rooms. These can be used to develop a network for parents, and in some areas provide parents with a safe and support-ive place to be. A basic requirement for such a room might be chairs, a fridge, a kettle and toys and books for any under school-age children accompanying the parents. Some schools use parent rooms as a forum for meetings, advice and adult learning. A parents' room may house a toys and games library and a collection of books for parents to borrow or be used for the exchange of second-hand clothes and equipment. Parents who are least likely to volunteer or spend time with teachers may be attracted into school if there is a parents' room.

Involving parents for whom daytime help is difficult

It is not always easy for parents to be involved during the school day and some may not feel that working in the classroom is their forte. However, all parents have skills that can benefit a primary school. Most parents, and many grand-parents, are happy to contribute in a variety of ways other than as classroom helpers, so it is useful for the teacher to get to know about their interests, skills and experience. For example, one local school that uses parent helpers exten-sively during the day also calls upon parents at weekends, in the evenings or for the occasional day. Help has included the laying of a pavement, pond clearance, production of a newsletter, additional adult help on school visits, the making of games and resources, including reading games and book bags, the building of willow cabins and fences, story-telling and country dancing. Other parents are happy to raise money and organize social events, or to give professional advice. Some parents might be willing to come into school to talk about the work they do or a project they have undertaken. Other parents can become involved through their membership of the PTA, as a school governor or by being involved in a parent support group.

The school in the community

Increasingly, schools are widening their role in the community through the provision of breakfast clubs, homework clubs, after-school child care and adult learning opportunities that cater for a range of parents' and children's needs. This is resulting in a breaking down of barriers between home and school. These developments are compatible with the conception of an EAZ (DfEE, 1997) where the school is a central location but it operates in partnership with families and other agencies and organizations. They also begin to meet the vision of a school as 'a centre of community learning' providing flexible learning opportunities for children and adults of all ages (RSA, 1998).

Involving Parents at Home

Homework

Homework in the primary phase is usually fairly informal and mostly takes the form of home tasks or 'joint learning tasks' (Bastiani, 1989). Formal homework is unlikely to be introduced until children are preparing for the national tests in Year 6. One of the most common forms of homework in primary schools is reading. Children in Key Stage 1 and the Foundation Stage take books home to read and enjoy with parents. For the youngest children the homework may involve parents reading to their child and talking about the book. More experienced readers may read to their parents, other adults or even a brother or sister. Parents of fluent readers may be asked to make sure that their child reads silently for 20 minutes a couple of times a week and may be asked to talk to their child about their reading. The nature of the homework will vary according to the age and needs of the child.

There are other forms of homework that children can be asked to undertake and, as far as possible, they should try to make use of the child's home and local environment. Well thought through homework tasks:

- help children make connections between school and the 'real world';
- help children appreciate the value of what they learn in school and see its relevance;
- are accessible to children of differing ages and abilities;

- can be used to initiate work that will be developed later in class;
- provide opportunities to develop class work;
- make the curriculum visible to parents; and
- invite parents to work with their children in enjoyable ways.

Such tasks could include, for example:

- collecting examples of the use of numbers in the home and the local environment;
- collecting names of shops and superstores and discussing their meanings and origins; and
- looking at food packaging to discover the country of origin of different foodstuffs.

Parents can be asked to give feedback on the homework that is given to children and to offer suggestions about other activities that schools may want try out in the future.

Games

Many schools send home games for children to play as homework. These are usually linked to reading and mathematics. The games themselves can convey useful messages about what the school expects and how children learn. They also provide a reason for parents and children to spend time together and to talk to each other. Parents can be involved in producing and organizing games and materials, and in running the loan system. The *East Anglian Daily Times* has developed a scheme with schools which provides a wide variety of activities connected with reading and writing using the local daily paper. Schools that have been involved in the scheme note a rise in reading levels, and parents and children seem pleased with the activities.

Home–school notebooks

Home–school notebooks are a method of communicating between home and school and providing information about what is going on in school and at home. They can be used in three ways:

- to convey general items of information, such as the teacher introducing him or herself;
- to provide specific information about the child, such as difficulties or successes the child is experiencing at school or at home; and
- to enable teachers and parents to collaborate on a joint task.

Comments on homework tasks or on tackling a behaviour problem might be examples of this. Teachers need to instigate and keep the notebook going.

Sometimes, parents may have few comments to make, but the notebook provides them with the opportunity to maintain a dialogue with their child's teacher about their child and schooling.

Meetings between Parents and Teachers

The annual parent–teacher interview is often described as taking place on 'parents' evening'. This is misleading as most schools now offer parents the opportunity to discuss their children's progress at a time to suit them. For parents who have young children a daytime appointment might be best; others may find an appointment immediately after school finishes most convenient. So, rather than taking place during one evening, parent–teacher interviews are likely to be spread throughout the course of a week towards the end of the summer term.

Parent–teacher interviews are a significant event in the school year. During the meeting teachers and parents discuss the important topic of children's academic progress and their strengths and weaknesses as learners, and ways of helping the child to continue to make progress in the future. Bastiani (1989, p. 76) summarizes the main purposes of parent–teacher interviews as follows:

School purposes
- to inform parents of the child's progress;
- to meet demands for accountability;
- to establish and maintain good relations with parents;
- to share with the parents the problems and difficulties the child has in school;
- to explain and justify the school's policies and decisions as they affect individual pupils;
- to critically review with parents the child's experience of schooling;
- to learn more about the child from the parents' perspective;
- to learn more about parental opinions on what the school is doing;
- to identify areas of tension and disagreement;
- to identify ways in which parents can help their children; and
- to negotiate jointly decisions about the child's education.

Parental purposes
- to get a report on the child's progress;
- to identify any problem;
- to confirm existing judgements;
- to find out ways of helping the child;
- to see the child's work and possibly compare it with that of other children;
- to meet the people who teach the child;
- to bring up problems identified at home;
- to learn more about the school and the teaching;
- to inform the teacher about a particular matter; and
- to question the teacher about issues of concern.

This is rather a long agenda on both sides, so it is no wonder that parents and teachers feel that parent–teacher interviews are never long enough. To avoid having to cover too much in too short a time, interviews should be seen as part of an ongoing series of formal and informal meetings that take place during the school year. For example, areas of tension or issues of concern should be dealt with when they arise, not just at the end of the school year. Parents should be able to see their child's work during open days. From time to time photocopied samples can be sent home. It is also useful if reply slips on invitations to parent–teacher interviews include space for parents to note any particular issues that they would like to discuss. This gives teachers time to prepare and gives a focus to the meeting.

During the school year many parents will meet teachers on a number of occasions. Apart from very quick questions and answers, meetings should be timetabled to take place before or after school or at lunchtimes, unless cover can be arranged to enable teachers to leave their classes. Meetings should be treated seriously and, so, they should take place away from pupils and be given sufficient time. It is good practice for schools that have parents who have a limited command of English to arrange for a translator to be present at meetings.

Sometimes parents may become distressed or angry when they are discussing their child with teachers. If they are angry it is never wise to get involved in confrontation. Instead, listen carefully for a few moments to see if they run out of steam, offer to let them cool down alone, and, if these strategies do not seem to be having any effect, tell them that you will ask the headteacher or another senior colleague to speak to them to see if they can calm the parent down and find out what is wrong.

Helping Parents Understand the Education System

Practical and written information

If parents are to support their children at home, they need to have some understanding of the curriculum and the methods used to teach it. Many schools provide booklets about the curriculum for the parents of new school entrants. Booklets about learning to read and reading with children are very common and their usefulness is extended if their distribution is combined with a workshop and a display of books. Curriculum workshops and open days when parents can watch children and teachers at work provide parents with insights into the curriculum and how it is learned and taught. Sometimes schools can give parents misleading messages about how children learn. For example, parents may see only written mathematics work and so may think that only recording represents learning in this subject. To make sure that parents appreciate that thinking, oral work and the use of practical materials play their part in learning, teachers can make videos that show different learning and teaching methods and show these to parents.

Sources of help for parents

The Internet is a rich source of help for parents and covers all kinds of needs, from specific help for parents with children with SEN to ideas for parties and outings. The DfEE has a number of websites that offer help to parents, a range of leaflets in English and other community languages, and a quarterly magazine, *Parents and Schools*, which contains all kinds of information. Local education authorities also offer help and most LEAs have an accessible website that includes information for parents.

Issues for Reflection

- How can schools make sure that parents feel that they are regarded as equal partners in the education of their children?
- Is it possible to involve all parents in school-arranged learning? Does it matter if some parents do not seem to be actively involved in their children's education?
- What are parent–teacher interviews for? How should they be organized to make the best use of time and to leave parents and teachers feeling satisfied that they have exchanged information and listened to each other.

Summary of Key Points

- There is now a large body of evidence to show that well-organized parental involvement has beneficial effects on pupils' learning.
- Parental involvement benefits children, parents and teachers.
- Parents provide children with rich and successful learning experiences before and outside school.
- Parents and teachers need to respect the contribution that each makes to children's learning and development in order to successfully work together.
- Contact between parents and teachers is established and maintained through meetings and written communications.
- Some parents choose to become involved in the life of the school.
- Some parents choose to work with their own children at home.
- Meetings between parents and teachers need to be prepared for and organized carefully in order to make the best use of time.
- To help their child most effectively parents may need guidance in understanding the curriculum and the education system.

Suggestions for Further Reading

Books

Hornby, G. (2000) *Improving Parental Involvement*. London: Cassell. This useful book has as its focus strategies to help teachers think through how they communicate with parents. It includes advice on interpersonal skills and improving communication as well as chapters on ways of approaching challenging situations and sensitive issues.

Merttens, R., Newland, A. and Webb, S. (1996) *Learning in Tandem: Involving Parents in their Children's Education*. Leamington Spa: Scholastic. This practical and straightforward book focuses on how teachers can help parents become constructively involved in their children's learning in mathematics and English. It includes plenty of practical strategies for work in maths, reading and writing.

Websites

National Confederation of PTAs website, www.ncpta.org.uk This website promotes partnerships between home and school; pupils, parents and teachers; parents, LEAs and other agencies. It provides advice and a channel for parents to inform the government about parents' concerns.

Parent Centre website, www.parentcentre.gov.uk This is a DfES site, illustrated by Quentin Blake, which is a series of leaflets offering suggestions for home-based activities related to all the curriculum areas and matched to different key stages. A site for an already confident and motivated parent.

BBC Schools website, www.bbc.co.uk/schools This is a BBC website which provides learning resources for home and school for children of all ages. It gives a summary of latest legislation, ideas for fund-raising, help with homework and learning games.

Acknowledgements

I would like to thank Gill Preece and Jenifer Smith for their contributions to this chapter, and Angel Road First School, Norwich, for the home–school agreement in Figure 7.1.

8

The Primary Teacher's Responsibility for Pastoral Care

Gill Blake

The following topics and issues are covered in this chapter:

- the responsibilities of the class teacher for the welfare and protection of individual children;
- primary school policies and structures for pastoral care;
- attendance;
- health and safety;
- child protection;
- physical contact with children;
- health and its relationship to the child's learning;
- children in care;
- bullying; and
- where sources of support can be found.

A concern for pastoral care is likely to permeate everything a teacher does in the primary classroom. Without a commitment by the teacher to the personal well-being of the children in their care, learning is at best greatly restricted and at worst fails to happen at all. For a primary school teacher pastoral care can range from creating a positive atmosphere for all the children in their class to meeting very individual and specific needs.

One dictionary defines pastoral care as 'the teacher's responsibility for the personal, as distinct from the educational, development of pupils' (*Collins Concise Dictionary*, 1999). In my experience, however, I have found that most teachers would not consider the two areas of personal development and educational development as being distinct at all. In practice these two strands are very much connected and dependent on each other. In the first half of this chapter we shall see that, although the personal needs of individuals within a class can be complex and far-ranging, the class teacher is not working in isolation but within a framework of policies, guidelines and support from teachers with special responsibilities. The important thing is to know who to ask and where to find the guidance. We shall then visit briefly some strategies that enable the class to grow and thrive as a group which provides mutual support. Throughout I shall draw on legislation and government policies in England and my experience as a headteacher of a first and middle school in Norfolk. However, the principles that underpin these will apply to the teacher's responsibility for pastoral care anywhere.

School Policies and Other Structures for Pastoral Care

Most teachers expect that care for the personal development and well-being of their pupils will come naturally to them. It is part of their vocation. Trainee teachers and newly qualified teachers, however, in their enthusiasm for this aspect of their role, may fall into the trap of believing that their particular brand of empathy and classroom organization will remove the need for more experienced and specialized professionals to become involved. Not only is this misguided, it is positively dangerous in an ever more litigious society where we all have to be answerable for our actions. For this reason familiarity with the legal framework for the teacher's responsibilities for care discussed in Chapter 5 is essential.

Schools and, possibly, LEAs have policies and guidelines which translate government directives into everyday routines. Individual schools often have an induction pack covering the important issues described in this chapter. The guidance provided in such a pack ranges from whole-school aims and ethos to practical steps to be taken in the case of specific concerns, such as child abuse. There should also be named staff responsible for each of these areas.

School aims for pastoral care usually include an expectation that the teacher and the school collectively will have a commitment to pastoral care. These aims will probably highlight such things as:

- the importance of the individual;
- the need to establish a positive and secure environment; and
- the importance of striking a balance between individuality and teamwork.

Each teacher's job description will point out their responsibility for the welfare of pupils in their particular class. However, this is not a task to be tackled alone but within the whole-school context, with experienced staff as support who in their turn will draw on outside professional agencies.

Attendance

A very basic level of pastoral care is to encourage children to come to school regularly and on time. Following the publication of *The Education (Pupil*

Registration) Regulations (DfEE, 1995a), guidance for schools in England on registering absence and encouraging good attendance was tightened up. The primary school teacher can expect, therefore, that within their school there will be a school policy on attendance, absence and registration. The responsibility for administering this will lie with the school office and the headteacher, who is the only person who can authorize absences. However the class teacher can play an important part in noticing and affirming good attendance. Children who have been absent should be welcomed back and helped to catch up with any missed work. They should also be brought up to date with any important information and given copies of paperwork missed, such as a parent newsletter.

The class teacher may be the first to notice patterns of absence, such as every Monday after a visit to an absent parent or every Friday when outdoor games is on the timetable. This could lead to an informal chat with the pupil or parent or a more formal concern expressed to the headteacher. Agencies such as the pupil attendance service and education social workers can be called on to support individual families. Having said all that, we should always remember, of course, that children are more likely to want to come to school if the classroom is a secure and stimulating place to be! Good teaching is always a prerequisite for good pastoral care.

Health and Safety

Pastoral care clearly involves ensuring – as far as is reasonable – the immediate physical safety of the pupils and the avoidance of any threats to their health. This aspect of the teacher's role complements that of 'health education' discussed in Chapter 14, where the emphasis is on promoting the children's long-term health and safety through their own learning. The teacher's concern for children's health and safety also operates within the legal framework of health and safety regulations (see Chapter 5).

Each school will have a fairly weighty tome entitled 'Health and Safety Policy' covering virtually every aspect of daily life in school. There will also be a designated health and safety officer on the staff to whom all concerns should be reported. Class teachers are required to exercise effective supervision of the pupils at all times and to know the emergency procedures in respect of fire, first aid and other emergencies. The 'effective supervision' question usually causes a great deal of discussion in staff rooms. Are the children allowed to stay in the classroom at playtimes without an adult in the room? And how do you manage a visit to the toilet when you have been on playground duty during break but must not now leave your class unattended for the five minutes you desperately need? Generally speaking there will be school procedures for such matters which it is advisable to follow, just in case a pair of scissors is waved around carelessly while you are absent from the classroom.

A primary school teacher who cares for the well-being of their pupils as a matter of course glances around the classroom each day wearing a metaphorical safety hat to check that the room is a safe place to be. This means, for example, checking that the escape doors are not blocked, that fire instructions are displayed clearly, and that there are no high objects liable to fall on heads or cables to trip over. Schools carry out regular fire drills and it is important to impose expectations for class behaviour at such times. These might be, for example, no talking, no running and lining up in a particular order. A culture where children follow oral instructions from their teacher without question obviously helps at such times. If the children trust the teacher to look after their well-being, any emergency procedures are likely to run smoothly.

Security and the screening of visitors is also taken very seriously in the present climate. There may be external classroom doors which have to be kept locked and a system of visitor passes which encourages children to challenge or report any adult not wearing the appropriate badge. This system is usually organized from the school office but staff and children need to be aware of the implications.

Other considerations under the safety umbrella include codes of practice for subjects with particular elements of danger such as science, physical education, design technology and information and communications technology. The subject co-ordinators are the sources of specialist advice on these matters. This is another area in which the enthusiasm of a trainee teacher or a newly qualified teacher to excite and engage the children may sometimes need to be curbed. Exciting pupil-activities which contain an unnecessary element of risk may have to be foregone in favour of something safe and boring!

Child Protection

Possibly one of the weightiest responsibilities for a class teacher lies in the field – or minefield – of child protection. Whilst unfounded suspicions can lead to trauma for innocent families and the breakdown of the relationship between school and parents, it is important to remember that a failure to take action can, at its most extreme, lead to the death of a child. It is not uncommon for schools to be criticized for lack of knowledge and inefficient procedures when cases come to court. As with other sensitive areas a member of the school's senior management, often the headteacher, will be the designated teacher for child protection. This role involves undergoing training and understanding the local arrangements laid out by the Area Child Protection Committee (ACPC). In England, LEAs have drawn up their procedures following DfEE Circulars 10/95 and 11/95 (DfEE, 1995b; 1995c). These circulars provide government guidelines on protecting children from abuse. Many schools base their own policy on the United Nations Convention on the Rights of the Child and the principles of the 1989 Children Act (DoH, 1989).

The class teacher has a responsibility to protect children while they are in their care during the school day and on trips out of school. This includes reporting to the designated teacher any concerns, worries or suspicions that a pupil is suffering neglect, injury or abuse. Signs and symptoms to look out for include personality changes, physical problems such as tummy ache, tiredness, bruises and burns, and a general failure to thrive. During health education and other discussions teachers aim to provide children with the relevant information, skills and attitudes to resist abuse and to prepare for the responsibilities of adult life. It is important that if a child wishes to discuss sensitive matters at such a time, including a possible disclosure of abuse, the teacher does not promise confidentiality. This may compromise the responsibility to activate child protection procedures should anxieties arise. If a teacher becomes involved in preparing a court statement, this is done with the support of the school's designated teacher and a social worker within LEA guidance.

Physical Contact

Government guidance for schools in England on the use of force to control or restrain pupils (DfEE, 1998b) sets the framework for school policies in this area. There are two main reasons for physical contact with children in school: first to offer comfort, reassurance and encouragement; and, second, to restrain them from some level of violence. It is very important that a teacher becomes acquainted with any school guidelines on physical contact as they will offer protection to the teacher who may be put in a personally difficult situation by the consequences of well-meaning actions. In today's climate children who may have an axe to grind can make allegations that can leave the teacher in a very vulnerable position. Personal, social and health education lessons on topics such as 'personal space' and 'saying no to touching' will give children a positive context from which to make judgements.

School guidelines on physical contact usually give advice on:

- appropriate and inappropriate touches;
- gender issues;
- the avoidance of private situations;
- the fact that some children find any kind of physical contact disturbing; and
- physical restraint.

Physical restraint is only justified in the following circumstances:

- to defend yourself or others from assault;
- to stop an assault already happening;
- to stop a pupil inflicting serious harm on themselves; or
- to stop a pupil doing serious damage to property.

If possible, physical restraint should be left to senior management or designated members of staff who have had specific training on how to hold children in such cases. The best reaction is usually to remove the rest of the children from the scene of the violence if at all possible and to keep their normal routines going in a temporary venue. It is important to remember that vulnerable children may find incidents such as this particularly disturbing, so the teacher should plan a debriefing and a sharing of thoughts with the rest of the class. They could also talk through how they will react if such an incident happens again. Later in this chapter I will refer to some strategies for helping a child who may resort to violence if feeling under threat.

Health and its Relationship to Pupil Development

As we all know, teachers are often held responsible for every aspect of a child's development, from their sleeping and eating habits to the frequency of head-lice outbreaks! Whilst acknowledging that children learn better if their physical needs are met, there is a limit to how much responsibility can be taken by an individual teacher. It is however appropriate to act as a channel of information, either to parents, such as in the case of head-lice, or to the special needs co-ordinator (SENCO) in the case of possible developmental problems impeding progress.

Many schools are taking the promotion of good health seriously, with water readily available in classrooms, healthy choices at lunchtime and healthy lifestyles promoted in relevant lessons (see Chapter 14). It seems self-evident that healthy pupils will learn better and enjoy happier lives in school. But not all pupils are generally healthy and physically well. As a pastoral carer the class teacher has the responsibility to be aware of any particular health problems suffered by children in the class so that appropriate protection and support can be provided. The school office will prepare a list of any health issues for the class such as asthma and allergies. Health issues should be managed in the same way as other classroom routines so that they do not stand in the way of day-to-day learning. Children with asthma will usually need access to an inhaler before or during PE lessons, so this routine will need to be established. Depending on the age of the child, the inhaler may be kept in the classroom or in a central medical area. The older the child the more responsibility they can take for their own regime.

Allergies

One area of increasing importance is the awareness of allergies among children, particularly those which could produce anaphylactic shock. The food technology curriculum includes the making and tasting of biscuits and sandwiches, and children often celebrate birthdays by bringing in goodies to share with the class. It is important, therefore, to make a mental note of potential problems, without becoming a total killjoy. Many teachers send letters home to parents to check the situation and to obtain written permission before embarking on any communal food-tasting. This would seem a sensible safeguard and will often be school policy.

Serious medical conditions

Children with potentially serious medical conditions will have an individual health plan drawn up with the help of the school nurse and with the agreement of the parents. The previously mentioned anaphylactic shock will involve staff training in the use of an epipen. Other conditions might include epilepsy, diabetes and severe asthma. Most schools have a designated first aid provider, often a learning support assistant, who is the key person for implementing any individual health plans. There will also be school guidelines for various first aid procedures. Individual health plans will include a recent photo of the child, which will – with parental permission – be displayed in the child's classroom and at other central areas for quick reference should an incident occur. This is particularly useful for supply teachers.

Supporting pupils with medical needs

Government guidance on supporting pupils with medical needs in school (DfEE, 1996a) states that there is no legal or contractual duty on school staff to administer medicine or to supervise a pupil taking it. This is a voluntary role and appropriate training must always be supplied for anyone taking on such a role. However, all teachers have a common-law duty to act as any reasonably prudent parent would.

Medical support and advice for a school is provided by the school's medical officer, usually a consultant paediatrician based at a local health centre. Any concerns a teacher may have about a child – for example, hearing or visual problems – can be referred to this medical officer, with parental permission. Often there is an overlap between medical and educational needs, with the school SENCO keeping a watching brief over both areas. It is sometimes more appropriate to refer parents to their own family doctor if a problem is suspected, but both routes should be considered, especially if there is any reluctance by the parent to follow up the school's concern. Any general failure to thrive or cases of poor attendance due to ill health could also be followed up in this way. In the case of a child with a potentially life-threatening condition such as diabetes or epilepsy, the school is usually given a specialist contact person for emergency advice. This is particularly useful if children become unwell on a school residential trip.

Speech problems

There is considerable debate about whether speech problems and the provision of speech therapy constitute an educational or a health matter. This usually depends on the nature of the speech problem; to put it simplistically, whether it is mainly about the production of sound or about the understanding of language. In either case, as speech is such a fundamental prerequisite for many basic skills such as reading, writing and social interaction, any problems must be identified and remedied at the earliest possible stage. Parents should be encouraged to keep speech therapy appointments and progress by the pupil should be celebrated. If programmes are implemented in school this becomes officially an educational provision which will be co-ordinated by the SENCO and may appear on an individual education plan (IEP). Some specialist speech therapists visit schools themselves to carry out programmes, to advise support staff and to monitor progress. Class teachers will be involved in liaison with such specialists.

Children who have English as a second language are also offered support from a specialist teacher as they develop their skills in the classroom. It is the responsibility of the local education authority to provide this additional support. The visiting teacher provides suggestions for follow-up activities in the classroom as time and resources allow. (See also Chapter 13.)

Children in Care

At some time in their teaching career all teachers encounter children in care (sometimes called looked-after children) within their class. Government guidance on the education of children and young people in public care (DfEE, 2000e) was designed to tackle the serious underachievement of children in residential and foster care. There are often negative attitudes and assumptions surrounding these children, with low expectations of their potential. Schools are required to appoint a designated teacher for children in care to be an advocate for them and to communicate with social workers and carers. Each child has a personal education plan (PEP) which includes clear goals, a record of their achievement, their right to particular services and support and, if appropriate, any special educational needs. The class teacher should become familiar with the plan and liaise with the designated teacher to discuss any implications for life in the classroom. Emotional needs may become evident on a day-to-day basis. Appointing a mentor for the child within the school, usually a learning support assistant (LSA), can be a very positive step. This can be a low-key arrangement but nevertheless having a special person with a particular interest in them can make a huge difference to a child who is feeling insecure.

Bullying

Children may be unhappy at school for any one of a number of different reasons. Usually this is obvious to the class teacher, but sometimes the unhappiness can be contained at school and only comes flooding out in the safety of home. Parents will express concern at a child's unwillingness to come to school and may not be able to establish the reason themselves. One of the possible causes may be bullying, because the control which the bully exercises may include a silence clause: 'If you tell anyone about this I will make it twice as bad for you.' Bullying is widespread and serious. Sonia Sharp (1996) reports that, at any one time, as many as one in four primary-aged pupils may be experiencing bullying at school. She also suggests that pupils who join a class part way through the academic year can become the targets of a bullying group.

Schools have guidelines for dealing with bullying, possibly as part of the behaviour policy. These guidelines might include a definition of bullying, such as 'any sort of deliberate physical or psychological intimidation by those in a position of power over those who are unable to defend themselves'. This definition implies a wilful, conscious desire to hurt, threaten or frighten someone, with the intention of causing distress. It is usually done for the bully's personal gain or gratification, sometimes aimed at impressing others.

The headteacher, backed by the staff team, should make it clear that bully-ing is not to be tolerated and what action will be taken if it occurs. It is helpful if all parents have a copy of the school policy on bullying incidents. The class teacher should be aware of the characteristics of bullies and victims, and the times and places where bullying may happen.

The unwillingness of a victim to reveal bullying in case of reprisals can put parents, friends and teachers in a difficult position. Children must be encour-aged to report incidents otherwise the bully may go unchecked. It is essential not to promise that nothing will be said directly to the bully. General class-room encouragement to be nice to each other is taken on board by everyone except the person it is intended to warn. Direct consequences for bullies, together with support for changing the behaviour, are the most effective sanc-tions. If a teacher is in doubt about the level and frequency of the bullying, they should record any observations over a period of time, enlisting the help of classroom support staff and midday supervisors. The headteacher may keep a specific log of bullying incidents in the office. This helps when confronting the bully with the serious nature of their actions. It also helps to sift out chil-dren who say they are being bullied but in fact are simply having an occasional clash with someone in their class.

Parents of both bully and victim should be informed of the problem and involved in the solution. Unless the teacher concerned knows both sets of parents fairly well and is convinced that a meeting between them will lead to positive results, it is better to meet with them separately, making it clear what action you are taking. This meeting should include a member of the senior management team, with whom discussions will have already taken place. As with previous issues discussed in this chapter, being clear about school proce-dures and staff responsibilities, recording carefully any observations and actions, and keeping open lines of communication with all groups involved will lead to the most successful resolution. The Circle of Friends strategy (described below) can be very helpful for both bully and victim. The victim can be trained to be more assertive, to change their body language and to express clearly their feelings. Bullying is one of the important issues tackled in PSHE lessons and undoubtedly in assemblies too. Kidscape, a charity supporting children being bullied, produces useful resources in this area.

Strategies for Developing Mutual Support

Pastoral support at its best is provided not just by the teacher but by the peer group within the classroom. With some groups of children this happens natu-rally but, on the whole, pupils in primary schools will need to be trained in strategies for mutual support, particularly if there are several complex needs within the group. Circle Time (see Chapters 14 and 15) is now well established in many primary classrooms and provides an effective strategy for developing a class commitment to care for each other. Circle of Friends has also proved very successful. This is when children with behavioural and social problems have a small group of established 'buddies' who give them regular (mainly positive) feedback and work with them to encourage positive models for behaviour and relationships.

Enabling a class to grow into a supportive group, taking one another's needs seriously, is probably the hardest task but also one of the most rewarding tasks for a teacher. Once class rules and structures have been discussed and agreed, with clear expectations and consequences for actions established, the class teacher can decide on the procedures which will be established for children to express their needs and opinions. These times of structured communication are essential for the mutual growth of the class.

In addition to Circle Time and Circle of Friends, many schools have developed school councils and class councils. These meetings provide opportunities for children to express their opinions but also, perhaps more importantly, to listen to the opinions of others. A class council meeting usually has an agreed format with rules that everyone understands. Children will chair the meetings with possibly other officers, such as a secretary, to help. They may have to give a signal when they wish to speak and be required to keep to the subjects on the agenda. Usually class representatives attend a whole-school council. This acts as a kind of parliament for the school, with adults attending meetings to contribute to particular subjects. The confidence gained by children participating in such meetings helps them to express themselves in other contexts.

The recent growth of philosophy sessions in primary schools is also contributing to the development of the speaking and listening skills that are essential for mutual support within a class. In philosophy children not only think through issues analytically and discuss and share ideas, but they are also encouraged to say specifically whether they agree or disagree with the opinions of others and why. This kind of reasoning and self-expression can be carried over into other classroom discussions including the unravelling of relationship and behaviour problems.

For children who still find it difficult to express their worries, or may be too shy to do so, a means of communicating with the teacher through a notebook or message box may be helpful, especially if confidentiality is assured. Drama and role-play can also provide anonymity while exploring personal difficulties and anxieties, as scenarios are acted out within the safety of a group and by assuming another identity.

The setting-up of classroom structures and training in how they work can be time-consuming, frustrating and – with some troubled classes – exhausting. But it is energy well spent as channels are provided for expressing and dealing with the many needs mentioned in this chapter.

Communication

To sum up my experience in this area, I would say that it is communication that must lie at the heart of pastoral care. The importance of communication between staff and children, child and child, teacher and parent, teacher and other teachers with particular responsibilities, school and external agencies cannot be overstressed. And what does a teacher who takes this role seriously do if they have to be away from their class for a day or longer? They leave a supply teacher's information file which includes notes on specific children, behaviour expectations and class procedures. Even when they are not there the professional teacher continues to communicate their personal standards of care.

Issues for Reflection

- What support might be available for a teacher considering a child protection issue?
- Once a case of bullying is confirmed within a primary school what measures should be taken and who should be involved in resolving the issues?
- What would a working classroom in a primary school look like if pastoral care has been taken seriously?
- Is the pastoral role of the class teacher more important than the educational role?

Summary of Key Points

- Pastoral care is not just an individual teacher's emotional concern for the children in a class; it is a practical and professional responsibility that must be exercised within the school's framework of policies.
- Class teachers will find support for issues of pastoral care from designated teachers and others with specific responsibilities within the school.
- Outside agencies are available to support the school with specific complex problems in the field of pastoral care; these agencies are usually accessed through the school's senior management.
- Bullying is a widespread problem, affecting the well-being of many pupils in primary schools; every school must have a policy for dealing with it.
- Children in primary schools have to be trained to care for and to support one another; class ethos, structures and specific procedures will help to achieve this.
- Vulnerable children need to be given strategies for expressing their concerns without the fear of being overwhelmed by children they perceive as more powerful.
- The complexity of this facet of school life makes communication the number one priority.

Suggestions for Further Reading

Rogers, B. (1990) *You Know the Fair Rule.* London: Pitman Publishing. This book, which provides down to earth advice on the subject of discipline, includes helpful chapters on rights in the classroom and strategies for building a positive classroom climate.

David, K. and Charlton, T. (eds) (1996) *Pastoral Care Matters in Primary and Middle Schools.* London: Routledge. This wide-ranging collection of contributions on the subject of pastoral care includes a survey of the pastoral needs of primary-age pupils and a useful section on working with agencies.

Calvert, M. and Henderson, J. (eds) (1998) *Managing Pastoral Care.* London: Cassell. This book asserts that the pressure placed on schools by the National Curriculum has threatened to squeeze out the teacher's commitment to pastoral care. It underlines the need for a school to have a planned approach to pastoral care, giving advice on both organization and resourcing.

9
Special Educational Needs in Mainstream Primary Schools

Ann Browne

The following topics and issues are covered in this chapter:

- defining special educational needs;
- the terminology of SEN;
- the SEN Code of Practice and its implications for schools;
- school policies for SEN;
- the role of the SENCO;
- working with outside agencies;
- SEN related to cognition and learning;
- SEN related to behaviour, emotional and social development;
- sensory and physical SEN;
- planning for children with SEN in primary classrooms;
- liaison with other adults in the classroom;
- working with parents and carers of children with SEN;
- discussions with pupils;
- observing individual children; and
- reviewing progress, planning and teaching.

This chapter provides information and some practical guidance on the teaching of children with special educational needs in mainstream primary schools. This is now a significant issue for trainees as well as qualified teachers. The practicalities and issues relating to children with SEN are common to teachers throughout the UK as well as in other countries. However in this chapter I will be drawing on official documents that relate to the education system in England. The policy of increasing the inclusion of children with SEN in mainstream schools in England has received additional impetus in *The Special Educational Needs Code of Practice* (DfES, 2001a). As the majority of children with SEN are provided for in mainstream schools and every primary or early years class is likely, on average, to contain three or four children who need some form of special provision, trainees and teachers will encounter children who need support that is additional to or different from that given to the majority of children in the class. Those who are training as primary school teachers in England have to work within a framework of standards for the award of QTS (DfES/TTA, 2002) that includes specific reference to SEN and requires that newly qualified teachers are able to:

- understand their responsibilities under the SEN Code of Practice;
- take account of and support pupils' varying needs (when planning);
- identify and support those who are working below age-related expectations, those who are failing to achieve their potential in learning, and those who experience behavioural, emotional and social difficulties; and
- differentiate their teaching to meet the needs of pupils including those with special educational needs.

This chapter will examine these issues and suggest further sources of information.

Definitions

Defining special educational needs

The SEN Code of Practice (DfES, 2001a, p.6) defines special educational needs clearly. It states that 'children have special educational needs if they have a learning difficulty which calls for special educational provision to be made for them'.

In the Children Act 1989 a child with a disability is defined as one who is 'blind, deaf or dumb or suffers from a mental disorder of any kind or is substantially and permanently handicapped by illness, injury or congenital deformity or such other disability as may be prescribed' (DoH, 1989, s. 17.11).

According to the Education Act 1996, children with learning difficulties are those who 'have a significantly greater difficulty in learning than the majority of children of the same age; or have a disability which prevents or hinders them from making use of educational facilities of a kind generally provided for children of the same age' (DfEE, 1996b, s. 312).

Disability is further defined as 'a physical or mental impairment which has a substantial and long-term adverse effect on the ability to carry out normal day-to day activities' (DfES, 2001b, s. 1.3).

Terminology

The way we use language when talking about pupils often reveals our attitude towards them. If the terminology of SEN is used incorrectly or insensitively it may damage children by being deficit focused and may interfere with the adult's ability to see the child beyond the special need. In order to use language appropriately it is worth having as clear an understanding as possible of some of the key words used in the definitions given in the Code of Practice. Three key words are explained below.

- *Impairment* refers to a loss of or abnormality in development or growth.
- *Disability* refers to the limitation of activity caused by an impairment.
- *Handicap* is the personal disadvantage that a person experiences in society as a result of their disability.

Teachers may not be able to do anything about a pupil's impairment, but they may be able to address the disability that arises from it and may be able to do many things such as adjusting the classroom environment or providing additional resources or support to ensure that the resulting handicaps are reduced.

Sometimes one hears a teacher or a trainee say 'he is a special needs child' or 'she is dyslexic'. The use of the word 'is' in these statements suggests that the child is little more than the label. It is also imprecise, tells us little about the nature or severity of the learning difficulty and can obscure other important aspects of the child. People may also incorrectly stereotype children with disabilities. Comments such as 'Dyslexic children are very bright' or 'autistic pupils are talented' are not helpful when thinking about how to cater for children's needs, and again obscure the unique traits of each individual who has dyslexia or autism.

A Summary of the SEN Code of Practice and its Implications for Schools

The Code of Practice (DfES, 2001a) sets out the procedures that schools and others must follow when making provision for pupils with SEN. Underpinning the Code of Practice are a number of principles that should inform the way schools treat pupils with SEN and how they interpret the statutory requirements.

Principles

The first principle is that children with SEN should have their needs met. This means that recognized needs should be addressed rather than left in the hope that they are attributable to a developmental delay that will be outgrown. Schools need to be proactive rather than reactive. The sooner the school takes action the sooner the child's difficulties can be reduced.

The SEN of children should in most circumstances be met in mainstream schools or settings. Only where the child's inclusion is incompatible with the efficient education of other children will a child be considered for education elsewhere (see Chapter 10). This means that provision in schools should be flexible enough to accommodate long- and short-term needs as well as the range of needs and differing degrees of severity of need. For example, schools should be able to support a child whose ability to learn has been affected by a family bereavement as well as a child with a permanent hearing loss.

Children with SEN have a right to participate in making decisions about the sort of help they would like. Their views need to be sought, listened to and taken account of, as they have a unique knowledge of their own needs and circumstances. They should contribute to such things as the setting of learning targets, individual education plans and the annual review. Although seeking the views of children, some of whom might be very young or have severe communication difficulties, may not be easy, schools should make arrangements to do this.

The role of parents is recognized as being crucial in contributing to their child's education and diagnosing their particular needs. Their knowledge and experience will contribute to the understanding of the child's needs and how the child can be best supported. To this end parents should be treated as partners and should be supported and empowered to make their views known. Parents must be told when a school is making special educational provision for their child.

The final fundamental principle is that children with SEN should be offered full access to a broad, balanced and relevant education. They are entitled to access the National Curriculum and the Early Learning Goals.

Level 2 procedures

The Code of Practice contains practical guidance on the procedures that schools should follow when making arrangements for educating pupils with SEN. This includes the procedures to be followed from the first identification of a special need, to requesting a statutory assessment. The process of providing for a child with SEN begins with the teacher's assessment that a child is not progressing satisfactorily. The teacher will be aware of this through observations and the analysis of the child's work. At this stage the teacher should consult the special educational needs co-ordinator to consider what strategies can be employed to help the child learn. If the teacher and the SENCO decide that the child needs help over and above that which is normally available within the class, they will consider helping the child through Early Years or School Action. Action can also be triggered by parental concerns. The criteria for considering action are that the child:

- makes little or no progress even when teaching approaches are targeted particularly on a child's area of weakness;
- shows signs of difficulty in developing literacy or mathematics skills which result in poor attainment in some curriculum areas;
- presents persistent emotional or behavioural difficulties which are not ameliorated by the behaviour management techniques usually employed in the school;
- has sensory or physical problems, and continues to make little or no progress despite the provision of specialist equipment; or
- has communication and/or interaction difficulties, and continues to make little or no progress despite the provision of a differentiated curriculum (DfES, 2001a, pp. 52–3).

Discussions about the type of action that is required should be informed by evidence collected by the teacher, information provided by parents and information from any other professionals involved with the child. This will enable the teacher to draw up a record of concern as illustrated in Figure 9.1.

The SENCO and the teacher should decide on the action that is needed and the parents should be informed about what is being done and invited to add to the teachers' picture of the child. The child's progress should be assessed regularly. The strategies that are employed should be recorded within an individual education plan. An example is provided in Figure 9.2. The IEP should include:

- the short-term targets set for or set by the child;
- the teaching strategies to be used;
- the provision to be put in place;
- when the plan is to be reviewed;
- success and/or exit criteria; and
- outcomes (to be recorded when the IEP is reviewed) (DfES, 2001a, p. 54).

The IEP should be reviewed at least twice a year. Ideally it should be reviewed every term, and parents and, wherever possible, the child should be involved in the review. New targets and strategies can be identified (see Figure 9.3). It is important that the targets that are set are realistic. Learning should be broken down into small attainable steps.

The second stage of the procedure, called Early Years Plus or School Action Plus, may result if, after a review, the conclusion is that the child:

- continues to make little or no progress in specific areas over a long period;
- continues working at an early years curriculum or at National Curriculum levels substantially below that expected of children of a similar age;
- continues to have difficulty in developing literacy and mathematics skills;
- has emotional or behavioural difficulties which substantially and regularly interfere with the child's own learning or that of the class group, despite having an individualized behaviour management programme;
- has sensory or physical needs, and requires additional specialist equipment or regular advice or visits by a specialist service; or
- has ongoing communication or interaction difficulties that impede the development of social relationships and cause substantial barriers to learning (DfES, 2001a, p. 55).

Early Years Plus or School Action Plus will begin with a new IEP that sets out revised strategies for supporting the child. External specialists may be involved in drawing up the new IEP.

If, after working with the Action Plus IEP for a reasonable length of time, the child continues not to make progress and demonstrates significant cause for concern, the school may request a statutory assessment of the child's SEN from the LEA. This may result in a Statement of SEN. After conducting the statutory assessment, the LEA will decide whether the child's SEN should

SPECIAL NEEDS ACTION RECORD
RECORD OF CONCERN

Personal Information		Other Information
Name of student	Philip	Health
DOB		EWO
Parent/Carer		Social Services
Class/Form		School Support Team
NCYG	Year 2	Other

Area of Concern	Date Identified	Date Resolved
Numeracy Philip has difficulty understanding the numbers from 11-30. He finds counting back difficult and has not yet understood what each digit represents. He has little understanding of the value of numbers.	Oct 02	
Writing When writing independently Philip finds constructing complete sentences difficult. His letter formation needs work. His handwriting is large. He needs work on spelling common words.	Oct 02	
Reading Philip has made progress but needs extra help to assist him with Year 2 work.	Oct 02	

THIS CAN BE ADDED TO AT ANY STAGE OF ASSESSMENT. WHEN A CONCERN IS IDENTIFIED IT SHOULD BE NOTED AND ADDED. THE DATE RESOLVED SHOULD ALSO BE NOTED WHEN ACTION IS SUCCESSFUL.

Figure 9.1.   Example of a record of concern

continue to be met from the school's existing resources, whether extra resources are necessary or whether the child needs a change of placement. The first of these options does not result in a statement and the school will be expected to continue to make provision through School Action Plus. If the second or third option is considered necessary, the LEA will draw up a statement. The statement will formally identify the child's needs, the full range of provision to be made and the review arrangements. When a child's needs are to be met in school the statement might result in additional resources such as regular teaching by a specialist teacher, daily individual support from a learning support assistant, specialist equipment or the regular involvement of non-educational agencies. The funding for this is provided by the LEA.

SPECIAL NEEDS ACTION RECORD

INDIVIDUAL EDUCTION PLAN STAGE 1 2 3 4 5

Name of student   Philip

Date of birth

NCYG   Year 2

Teacher responsible

Date this plan started 10.01.03

Class/form

Parental contact (date/method)

Targets ... will be able to	Action	Outcome Date of review
Use initial consonant clusters when reading and spelling (cr, cl, dr, br, fl, fr, gr, gl, pl, pr, sl, sm, sn, sp, spl.) (words overleaf)	Learn 5 simple spellings weekly as homework. Early morning work (look, cover, write, check) with weekly spellings.	
Read common high frequency words (listed overleaf)	Guided reading in a small group once a week. Individual reading twice a week. Learn words through games. Learn words using ICT programmes.	
Write a simple sentence independently remembering to include a full stop and capital letter	Write sentences linked to guided reading. Write sentences including spelling words each week.	
Form a,c,d,g,b correctly	Practise writing as homework. Early morning work practising handwriting. Small group work on letter formation.	
Comments/future action		External agency/school support team involvement.

Figure 9.2. Example of an IEP

SPECIAL NEEDS ACTION RECORD

INDIVIDUAL EDUCTION PLAN STAGE 1 2 3 4 5

Name of student	Philip	Teacher responsible	Parental contact (date/method)
Date of birth		Date this plan started 10.10.02	
NCYG	Year 2	Class/form	

Targets ... will be able to	Action	Outcome Date of review
Construct a complete sentence with greater independence	Write sentences linked to guided reading with support. Simple repetitive writing activities to encourage the use of sentences e.g. news, weather diary.	Able to write simple sentences with support. Still needs reminding about letter formation and size. Unable to punctuate independently.
Spell common words (listed overleaf)	Simple spellings learned weekly as homework. Early morning work practising spellings of common words. Use try book to assist with spelling.	Spelling assessed 10/01/03. Results overleaf. Progress has been made with sh, ch, st, th. High frequency words still need practice.
Read common words (listed overleaf)	Guided reading in a small group once a week. Individual reading twice a week. Learn words through games. Learn words using ICT programmes.	Reading of common words assessed on 7/01/03. Results overleaf. Progress has been made with reading. Confidence has improved.
Comments/future action		External agency/school support team involvement.

Figure 9.3. Example of a reviewed IEP

School policies

All schools must have a SEN policy which should contain information about:

- the SEN provision made by the school;
- how the school identifies, assesses and provides for children who have SEN; and
- the school's policy on staffing, working with outside agencies and parents.

The policy and the provision for children with SEN is reviewed annually by the governors and the headteacher and a report on the effectiveness of the policy is distributed to parents as part of the Governors' annual report to parents.

The role of the SENCO

Although all teachers are teachers of children with SEN, all schools must have a SENCO or a group of staff who form a SEN support team. The SENCO will have particular knowledge of SEN and can advise colleagues, including trainees, about their work with SEN pupils. The SENCO has a number of duties, which include:

- developing the SEN policy;
- developing the provision for SEN;
- responsibility for the day-to-day operation and implementation of the SEN policy;
- co-ordinating provision for pupils with SEN;
- working with and advising colleagues;
- managing learning support assistants;
- liaison with parents of children with SEN;
- contributing to the in-service training of staff;
- undertaking assessments of pupils' needs;
- monitoring the quality of teaching;
- overseeing the records of all children with SEN; and
- liaison with external agencies, including the LEA's support and educational psychology services, health and social services, and voluntary bodies.

Outside agencies

A number of outside agencies can provide schools and teachers with advice and help, as well as providing direct support for pupils with SEN. It is most likely that schools will consult specialists when they take action on behalf of a child through School Action Plus. However, outside agencies can also play a part in the early identification of SEN and in advising schools about effective provision designed to prevent the development of more significant needs. They can act as consultants and provide in-service training for teachers.

Support services provided by the local education authority include specialist teachers of pupils with hearing, visual and speech and language impairments, teachers providing general learning and behaviour support services, counsellors, educational psychologists, the education welfare service and advisers or teachers with knowledge of ICT for children with SEN.

The educational psychology service can be a very important resource for a school. It can provide a range of support including:

- carrying out specialized assessments;
- advising on behaviour management techniques;
- evaluating individual pupil progress;
- assisting with the development of SEN and behaviour policies; and
- helping to develop the knowledge and skills of staff.

Health services may also be involved with children with SEN. The range of health professionals who can provide support for children with SEN includes speech and language therapists, occupational therapists, physiotherapists, doctors and the school nurse. Social services departments have a designated officer responsible for working with schools and LEAs on behalf of children with SEN. Social services might be involved in contributing to the non-educational provision specified in a statement.

When schools work with visiting professionals, their effectiveness is helped when there is:

- active support from members of the senior management team;
- time for regular, formal and informal discussions;
- joint planning, problem-solving and decision-making;
- an understanding of, and respect for, the roles and goals of other professionals;
- the use of a common, easily understood language; and
- in-service training in teamwork.

A Brief Guide to Some of the Special Needs Commonly Encountered in School

The Code of Practice (DfES, 2001a) identifies four general areas of SEN. These are:

- communication and interaction;
- cognition and learning;
- behaviour, emotional and social development; and
- sensory and physical.

Children with SEN will have needs and requirements which may fall into at least one of these areas. However, individual children may well have needs that span two or more areas. In particular, children with a special educational need that leads to learning difficulties may become frustrated and manifest behavioural and emotional difficulties as a result. Aggression, lack of concentration or temper tantrums might lessen if the child is given work that is at an appropriate level so that the child can succeed and that is motivating and relevant to the child's interests.

Very often children with SEN have a primary condition such as autism or dyslexia and this is what practioners want to know about. For this reason I have arranged these commonly encountered conditions under the headings used in the Code of Practice. Understanding the particular characteristics of different SEN helps teachers to think about how they can best plan, teach and support pupils, and guide their responses to pupils in the classroom.

Communication and interaction

Autism

Autism is a lifelong developmental disability that affects the way a person communicates and relates to people around them. There is no known cause. Boys are affected more often than girls. It is twice as common in males than in females. Children with autism have difficulties with social relationships. They lack awareness of others, avoid eye contact and prefer to play alone. They may be aggressive and show little interest in making friends. They have difficulty communicating verbally and non-verbally. They may talk incessantly about one topic or engage in echolalic speech where they copy or repeat what is said to them. Their language develops slowly or not at all, gestures may be used instead of words or words may be used but in an apparently meaningless way. Statements or questions may be interpreted in very literal ways – so teachers need to be careful about how they use language. Children with autism may have difficulty with imaginative play, with using their imagination and with abstract thinking.

Further, children with autism may have difficulty concentrating and often dislike or are disturbed by changes in routine. They may manifest bizarre behaviour such as abnormal body movements including arm-flapping, rocking and grimacing. They may produce inappropriate noises such as laughter or screams. Some children display self-harming tendencies such as head-banging or hand-biting. Some can do some things very well and very quickly. They may have an isolated special skill such as drawing or music or have an outstanding rote memory.

Autism is a complex disorder and the needs of children with this condition can vary enormously along the autistic spectrum. The condition can vary from mild to severe. The more able autistic child is often diagnosed as having Asperger's syndrome.

Dyslexia

This is a reading problem, where the child has great difficulty in learning to read despite conventional instruction, adequate intelligence and sociocultural opportunity. There is no obvious reason for this disability. Children with dyslexia may become frustrated, angry and disruptive. There are other SEN associated with difficulties with using symbols. These include dyscalculia where children have problems with arithmetical calculation, disgraphia or problems with writing, and dysorthographia, meaning problems with spelling.

Dyspraxia

Dyspraxia is an impairment or immaturity of the brain which results in messages not being properly transmitted to or from the brain. Children with this condition sometimes appear thoughtful but seem to have difficulty in putting their thoughts into action. They are often clumsy and have difficulty in controlling material such as paper and pencils. They may have a poor short-term memory, be sensitive to touch and have little sense of direction. Language delay may occur with dyspraxia and children may be unable to answer simple questions, even if they know the answers. Their behaviour may be immature and they may have temper tantrums.

Shyness

Children who are extremely timid or withdrawn may lack the social skills necessary to make friends or work with and learn from others. They may be lonely and rejected by other members of the class. Carefully planned group and paired work that leads to positive and productive outcomes will provide opportunities to develop verbal and social skills.

Other disorders that lead to difficulties with communication and interaction

It is important that teachers are aware that speech and language impairment can be caused by many factors. It can occur as a condition on its own or it can be the result of other conditions such as cerebral palsy or hearing impairment.

Cognition and learning

Giftedness

Gifted children stand out from their peers by virtue of an outstanding ability in an academic, artistic or physical skill. They may also have an unusually high IQ score. Gifted children may need to be motivated to complete routine tasks. They may become bored with school work and become disruptive. They may manifest anxiety about succeeding in areas in which they are gifted and about failing at other work. See Chapter 11 for further information about gifted children.

Other disorders that lead to difficulties with cognition and learning

Conditions such as autism, dyslexia and dyspraxia will lead to problems with cognition and learning which will need to be addressed through specific programmes to help with language, literacy, memory, motor and reasoning skills.

Behaviour, emotional and social development

Attention deficit disorder (ADD) and attention deficit hyperactivity disorder (ADHD)

Attention deficit disorder and ADHD are conditions related to problems of attending to or concentrating on tasks. If lack of attention is more evident than overactivity, then the term attention deficit disorder is used. When both lack of attention and overactivity are present then ADHD is used. Children with these conditions may experience great difficulty in controlling their motor responses and exhibit high levels of inappropriate activity at school. They may have poor co-ordination, appear disorganized and experience problems with peer relationships. Children with ADD/ADHD are not necessarily below average intelligence, but often achieve poorly. Their poor concentration span and restlessness may seriously impede progress. This condition is usually treated with medication, either with drugs such as Ritalin or homoeopathically, but it is important that children are also given support mechanisms that will help them to control their behaviour.

Behavioural difficulties
There is a range of behavioural, emotional and social difficulties which can impede learning, such as withdrawn, isolated and disruptive behaviours. Children who present challenging behaviours will need help to develop social competence and emotional behaviour and to adjust to school expectations.

Sensory and physical

Asthma
Children with asthma experience problems with breathing. They may be allergic to substances such as pollen, some foods and dust, all of which could bring on an asthma attack. The severity of the condition varies. Children with asthma usually have an inhaler. Some schools make arrangement for the storage of inhalers and expect children to access their inhalers when they need them. Asthma may limit the extent to which some children can participate in physical activities. During an attack children's breathing should not be restricted, for example, by being held.

Cerebral palsy
This is a term for disorders of movement and posture resulting from damage to a child's developing brain in the later months of pregnancy, during birth, in the neonatal period or in early childhood. Cerebral palsy jumbles messages between the brain and muscles. The muscles of one or more limbs may be permanently contracted and stiff, leading to disordered movement. Children may manifest frequent involuntary movements and when they have difficulty controlling their tongue and vocal chords their speech may be difficult to understand. Balance may be affected causing an unsteady way of walking, shaky hand movements and jerky speech. Cerebral palsy may cause visual perceptual problems and children may tire quickly with tasks that require controlled eye movements such as reading. It can affect spatial perception and may cause hearing difficulties. Epilepsy is also associated with cerebral palsy. Some children with cerebral palsy have learning difficulties, some have average intelligence and some have higher than average intelligence. Their problems may cause some children to become frustrated and lead to behavioural difficulties.

Cystic fibrosis

This genetic disorder is characterized by an inability to absorb nutrients from food, lung infections, liver problems, diabetes, pancreatitis and gallstones. The treatment and care of those who have cystic fibrosis involves physiotherapy, a special diet and food supplements. Children with cystic fibrosis may be absent from school due to ill-health. This can interrupt their schooling and so they may need extra support with their learning.

Down's syndrome

This is a chromosomal abnormality. There are different degrees of severity and children with Down's syndrome have widely varying abilities. Characteristics of the condition include short stature, learning difficulties, which can be moderate or severe, hearing and visual problems, heart problems and an increased susceptibility to infection. The child's parents are the best source of information about the severity of the child's difficulties and how to keep the child safe and comfortable. Children with Down's syndrome usually have enlarged tongues and this can make speech difficult. Speech therapy may help.

Epilepsy

This is caused by abnormal electrical discharges from the brain which can lead to seizures. With a minor condition the characteristics may display themselves as a fainting fit and should be treated as such. Major epileptic fits may be accompanied by feelings of strangeness, a headache, irritability, restlessness or feelings of lethargy. Children who suffer from epilepsy should be protected from danger and allowed to sleep. During a seizure something soft should be placed under the head to prevent injuries and any sharp items removed. The child should not be moved. When the seizure has finished, the child can be placed in the recovery position. Epilepsy is often controlled with medication. This can lead to drowsiness which will affect children's ability to concentrate.

Hearing impairment

There are two types of deafness: conductive, meaning faulty transmission of sound from the outer to the inner ear; and sensorineural, when sounds that reach the inner ear fail to be transmitted to the brain. The most common causes of hearing impairment are infection and glue ear. Glue ear particularly affects children below the age of eight years. Children can be helped by surgical correction, speech therapy, the use of British Sign Language and hearing aids. Children who have a hearing loss may have speech difficulties as a result of their inability to hear voices and sounds. They may manifest anxiety and coping difficulties, and experience loneliness because of reduced social interaction. They may not respond to instructions or respond incorrectly. They might communicate in a noisy way and appear to be ignoring normal turn-taking conventions. These are not behavioural problems. They benefit from links between visual and aural cues so, for example, using story props or physical actions when reading a story will help children to understand and attend.

HIV

A child with HIV may have frequent absences from school due to illness. He or she is very vulnerable to infection and, so, parents need to be notified if there is an outbreak of common childhood illnesses such as chicken pox. HIV is a communicable disease and, so, precautions need to be taken in order to protect staff and other children. Disposable gloves should always be worn when dealing with open wounds or blood spillage, for any person within the school community. Blood should be cleaned up immediately. Confidentiality about a child with HIV is essential. Information about the child should be passed on only to those who need to know.

Muscular dystrophy

This is an inherited muscle disorder in which there is slow but progressive degeneration of muscle fibres.

Sickle-cell anaemia

This is sometimes known as thalassemia. It is an inherited blood disorder which impedes normal blood flow and causes anaemia. Children with this condition may experience severe pain in the arms, legs, back and stomach, infections such as coughs, colds, sore throats, fever and jaundice. They may need to take time off school for hospital visits and it might be necessary to plan opportunities for the child to catch up on missed learning due to absence. If the child suddenly becomes unwell or complains of severe pains they may need hospital treatment. Children with sickle-cell anaemia should always be kept warm and dry. For example, they should not be allowed to become chilled after swimming. They should not become dehydrated and may need to drink greater quantities and more frequently than normal.

Visual impairment

More than 55 per cent of visually impaired children attend mainstream schools. They will have a statement of educational need which will detail the support and special equipment they need. They may benefit from people who will read school material to them and the use of tape recorders to record ideas or computers set up with a very large font. Tactile and auditory resources will be helpful and thought should be given to positioning the child in the class so that they can make best use of their vision. It will be necessary to think about safety issues, such as how to protect children from unnecessary bumps in the classroom.

Planning and Teaching

Planning for children with SEN

When planning for children with SEN it is useful to think first about the characteristics of the special educational need and the learning behaviour and preferences of the child. This can help the teacher identify subjects and teaching strategies that might cause problems and help the teacher to think about minimizing these difficulties. Failure can often be reduced through adapting the environment and using resources to benefit the child. Figure 9.4, for example, is a preliminary planning sheet for a child with dyspraxia. It shows how one can begin to think about how to cater for the learning of children with a particular special educational need.

The information on this sheet will help the teacher to plan and organize teaching sessions that enable the child to learn more successfully. It will also help the teacher to differentiate work by allocating resources and devising suitable activities. This will help to ensure that the child is included in the work that is prepared for the class as a whole and will avoid differentiating merely by having different expectations about the amount or quality of the work that is produced.

There are some general strategies that can be helpful to think about when planning for children with SEN. These include:

- working closely with parents and carers;
- liaison with medical and advisory services;
- observing the child closely to recognize patterns and see where the child succeeds and where support is needed;
- breaking down long-term curriculum goals into small, attainable steps;
- differentiating work;
- building self-esteem and confidence; and
- celebrating achievements.

Liaison with other adults in the classroom

Learning support assistants often work with children with SEN. Some children will have been allocated an LSA for a number of hours each week. In order to work most effectively with the child, the LSA needs to:

- be aware of the learning implications of the child's SEN;
- understand the learning objectives for the pupil and the session;
- be familiar with the resources and materials that are used;
- know the role that they are expected to play;
- participate in planning for the child; and
- share observations about the child's needs, interests and progress with the teacher.

The teacher and the LSA need to work together to exchange information and discuss learning opportunities. The close relationship that LSAs have with their designated children means that they have a good understanding of the their needs and interests, and this information can be considered when planning future work.

Although LSAs will focus primarily on the needs of the designated children, they may also work with other pupils when appropriate. This flexibility means that sometimes the teacher can work closely with children with SEN

Planning for Children with Special Educational Needs

Dyspraxia
Subjects that the child might find difficult
Language and literacy
PE
Anything involving recording

Teaching methods that might be difficult for the child
Question and answer sessions
Writing sessions
Handwriting sessions
Copying from the board
Reading from left to right without help
Following instructions

Things to avoid
Copying from the board
Too much writing with paper and pencil
Competitive tasks

Aspects of existing provision which might be successful
Use of the computer for writing
Computer reading programmes where direction is clearly indicated
Paired work with an understanding child or friend where written tasks can be shared
Paired reading
Taped stories
Shared reading
Shared writing
Matching writing activities and reading books to children's interests

How to help
(use of resources, additional adults, differentiation etc.)
Some one to one work with an additional adult
Computer
Tape recorder
Reminding about the task in hand
Short achievable tasks
Help the child to feel successful perhaps by having an adult doing part of a task
Giving time to answer questions
Recording through pictures or a limited number of words
Handwriting practice through play activities, chalk, water
Adult pointing while reading
Lots of practice through repetition
Practice in tasks that need co-ordination

Figure 9.4.   Planning sheet for a child with dyspraxia

and get a greater understanding of the progress they are making and how they are responding to the work that has been planned for them.

Working with parents and carers

Teachers understand that positive relationships with parents can have a crucial bearing on all children's progress at school. Constructive relationships are even more important with parents of children with SEN. A specific requirement of the Code of Practice (DfES, 2001a) is that parents should be involved in the assessment of children with SEN, reviews of progress, the process of statutory assessments and the annual reviews of statements.

Parents know their children well and, if the information they have is shared, teachers will have a much more complete picture of the child's strengths and difficulties. Teachers should also share their views of the child with the parents. Parents can provide information about their child's:

- health;
- physical development;
- communication;
- work habits such as concentration and memory;
- play and leisure interests;
- likes and dislikes;
- behaviour; and
- relationships.

This will help teachers to plan more effectively to meet the child's individual needs in ways that are appropriate.

Involving pupils

Discussions with pupils can be revealing and can help the teacher to cater more effectively for their learning. Questions that might help the teacher understand the child's needs might include:

- What is your favourite subject? Why do you like it?
- What is your favourite way of working; with other children, with an adult, on your own, with the whole class? Why?
- What subjects or ways of learning are boring or frustrating?
- How have your teachers helped you?
- How could your teachers help more?
- What do you think you do well?
- What would you like to be able to do better?

Involving pupils in reviewing their learning and setting future targets helps them to be clear about what is expected from them and can contribute to a more positive self-image and greater self-confidence.

Observing individual children, reviewing progress, planning and teaching

Observation of children is crucial in order to plan for their learning and to meet their needs. Observation can be structured or unstructured and can take place when working with the child or while remaining distanced. The nature of the observation will depend upon what one wants to find out. Learning support assistants can also undertake observations. When undertaking observations the teacher might want to find out:

- the kinds of activities in which the child concentrates well or poorly;
- the typical length of time that the pupil concentrates for;
- the activities in which the child appears most confident;
- the resources that motivate the child;
- the times of day when the child works well or poorly;
- other children that work well with the child; and
- the activities that the child chooses to do.

This information can be built on by the teacher so that the classroom fosters rather than hampers learning.

In order to review the child's progress against the targets set on the IEP or to prepare for a statutory assessment, the teacher might want to observe the child working on the activities that are detailed on the plan. For example, rather than just looking at a finished sample of work to see if the child has used punctuation to demarcate sentences, one might observe the child writing. This will help the teacher to see the choices the child is making. Does the child alter the work or reread it to insert capital letters and full stops? Is it used at the start of his writing and then, because the child is so involved with the content of what is written, is it forgotten later on? Does the child ask friends for help? Is the child distracted by others while writing and so does not concentrate? The information that the teacher gathers from an observation on a specific activity can be checked out by talking to the child later and then can be used to verify judgements about progress. It can also be used in future planning. For example, the child could be reminded to read the writing through to check for punctuation or the child could work at a quieter table.

Issues for Reflection

- Select a primary school child with SEN from a class that you are teaching or involved with. Find out about the child's interests and friends. Discover what the child finds easy and difficult. Find out about the child's particular SEN. Observe the child's responses in a literacy session. Select another curriculum area if you wish. How far did the child achieve the learning objectives that were set for him or her or achieve the learning objectives for the session? How was the child supported during the session? How was the work tailored to meet his or her needs? How did the outcome, the resources, the support or the activity differ from those given to the majority of children in the class? What future follow-up work would be appropriate to achieve or consolidate the learning objective? How could this be presented? Discuss your observations and suggestions with your teacher or the LSA. Note his or her comments.

- Look around or bring to mind a primary classroom with which you are familiar. Select a special educational need from those discussed in this chapter and ask yourself what it would be like to be a child with that special educational need in this environment. Imagine that you are the child. Are there images of children like you? Do you find it easy to move around the room? Are resources or activities that will interest you available and accessible to you? What would you ask your teacher to change to make the classroom more welcoming and more inclusive for you?
- Identify a child with SEN that you know. Using the planning sheet, Figure 9.4, given in this chapter, list the subjects and teaching methods that might cause the child problems and teaching methods and resources that will help the child. Use this to plan a writing session for the child.

Summary of Key Points

This chapter has provided a framework from which trainees and teachers can develop their teaching of pupils with SEN. It has introduced them to:

- the Code of Practice;
- some commonly encountered special educational needs;
- planning for teaching pupils with SEN; and
- working with adults and involving pupils in planning and teaching.

Suggestions for Further Reading

Books

Farrell, M. (2003) *The Special Educational Needs Handbook*. 3rd edn. London: David Fulton. This book is a collection of useful explanations of terms related to SEN arranged alphabetically. Each entry contains suggestions for further reading.

Gross, J. (2002) *Special Educational Needs in the Primary School: A Practical Guide*. 3rd edn. Buckingham: Open University Press. This Open University textbook contains comprehensive, practical guidance on planning for and teaching children with SEN.

Porter, L. (2002) *Educating Young Children with Special Needs*. London: Paul Chapman Publishing. Porter gives some excellent advice about how to work with children with SEN and the nature of SEN.

Websites

DfES website, Special Educational Needs section, www.dfes.gov.uk/sen This is a good first stop for finding out about SEN, statutory requirements and provision.

National Association for Special Educational Needs website, www.nasen.org.uk This site provides useful information about professional development for teachers working with children with SEN.

National Grid for Learning website, www.inclusion.ngfl.gov.uk The inclusion section of this site has a range of resources to support inclusion of children with SEN in mainstream classes.

Centre for the Study of Inclusive Education website, www.inclusion.uwe.ac.uk/csie/csiehome.htm This is the website of an academic centre promoting inclusive education.

10
Teaching and Learning in Special Schools

Maggie Woods

The following topics and issues are covered in this chapter:

- current trends in special education;
- the main types of special need accommodated in special schools;
- types of special schools;
- the distinctive nature of provision in special schools;
- curriculum and pedagogical approaches;
- the future for special schools;
- working within a team; and
- assessment issues for special schools.

No doubt there are those who will find it somewhat surprising to be reading about special schools at the beginning of the twenty-first century but, in reality, they still make a significant contribution to educational provision in many LEAs and could be viewed as one of the better kept secrets of the educational world. This chapter sets out to reveal some of those secrets, assuming that for many teachers and trainee teachers in this country the world of the special school is outside their experience.

Current Trends

The report of the Chief Inspector of Schools (Bell, 2002) states that there are approximately 1,300 special schools in England providing education for about 90,000 pupils. However, this report informs us that: 'The number of pupils in special schools has fallen by about 4% over the last four years. In contrast to this general trend, the number of pupils in schools for those with emotional and behavioural difficulties has risen slightly, as has the number of schools catering for them' (Bell, 2002, para. 239). This might reflect a growth in the number of emotional and behavioural difficulty (EBD) pupils, a shift in schools' ability or willingness to work with them, or the impact of a changing culture. It is often attributed to the present greater focus on, and public accountability for, standards. It does not reflect a decline in numbers of pupils with other special needs, since more children with learning difficulties now survive birth to reach school age.

The Main Groups of Special Need Accommodated in Special Schools

The following classification of types of special need that may be found in a special school is based on the DfES consultation on classification of SEN and the classification devised in Hertfordshire (Harman, 2001).

Moderate learning difficulty

Moderate learning difficulty (MLD) is a developmental delay with attainment below age-related levels in most curriculum areas. Pupils have difficulty in learning basic literacy and numeracy skills. Their cognitive delay may be reflected in speech and language difficulties. Their rate of progress in learning is therefore slower than would be expected for pupils of the same age. Pupils with moderate learning difficulties may also have low self-esteem and lack confidence. Their social skills may be underdeveloped and there might be an accompanying physical difficulty such as epilepsy.

Severe learning difficulty

Severe learning difficulty (SLD) is a significant developmental delay that may include mobility difficulties, communication difficulties and, sometimes, challenging behaviour. These pupils will find access to all areas of the curriculum difficult. They need support to develop social skills and to become independent.

Profound and multiple learning difficulty

Profound and multiple learning difficulty (PMLD) is a severe developmental delay. Such pupils are likely to have a combination of very significant difficulties that include physical/medical as well as cognitive difficulties. They have difficulty with communication and with their connection to their environment. Some pupils will have regressive conditions. They need a high level of support in order to learn and for personal care. They may be passive or challenging through anxiety.

Emotional and behavioural difficulty (EBD) or behavioural, emotional and social difficulty (BESD)

These terms are used to describe pupils whose difficulties in the area of behaviour impede their learning. They may have additional cognitive learning difficulties but can be average or able learners. The difficulties may manifest themselves in poor co-operation with others, inability to cope in unstructured time, poor concentration, outbursts of temper and physical or verbal aggression. Such pupils often have low self-esteem. They are frequently off task and may be unable to accept praise or take responsibility for behaviour. These are often pupils with poor literacy skills whose behavioural difficulties are significantly exacerbated by their inability to meet the literacy demands of the curriculum.

Hearing impairment

The educational definition of hearing impairment is based on the need for adaptation to the environment or the need for support through hearing aids to access the curriculum. A moderate hearing impairment may affect the ability to access the language of the curriculum, particularly in a whole-class setting. Such a pupil would be helped by the use of a radio aid. A severe hearing impairment would require more specialist equipment such as auditory training or subtitling facilities. It would be difficult for a child with a severe hearing loss to manage independently in a small group and to follow verbal instructions. The intelligibility of speech may be reduced. There may also be difficulty with written language. A pupil with a severe or profound hearing loss may have significantly delayed language and communication. They may require a range of specialist equipment including hearing aids, cochlea implant, radio hearing aid, auditory training unit, overhead projector and subtitling facilities. They may need considerable help to manage in a small group and may find it difficult to follow instructions or participate in classroom interactions. Such a pupil would need a visual means of communication and differentiated materials. Their speech may be intelligible to familiar listeners. There may be significantly delayed written language.

Visual impairment

The educational definition of visual impairment is based on the need for adaptations to the environment and/or physical support through the provision of vision aids and additional learning support in order to access the curriculum. For pupils with a moderate visual impairment there may be some difficulty with handwriting and printed materials will have to be modified. It may be difficult to manage in an unfamiliar environment. A severe visual impairment will have a significant impact on development and curriculum access. Printed material will need to be very large and mobility in unfamiliar environments will be very difficult. A profound visual impairment will mean that a child is unable to read printed material or communicate through handwriting. Mobility will be difficult in both familiar and unfamiliar environments. A blind pupil is usually defined as needing mainly non-sighted methods for learning, for example, Braille and use of hearing.

Multi-sensory impairment (MSI)

This is sometimes referred to as deaf-blind and also includes profound and multiple learning difficulties. The pupils' perception of their environment will be profoundly affected. This may make them extremely anxious and create some challenging behaviour. Communication is developed through using the other senses with support for any residual hearing or vision.

Autistic spectrum disorder

This term covers the range of difficulties within the autistic spectrum and should be used only where there is a medical diagnosis of autism. All pupils with autistic spectrum disorder (ASD) have difficulties on a triad of impairments. These are the understanding and use of social non-verbal and verbal communication; interaction – the understanding of social behaviour which affects the ability to interact with others; and imagination – the ability to think and behave flexibly, which may manifest itself in obsessional or repetitive activities. Such pupils will have a narrow and repetitive pattern of activities. The term *Asperger's syndrome* is used to describe pupils who have the triad of impairments but with a higher level of cognitive ability and better language development. They are more likely to be found in mainstream schools.

Specific learning difficulty (SpLD)

This term is used to cover a range of conditions that occur at different levels of severity and may be combined with other difficulties such as MLD or EBD. *Dyslexia* is the most common. It includes difficulties in learning to read, write and spell. It may also involve short-term memory, concentration, personal organization and sequencing. *Dyscalculia* involves difficulty with numbers and mathematical operations. There may also be difficulty with concepts of time, direction and sequences of events as well as with mathematical concepts. *Dyspraxia* involves an impairment or immaturity in organization of movement which often seems to be clumsiness. Pupils may have poor balance and co-ordination. They have difficulty with gross and fine motor movement which they find hard to learn and retain or generalize. They may also have immature speech and late language development. They may have poor body awareness and poor social skills.

Physical difficulty (PD) or physical and neurological impairment (PNI)

This covers a wide range of physical difficulty from pupils who are able to walk with aids to those who are unable to function independently. Pupils with physical disabilities may also have sensory impairments and learning difficulties. There are a large number of medical conditions which result in physical difficulties, including cerebral palsy and spina bifida. Some pupils with physical difficulties will have no problem with learning or curriculum access, while others will need a high level of support.

Special School Provision

When a child is placed in a special school their main presenting need will be identified in order to ensure that they are appropriately placed. All pupils in special schools have a statement of special educational need.

The spectrum of special needs that may be accommodated in special schools has resulted in a range of types of special school, some of which are LEA-maintained special schools, some are non-maintained special schools and others are approved independent schools. Since 1972, when all children were deemed capable of benefiting from education and should therefore be in schools, there have been a wide range of special schools. Schools for low-incidence disabilities are likely to offer regional provision with a high proportion of pupils from other LEAs. The three largest groups of schools are those for moderate and severe learning difficulties and those for pupils with emotional and behavioural difficulties. There are also independent schools, which are often for the small numbers of extremely complex and challenging pupils for whom the supportive environment of an ordinary special school is not sufficient to meet their needs. These are small schools with very high levels of staffing, organizational structures and accommodation suitable to meet the needs of these young people. They are usually residential. Placement in these schools must be individually approved by the Secretary of State for Education and Skills. Some maintained special schools have the facility to offer residential provision.

As the inclusion agenda is having greater impact, more pupils with mild or moderate learning difficulties are being successfully educated in mainstream schools (see Chapter 9). This is having an impact on special schools for pupils with moderate or severe learning difficulties which are now meeting the needs of a wider population of pupils with more complex learning difficulties across a broader range of need. There is a blurring of the distinction between SLD and MLD as well as EBD. There are now some schools whose designation is to meet the needs of pupils with both moderate and severe learning difficulties as well as ASD and PNI. This involves a very wide range of disparate need in one relatively small institution (100–200 pupils) and may involve mixed classes encompassing the whole range of need. Such schools have a very large staff, with class sizes in the region of six to 10 pupils, often supported by two or three learning support assistants in addition to the teacher. Pupils with emotional and behavioural needs may also be accommodated in these generic schools.

There is currently energetic debate within the special school community about the wisdom or otherwise of creating schools to meet such a wide range of need. The view expressed by Her Majesty's Chief Inspector of Schools (HMCI) in his 2002 report is that:

> While a small number of schools have encountered serious problems in coping with additional learning and behavioural difficulties, those provided with the necessary training and resources have met pupils' needs well. In particular, the majority of schools for pupils with severe learning difficulties and half of those for pupils with moderate learning difficulties now make provision for groups of pupils with autism. It is to their credit that the schools have maintained the improvement in standards despite meeting an increasing range of needs.
>
> (Bell, 2002, para. 242)

The statutory framework within which special schools operate is embodied in the Education Act 1996 (DfEE, 1996b) and the Special Educational Needs and Disability Act 2001 (DfES, 2001b), which set up the present system of statements of special educational need. The detailed framework that arises from this legislation is then contained in the Code of Practice for SEN (DfES, 2001a). This provides a 'focus on preventative work to ensure that children's special educational needs are identified as quickly as possible and that early action is taken to meet those needs' (ibid., p. (i)). It is a framework for school-based support with a minimum of bureaucracy. It emphasizes partnerships between parents, schools, LEAs, health authorities and social services as well as voluntary organizations. A new aspect of this revised code of practice is its stress on the importance of giving pupils a right to express a view about decisions that affect their education (See Chapter 9 for more detail about the workings of the SEN Code of Practice.)

In a special school, in which there are in-built strategies and mechanisms to support children with special needs, an individual education plan focuses on three or, at most, four key targets which will facilitate curriculum access. The group IEP is sometimes used for a small group of children needing the same support strategies to access curriculum. The IEP does not contain learning objectives for curriculum, which should be in the scheme of work for the subject, but it focuses on that which is additional or different. In a special school this scheme of work will, of course, already have been designed to meet the learning needs of pupils in the school.

What Makes Special Schools 'Special'?

Size

Special schools have several distinctive characteristics that make them different from mainstream schools. It seems almost too obvious to note that they are small schools, but this is a key feature of the provision that they offer. So special schools provide their pupils with the opportunity to learn in significantly smaller groups than would be possible in mainstream schools. It is risky to generalize but, typically, a class group would be in the region of six pupils in an SLD or PNI school and about 10 pupils in an MLD school or EBD school. The pupils accommodated in the school are those who need high levels of support and individual attention because they are very dependent. As a result of their needs, some may not be able to cope in a large, busy group where pupils are competing for attention and some would become a risk to others if there were not a high level of supervision. There will be pupils who cannot easily form relationships and, therefore, their free time needs to be as well organized as their lesson time because they need to learn how to play or occupy themselves. Some pupils will need regular therapy input in order to survive or to maintain their level of functioning. In a small environment there is more flexibility to accommodate the inevitable interruptions that this will bring and to enable pupils to catch up on any work missed, or indeed, to carry on working while a routine procedure is being carried out. A child who is being tube-fed may be at the side of a classroom still participating in a lesson. There are also more opportunities for pupils to shine by being able to take part in assemblies or presentations which will enhance their self-esteem. Children with limited concentration who are not able to focus during a group turn-taking session can be engaged in the session more effectively and learning styles can be more effectively accommodated in small groups. Children with difficulties in the area of social skills, including speaking and listening, can be more frequently and effectively given opportunities to practise these skills in a supportive and encouraging environment. There can be a greater focus on setting individual targets and regularly monitoring progress towards them.

Curriculum and pedagogy

A second characteristic of special schools is their curriculum and pedagogy. A balance has to be achieved between the pupils' entitlement to the National Curriculum plus RE, which is exactly the same as for any other child and meeting the additional learning needs which pupils will have. Special schools have become very skilled at developing schemes of work which meet the learning needs of their pupils within the frameworks of the literacy and numeracy components of the primary literacy and numeracy strategies. Some schools have devised their own literacy or numeracy framework which is derived from the NLS and NNS and reflects the model, but concentrates on and amplifies the aspects which most pupils will be working on. This is usually doing more detailed work at the earlier levels. There are also supplements to the national frameworks designed to meet the curriculum needs of special schools (for example, DfES, 2003d).

Since 2001 special schools have had non-statutory guidance on planning, teaching and assessing the curriculum for pupils with learning difficulties provided by QCA (2001). This guidance is designed to apply to pupils achieving significantly below age-related expectations. These are pupils who are unlikely to achieve above National Curriculum Level 2 by the age of 16. The curriculum lies within the framework of the existing National Curriculum and the inclusion statements are concerned with the 'statutory entitlement to learning for all pupils' (ibid., p. 4). The guidelines plan for lateral as well as vertical progress, learning in age-appropriate contexts and a widening of experience for pupils as they get older. They offer general guidance on developing skills across the subject curriculum and separate guidance for PSHE, for Citizenship and for RE. The QCA guidelines define progress for all pupils as 'about change and development' (ibid., p. 21). This may be in the area of increasing knowledge, skills and understanding, as for all children. Some pupils may follow the same developmental pattern as other children but not always at the same age or speed. Some pupils may progress more in some areas of the curriculum than others, while for other pupils, progress may be apparent in particular environments or with certain people or resources.

The QCA guidelines acknowledge the importance of IEP targets in the areas of communication, behaviour and social skills, literacy and numeracy. The guidance therefore gives schools permission to structure an individual's curriculum to their particular needs in the context of the subject curriculum as a vehicle rather than an end in itself. It also recognizes the importance of physical skills, therapy input and personal independence skills for daily living. There is guidance about access to each subject for pupils with learning disabilities and about expectations of pupils' learning according to their level and complexity of need. The booklets in this series include useful guidance on assessment and achievement. The concept of progress is expanded to include not only development of knowledge, skills and understanding, but also, for example, reduced support needs. The P levels (Pre-level 1) framework which is included in the booklets for each subject is based on the framework of attainment produced by Brown (1992). This framework identifies the following levels of response:

- encounter;
- awareness;
- attention and response;
- engagement;
- participation;
- involvement; and
- gaining skills and understanding (Brown, 1992).

This is not necessarily a hierarchy of response and may vary for an individual between activities and on different days. It is a model that may apply to all learning and all learners.

The different types of special school offer their pupils a different emphasis in their curriculum and pedagogy. The National Director for SEN has outlined the DfES curriculum model for special schools (Bainbridge, 2002). This is based on the six areas of learning from the Foundation Stage (DfEE/QCA, 2000) which also forms the basis for work in Key Stages 1 and 2. The six skill areas are embedded in the National Curriculum subjects. The development of skills is drawn up through the Key Stage programmes of study. This model of skills delivered through curriculum content continues through Key Stage 3 but in new contexts and with new materials.

The SLD curriculum

In an SLD school the formal curriculum will be used partly as a vehicle to deliver individual targeted learning. The subject content will be presented in ways that encourage some pupils to participate, take turns or develop independence. There will be use of signing and symbol to support access to communication and literacy, with further support from visual cues and objects of reference used to facilitate cognitive understanding. Learning will be accessed through practical experience rather than through literacy although based on the model of the National Curriculum. There will be emphasis on the creative arts as a means of expression and creativity and also as therapy. Communication skills are specifically taught, sometimes in class or group sessions delivered by speech and language therapists. There is a focus on developing personal independence and independence as a learner.

The MLD curriculum

In MLD schools curriculum delivery is closer to that in mainstream but with slower pace, at lower National Curriculum levels and with more reinforcement and repetition in order to establish concepts. There is less focus on accessing learning through literacy. There is also more support given through the use of visual cues to help those who are visual learners. In both MLD and SLD primary special schools the Foundation Stage curriculum is increasingly being used as a framework for curriculum into Key Stage 1 because it is appropriate for the developmental needs of these pupils. The issue for the school is then to make the smooth transition from the Foundation Stage model to National Curriculum so that pupils are on course by the time they are into Key Stage 2.

The EBD curriculum

The EBD curriculum again reflects that of the mainstream environment but with a strong focus on developing literacy skills which are often a particular need for pupils with this type of learning difficulty. There is focus on clear structures, routines and expectations of classroom behaviour supported by the school's framework for behaviour management. The aim is for achievement within the mainstream range, although often at lower levels.

Curriculum for autism

In provision for autism, use is made of very structured approaches, such as that promoted by the University of Carolina's Treatment and Education of Autistic and Related Communication Handicapped Children department (TEACCH website). This has individual programmes of work prepared for pupils in their work tray and a tight system of symbol timetables to clearly map out the day for them so that they know exactly what to expect, can check what is coming next and be directed through the activities of the day. It is thought that this structure and organization in the classroom will reduce problems characteristic of autism. The TEACCH approach emphasizes physical organization of the classroom, timetabling and teaching methods each planned for the individual pupil. The picture exchange system (PECS) is also used successfully for pupils with autism (Pyramid Educational Consultants UK Ltd website). The system has the capacity for developing more advanced language structures. It has been found to facilitate the development of speech for those with a wide range of communication difficulties.

Staffing

It is a particular characteristic of special schools that their level of staffing is greater than that in a mainstream school in proportion to the number of pupils in the school. There are usually teaching assistants working within each class as well as a range of health professionals working in the school. In SLD, PMLD or PNI (PD) schools there is a blend of professionals focused around the physical and care needs of the pupils, while in EBD schools the focus is around behaviour, social and mental health needs.

Support for SEN provision in mainstream schools

A further distinctive characteristic of special schools is their developing dual role in providing expert advice, support and resources to mainstream schools which accommodate an increasing number and range of pupils with learning difficulties. Some special schools have already been providing this service for a number of years and it is now developing as a formal aspect of the role of a special school. Local education authorities may provide training for staff who undertake this outreach work, which could include observing teaching and offering feedback, demonstration teaching at the special school, advice on strategies and resources for identified pupils, contributions to staff meetings and training activities run at either special or mainstream school.

Quality of education

The final attribute of special schools that makes them *special* is their commitment to providing high-quality education for their pupils which reflects their entitlement to the National Curriculum as well as meeting their individual special needs. The 2002 annual report from HMCI stated that: 'Standards continue to rise in most special schools and are good or better in eight out of ten. Schools are meeting a wider range of types of special needs than ever and the continued improvement reflects positively on the responsiveness and expertise of their staff' (Bell, 2002, p. 43).

The Future for Special Schools

There has been much speculation in recent years about the possible future of special schools. This is a result of the strong commitment by government to the inclusion of as many pupils with special needs in mainstream schools as possible, although official government policy has never stated that special schools should disappear completely. As LEAs have implemented this policy, the number of special schools has inevitably fallen as a result of closures and amalgamations. In the main, MLD schools and PD schools have been most vulnerable to closure, because it is less difficult to include their pupils in mainstream than it is for pupils with more complex needs. Some generic special schools have been formed, while other LEAs have continued to support their special schools. As a result there is a range of practice and different arrangements across the country.

Those who support a strong special school sector argue that there should be a genuine choice for parents who should be able to choose a special school as a positive option for a child with special needs. It is argued that special schools provide a higher quality of education for such children who will achieve more highly and gain confidence and self-esteem in an environment in which they are no longer always at the bottom and marginalized by those around them, who are quicker and more confident. Proponents of special schools point to the evidence from parents and pupils that the child is happier and keen to attend school in a way that they were not when at a mainstream school. There is also an argument put forward about the effect of pupils with special needs on the overall national test results of mainstream schools with special needs pupils. Special schools may be seen as providing a higher level of resource and individual support for their pupils than mainstream schools can. They offer small classes, high levels of individual attention and the opportunity to focus on the aspects of personal development needed by these pupils but not easily accommodated in mainstream schools.

The opposite school of thought, that which argues for inclusion, maintains that pupils who are sent to special schools are being segregated from other children and are not being offered an equal opportunity for the same educational provision. They argue that their horizons are limited by the narrower range and level of curriculum in the special school. It is argued that, since adult life is not segregated, so education should not be, but should reflect the inclusive world in which we aspire to live. They maintain that both pupils with and those without special needs will benefit from working together, supporting and encouraging each other. There is an argument that, in principle, segregation is unacceptable in an egalitarian and inclusive society.

There is now a clear statement of intent with regard to the future of the sector with the publication, in March 2003, of the report of the Special Schools Working Group chaired by Baroness Ashton. Although this is a consultation document, it makes a clear policy statement that special schools are to remain a viable element of the whole range of educational provision available. Baroness Ashton's foreword states that 'the Government is strongly committed to the sector and wants to work in partnership with them to ensure the have a secure long-term future … . The special schools sector enjoys the Government's full support' (Ashton, 2003, p. 1). The report proposes that special schools cater for:

the growing population of children with severe and complex special needs; that they should be outward looking centres of expertise and work more collaboratively with mainstream schools; and that the sector should go through a process of change in terms of leadership, teaching and learning, funding and structure and in the way in which they work with health, social services and other agencies to provide support beyond the classroom.

(Ashton, 2003, p. 1)

Working with a Team of Adults in the Classroom

One of the aspects of teaching in a special school which sometimes daunts new teachers in this sector is the number of other adults working in the classroom alongside the teacher. It is the role of the teacher to manage the work of, usually one and often more than one, teaching assistant (TA). This involves the teacher in careful planning to ensure that all pupils' needs are met and that the TA has clear guidance about what they are required to do when delivering part of a lesson to a group of pupils. There is also a need to ensure that the TA, being an expensive and valuable resource, is well deployed and not left as a spectator on the periphery while the teacher performs to the whole group.

There are many successful strategies employed by teachers to work well with their team of support staff. Some of these are listed below.

- There should be opportunity for regular discussion to ensure that TAs have a clear understanding of the learning that is planned for pupils and will therefore be able to support achievement of this end goal, rather than too much focus on the process through which it is to be achieved and the quality of the end result.
- Teaching assistants will be empowered to fulfil their role well if they have received training, along with all staff in the school, on effective strategies for managing pupils' behaviour so that there is complete consistency among all the adults with whom pupils come into contact.
- Many support staff in special schools have developed great skill in communicating with pupils with special needs and may be very skilled signers, using Makaton, for example, to the great benefit of pupils.
- The model of room management which identifies specific roles for members of classroom staff can also be helpful since it ensures that all the adults in the room are clear about what they are to do and will not overlap with each other or hold back through uncertainty.
- Teaching assistants have a valuable role in recording pupils' responses and achievements during the course of a lesson in order to free up the teacher to concentrate on interaction with pupils.

There are also other adults who work with the teacher in the classroom. These include the midday supervisory staff who cover an important part of the pupils' school day. It is valuable for them to be included in training, particularly in management of behaviour according to the school's policy and in organizing activities and play for pupils. The drivers and escorts who transport pupils to and from school each day are also part of the whole team of adults with whom pupils may spend a significant amount of time. It is beneficial for them to be included in some of the communication about pupils' needs and effective ways of managing them successfully.

In working in teams with all adults who contribute to the work of the school the key is, not surprisingly, clear, regular and meaningful communication. It is therefore important to ensure that time is planned in to allow this to happen on a regular basis and that there are mechanisms in place so that planning, recording and evaluation of pupils' ongoing progress is made available to all members of the team.

Assessment Issues – P Levels and Use of Data

The QCA guidance on the curriculum for pupils with learning difficulties (QCA, 2001) provides a framework for understanding and mapping the progress of pupils with learning disabilities in the form of the P levels. There are P levels for each of the National Curriculum subjects as well as PSHE, citizenship and RE included in the guidance, with advice on their use. They are expected to be used for summative assessment on a best-fit basis which will give a profile of achievement for an individual child. P levels 1 to 3, the earliest developmental level, are divided into two sublevels each and are generic across all subjects. In the guidance there are therefore examples of generic attainment within the context of each subject, based on the belief that attainment could vary between different subjects because a child may show a different response in a different subject context. The remaining P levels, 4 to 8, are subject specific. When originally devised, the P levels were expected to be used for tracking progress. For example, this could be at the end of a school year, for making best-fit summative judgements, for whole-school target-setting and to support routine assessments throughout the year. The P scales were not originally intended to facilitate formative assessment, which should be based on teachers' professional judgement. However, there are now several models of tracking of progress based on P levels that can be used to collect, collate and analyse data. There are also many examples of the use of P levels to provide a structure for the curriculum.

Issues for Reflection

- How can special schools contribute to the whole educational system? What are the benefits and drawbacks of their continued existence?
- How can special schools support and enhance provision for pupils with special educational needs in mainstream schools?
- How can teachers maintain a balance between learning and behaviour management in the classroom?
- What can the special school teacher do to manage effectively a team of adults working together in the classroom?

- What might be done to manage the growing number of pupils with EBD moving into the special school sector?

Summary of Key Points

- The special school population has fallen by about 4 per cent since 1998 but the number of pupils in EBD schools has risen slightly along with the number of such schools.
- Some LEAs have reduced their number of special schools. This has included amalgamations to create larger schools for a wider range of need.
- There is a range of significant learning difficulties, including cognitive, physical or emotional/behavioural, which may require special school provision. These difficulties may occur in any combination with each other.
- The impact of the inclusion agenda means that special schools now meet the needs of a wider population with more complex and challenging difficulties across a wider range of need. There are strong views for and against this trend.
- The statutory framework providing the context in which special schools operate is the Education Act 1996 and the SEN and Disability Act 2001. The SEN Code of Practice provides guidance on implementation of the SEN and Disability Act.
- The distinctive characteristics of special schools are their small size, their curriculum and pedagogy, level of staffing and their dual role.
- There is ongoing debate about the need for a strong special school sector.
- The government has now clearly stated its commitment to a 'secure long-term future' for special schools. This will include development of a dual role.
- The role of the special school teacher includes management of the often large team of adults working in the classroom.
- There are particular issues for assessment of learning for pupils working for most of their school career at low developmental levels and making progress in small steps. The P level framework has been devised to facilitate tracking of pupils' progress and achievement at this level.

Suggestions for Further Reading

QCA (2001) *Planning, Teaching and Assessing the Curriculum for Pupils with Learning Difficulties: General Guidelines.* London: QCA. This QCA guidance provides a clear framework for curriculum entitlement for pupils who have learning difficulties such that they are unlikely to achieve above level 2 at Key Stage 4.

DfEE/QCA (2001) *Supporting the Target Setting Process: Guidance for Effective Target Setting for Pupils with Special Educational Needs.* London: DfEE/QCA. The focus of this booklet is on the setting of targets in the context of the school improvement cycle. It includes a helpful explanation of the development and potential use of P scales in mathematics, language and literacy and science.

Berger, A. and Gross, J. (1999) *Implementing the Literacy Hour for Pupils with Learning Difficulties.* London: David Fulton.

Berger, A., Morris, D. and Portman, J. (2000) *Implementing the National Numeracy Strategy for Pupils with Learning Difficulties.* London: David Fulton. These two books give helpful guidance on implementing the NLS and NNS for pupils with learning difficulties. They offer detailed practical advice about activities and planning lessons.

The *British Journal of Special Education* and *Special Children* are the journals of the National Association of Special Educational Needs (NASEN) and contain articles and reports that are relevant to those concerned with SEN.

11
Gifted and Talented Pupils in Primary Schools

Derek Haylock

The following topics and issues are covered in this chapter:

- the nature and range of giftedness and talent in primary school children;
- personal and social characteristics of able children;
- general cognitive characteristics of able children;
- different categories of intelligence;
- recognizing high ability in English, in mathematics and in science;
- the acceleration/enrichment debate and the notion of 'stretching them sideways';
- activities outside of the class lesson for gifted and talented pupils; and
- further support and guidance.

This chapter is about the pupil who turns up from time to time in a primary school year group, for whom an intelligent and thoughtful teacher will recognize that the provision in one or more curriculum areas which is appropriate for the normal range of pupils in that year group is nothing like sufficiently demanding and challenging. The chapter starts by emphasizing the broad range of exceptional ability, giftedness and talent that teachers may encounter in their pupils. A number of models for describing the characteristics of such pupils are outlined. Within the core subjects of the curriculum – English, mathematics and science – in addition to exceptional achievement in conventional terms, there usually will be evidence of qualities that can be recognized in some way as being indicative of creativity.

The Nature and Range of Giftedness and Talent

A quick glance along the section of the library that contains books about this subject reveals a variety of terms by which authors and teachers refer to pupils who do outstandingly well in school in one or more areas of the curriculum.

Various titles refer to children who are identified as 'able', 'more able', 'very able' 'of exceptional ability', 'gifted' and 'gifted and talented'. The last of these seems to be the current favourite. It is clear that none of these terms is used consistently within the profession with any real precision, and both authors and teachers will often use different terminology at different times to refer to the same pupils. In this respect, this chapter will not be an exception. The view is taken in the discussion that follows that there is little to be gained by trying to provide precise definitions of various degrees of high ability, or fine distinctions between giftedness and talent.

The opening sentence of this chapter provides my own pragmatic description of the pupils that are being discussed here. Primary school teachers have to cope all the time with a range of competence within every curriculum area they teach and they develop a variety of strategies for differentiating between pupils in their planning and teaching. They often group pupils within their classes according to their ability in certain subjects. For example, they might have a group of three or four high attainers sitting and working together in mathematics. They have in their resources additional material for these more able pupils, to ensure that they are challenged sufficiently and achieve their potential. But now and again they will come across a pupil for whom their normal stock of additional material seems hopelessly inadequate and insufficiently demanding. Such pupils are the main focus of this chapter.

Sometimes this type of pupil will be one who shows exceptional ability in just one particular curriculum area, such as mathematics or sport or music. At other times it might be a pupil who seems to show generally high ability across a range of academic subjects, with, for example, exceptional language skills, outstanding scores in mathematics tests and a knowledge of science that makes their teacher feel inadequate! Some pupils stand out because they are exceptionally creative. Creativity is an umbrella term, used in educational discourse to cover a broad range of behaviours, such as fluency in generating ideas, flexibility in thinking, the willingness to deviate from routines and stereotype procedures, or the production of original and nonconformist material. Porter (1999, p. 28) notes that for some writers 'it is the ability to think creatively that distinguishes giftedness from precociousness'. Again this creativity might show itself in just one area of the curriculum, for example in exceptionally imaginative use of language in written English or in creative problem-solving in design and technology. Or it might appear as a more general trait demonstrated in several areas of the curriculum in which a nonconformist and original thinker can be given the opportunity to break away from conventional approaches to tasks and to express their individuality. Then, in addition to exceptional cognitive abilities and subject-associated talent, a definition of giftedness might include 'a less easily acknowledged talent such as leadership, social maturity' (Hymer, 2002, p. 10). Freeman (1998, p. 2) notes that in formal school education, 'social or business talents are rarely considered'.

So, when we are thinking about provision in primary schools for the occasional exceptionally gifted or talented pupil, we have to start by recognizing that we are dealing with a very varied group of highly individual children. These are pupils who should demand of their teachers as much individual attention to their special needs as those at the other end of the spectrum of school achievement, if they are to develop their gifts and talents to their full potential.

Characteristics of Exceptionally Able Pupils

In spite of the range of curriculum contexts in which pupils' giftedness will manifest itself and the variety of individual needs that such pupils may have, it is nevertheless possible to identify some characteristics that are often associated with exceptionally able pupils and which are of relevance to the primary school teacher. These are discussed below in terms of personal and social characteristics, general cognitive characteristics, different categories of intelligence and subject-specific behaviours.

Personal and social characteristics

We ought to mention this area to begin with, because there is a common misconception that gifted and talented pupils are more likely than others to be emotionally disturbed and introverted and to have ongoing social problems in relation to their peers. It may be the case that a number of high-profile adult geniuses, such as John Nash (Nasar, 1998), featured in the film *A Beautiful Mind*, have been emotionally disturbed and at times had desperate difficulty in forming normal human relationships. But it would be quite wrong to extrapolate such examples back to our expectations and perceptions of bright and creative children in primary schools. My experience of working with high-ability pupils in mathematics in primary schools would certainly contradict this view. These pupils have as often as not been stable young people, lively and extrovert, with a cheerful disposition and popular with their classmates. Freeman (1998, p. 27), summarizing the research findings in this area, assures us that very able pupils are emotionally normal: 'There is no reliable scientific evidence to show that exceptionally high ability *per se* is associated with emotional problems ... in fact, some studies of the gifted have shown them to be emotionally stronger than others, with higher productivity, higher motivation and drive, and lower levels of anxiety.' Additionally, Freeman notes that most research studies have found that highly intelligent youngsters have better all-round social relationships.

Drawing on a number of checklists produced by other researchers and writers, Leyden (2002, p. 109) suggests that, along with a number of distinctive intellectual faculties, exceptionally able pupils in primary schools may show some of the following positive traits: curiosity, persistence, initiative, independence, close attention to detail, a highly developed sense of humour, high expectations, a wide range of interests and a preoccupation with matters of philosophical and universal concern. However, in a group situation they may want to be in charge and can sometimes be intolerant of less able pupils. On the negative side, their written work may not always be neatly presented and well organized, they may be restless and inattentive, they may exhibit non-conformist, uncooperative or unconventional behaviour, and at times may appear hypercritical of teachers and other pupils. Most of these qualities may be true of a wider range of pupils, but they present a different kind of challenge for the teacher when they are combined with the greater ability, awareness and knowledge of the exceptionally able child.

General cognitive characteristics

Most teachers will often recognize the exceptionally able child as much by their distinctive ways of thinking, reasoning and problem-solving, as by their actual achievement or output. In general, these cognitive characteristics are often a combination of high intelligence and creativity. The checklists provided by Shore (quoted in Montgomery, 1996, p. 53), Freeman (1998, p. 12) and Leyden (2002, p. 109), for example, would suggest that there is research support for associating the following generic cognitive behaviours with pupils who show high ability in a particular curriculum context:

- they will have excellent memories and knowledge and be able to draw on this impressively in solving problems;
- although they may spend longer on planning their approach to a problem or task, they will reach decisions more speedily and will often condense the steps in a solution to a problem;
- they will show high levels of analytical thinking in tackling a problem, showing awareness of what information is needed and what is irrelevant;
- they will tend to generalize methods and principles and apply them readily to new situations;
- they will show flexibility in their thinking and can often see and will opt for alternative, non-routine approaches to learning and problem-solving;
- they will show a tendency to embrace complexity as a way of making tasks more stimulating; and
- they may show an ability to concentrate on extended tasks over a period of time from an early age.

It will often be characteristics such as these demonstrated in one or more areas of the curriculum that may alert a primary school teacher to the possibility that a particular child has a need for special provision in order to ensure that these kinds of thinking and reasoning are given substantial opportunities to develop and to be employed.

Different categories of intelligence

For many teachers, advisers and authors addressing the issue of curriculum provision for exceptionally able pupils, Gardner's model of multiple intelligences (Gardner, 1983) has resonated strongly with their experience of such pupils. Gardner has argued for there being at least seven distinct kinds of intelligence, which are relatively autonomous and independent of each other.

Any given exceptionally able pupil may then be identified as showing exceptional performance in one or more of these kinds of intelligence. In this model,
human ability can be evidenced in the following ways:

- linguistic intelligence, which involves the use of spoken, written or signed
  language;
- logical-mathematical intelligence, which includes both analysis – systematic
  and logical reasoning – and synthesis – recognizing patterns and articulating generalizations;
- spatial intelligence, including the ability to interpret and manipulate spatial
  information in two and three dimensions;
- musical intelligence, which shows itself through the ability to discriminate
  sounds and to respond to ideas and emotions in both musical performance
  and musical appreciation;
- bodily-kinaesthetic intelligence, physical co-ordination in sports and gym-
  nastics;
- interpersonal intelligence, showing itself in sensitivity to social cues and
  effective social behaviour; and
- intrapersonal intelligence, which is an awareness of yourself, your own
  needs and emotions, your personal strengths and weaknesses.

Subsequently, Gardner has expanded this list to cover comprehensively all
human endeavour, including, first, naturalistic intelligence (which allows
people to distinguish among, classify and use features of the natural environment), and then, later (Gardner, 2000), spiritual intelligence (dealing with spiritual awareness and response) and existential intelligence (showing concern
about fundamental questions of existence). These (seven, eight or ten) different 'ways of knowing' – as they are often referred to – have become immensely
influential in structuring educational provision in the USA particularly. In
Britain, too, it is not uncommon to see this model featuring in school and local
education authority policy documents and guidelines for provision for very
able pupils (for example, Norfolk Education and Advisory Service, 2003).
Teachers find it helpful to be able to focus on a child's particular ability by
referring to it as, say, high linguistic intelligence or high logical-mathematical
intelligence, and then to target the nurturing of the characteristic features of
that particular kind of intelligence.

The model also gives recognition to a broader range of exceptional ability
than might normally be taken into consideration in a school's provision for
more able pupils, by inclusion of special performance in areas like music and
sport, which traditionally have been identified as special talents, and also in
aspects of social, personal and spiritual development, which have not. Readers
may find it surprising to describe exceptional performance in areas such as
sport or social relationships as an 'intelligence'. Yet, one has only to consider
the way in which the mind of a top sportsperson – think of the footballer
David Beckham or the cricketer Sachin Tendulkar – is able to process rapidly
a complex set of spatial and kinetic relationships, to predict and evaluate
instantly the outcomes of a set of available choices and then to co-ordinate

their physical actions to produce the optimum effect, to realize that this is behaviour that is worthy of the adjective 'intelligent'. Yet, all too often teachers will not hold such outstanding performance in the same regard as outstanding achievement in academic areas of the curriculum. Gardner's theory at least has the merit of challenging such an attitude and recognizing intelligence in all its different manifestations.

Subject-specific behaviours

In practice, recognition of special talents in music and sport is usually the responsibility of experts in the fields – such as private music teachers and coaches in sports clubs – rather than that of the primary school teacher. By contrast, all teachers in primary schools will from time to time find themselves involved to some extent in the recognition of exceptional ability in language, mathematics and science, the core subjects of the curriculum. In these cases it is not just a matter of the pupil's attainment and scores in tests or examinations being at a higher level than their peers. It is also to do with recognition of the characteristic behaviours within each of these subjects that are the most significant indicators of exceptional ability. It is important therefore that each primary teacher should be aware of the key subject-specific behaviours associated with special ability in these core subjects. For the teacher, this awareness will provide not only a means of recognizing high ability in these subjects, but also a framework for the development and fostering of that ability.

High ability in English

Evans and Goodhew provide the following set of behaviours associated with the child with exceptional language ability, which forms a useful starting point for a primary school teacher:

- demonstrates a high level of technical correctness;
- writes complex sentences using extensive vocabulary;
- is able to write and speak in a variety of registers and styles to suit audiences;
- achieves excellence in creative writing;
- can identify and demonstrate irony, humour, absurdity, implied meaning;
- experiments with plot and character;
- displays originality;
- demonstrates speed and depth of understanding in the spoken and written word;
- is able to express and debate ideas in discussion;
- displays enthusiasm for the subject;
- is able to select, extract and synthesise facts from a passage of writing; and
- is a sustained reader from a wider range of materials (Evans and Goodhew, 1997, p. 20).

Clearly, many of the items in this list are simply a matter of doing at a higher level what we would aim for all pupils in primary schools to learn to do, such as handling spelling and sentence construction accurately and writing and speaking in a variety of registers. Pupils who are especially able in language will stand out because of their understanding and use of extensive vocabulary and their fluent reading and writing. But there are some primary school pupils who are able to do this in a stunning fashion, adding to technical correctness and skilful use of the architecture of language the creative elements of originality and a willingness to experiment and play with language. Here is an example of a highly able language-user starting an imaginative story:

> The bonfire crackled away merrily, its flames dancing and leaping upwards. Sparklers shimmered and Catherine Wheels whizzed. Snatches of conversation could be heard as people arrived and departed from the park. Sam wandered around, looking at the bonfire and licking a toffee apple. He was getting rather bored and wished that something exciting would happen. Suddenly he was aware of someone looking at him. An old lady, with tangled grey hair and a flowing black dress, beckoned him towards her. She gave him a firework, which she lit for him with a cigarette lighter. It crackled away excitedly for a few seconds, shooting out sparks and smoke like a jet engine, then fizzled out. Sam was suddenly aware that his whole body felt weird and that he seemed to be much closer to the ground. He had turned into a cat. He looked around for the old lady, but she had disappeared. He ran to his Dad, but he never did like cats and he just kicked him away. So he ran to his Mum, but when she saw him she just started to scream and to sneeze violently. Then Sam remembered. She was allergic to cats ...
>
> (Hannah, age 9)

Technical aspects such as accuracy in spelling, syntax and punctuation, the use of connectives, the choice of vocabulary and use of alliteration, the mix of simple and complex sentences, and the use of adjectives and adverbs are easily identified in this piece of writing. But teachers who are willing to embrace creativity in children's writing as a key factor in recognizing linguistic ability will need to be able to articulate what it is that makes a piece of writing like this 'creative'. For example, the use of original humour in writing and speaking is an early indicator of genuine creativity in language use. The deliberate use of irony, absurdity, puns, hyperbole and understatement are all facets of this kind of creative act in using language, making the reader respond with at least a smile. The fluent use of simile, metaphor and imagery – all of which begin to emerge in the writing of more able pupils in the primary years, as in the example given above – should also be highlighted as key indicators of highly creative ability in language.

Guidance for teaching gifted and talented pupils provided by the QCA suggests that the characteristics of pupils with special ability in English can be grouped under six headings: creative flair, stamina and perseverance, communicative skills, the ability to take on demanding tasks, arguing and reasoning, and awareness of language.

- Creative flair is shown by writing or talking in imaginative and coherent

ways, elaborating on and organizing content to an extent that is exceptional
for their age.

- Stamina and perseverance is shown by taking opportunities to produce
  work that is substantial and obviously the product of sustained, well-
  directed effort.
- Communicative skills include involving and keeping the attention of an
  audience by exploiting the dramatic or humorous potential of ideas or situations in imaginative ways, writing with a flair for metaphorical or poetic
  expression, grasping the essence of particular styles and adapting them to
  their own purposes, and expressing ideas succinctly and elegantly, in ways
  that reflect an appreciation of the knowledge and interests of specific
  audiences.
- The ability to take on demanding tasks involves researching, comparing
  and synthesizing information from a range of sources, including ICT, and
  engaging seriously and creatively with moral and social themes expressed
  in literature;
- Arguing and reasoning includes creating and sustaining accounts and rea-
  soned arguments at a relatively abstract or hypothetical level, in both
  spoken and written language, grasping the essence of any content and reorganizing it in ways that are logical and offer new syntheses or insights, justifying opinions convincingly, using questions and other forms of enquiry to
  elicit information and taking up or challenging others' points of view.
- Awareness of language is shown, for example, in understanding the nature
  of language and having a special awareness of features such as rhyme,
  intonation or accent in spoken language, and the grammatical organization of written texts (adapted from the National Curriculum website,
  Gifted and Talented Guidance).

High ability in mathematics

Mathematics is the core subject in the curriculum where exceptional ability
can be most marked. It is within this subject that we hear about 7-year-old
prodigies who can solve quadratic equations and 12-year-olds passing A level
examinations and embarking on their first degree! Even within a normal
range of pupils in a primary school class the clearly observable range of facility in mathematics will lead teachers to make separate provision for the more
able and less able pupils more often that in other subjects. In a typical Year 2
group (ages 6 to 7 years) a primary teacher will have to cope with some pupils
who struggle to calculate mentally, say, 8 + 9, and others who can successfully
treble a three-digit number like 298. Not surprisingly, therefore, there has
probably been more attention in educational research into the nature of high
ability in mathematics than there has in other subject areas.

Consequently, various lists of characteristics of high mathematical ability
have emerged in this field. Most influential has been the work of the Russian
mathematics educator, Krutetskii (1976), who used a problem-solving model
to identify the distinctive ways in which mathematically capable schoolchild-
ren respond to problems, process information in obtaining solutions, and learn
from the experience. Straker (1983) provided a checklist for teachers of young

children to identify mathematical potential, using criteria related to logical reasoning, recognizing and articulating pattern, and classification. In England, the Excellence in Cities programme (DfEE, 2000b), and guidance provided by the National Numeracy Strategy (DfEE, 2000c; 2000d) also provide lists of key characteristics of mathematically able pupils, highlighting again their ability to generalize patterns and to develop logical arguments, as well as their flexibility and persistence in problem-solving. Kennard provides a synthesis of some of these sources, indicating the following characteristic abilities associated with mathematically able pupils in primary schools:

- grasping the formal structure of a problem;
- generalising, initially through the recognition of instances of a general rule and later from the study of examples;
- generalising approaches to problem-solving;
- leaving out intermediate steps when solving familiar problems;
- thinking flexibly as a consequence of appropriate teacher intervention;
- using mathematical symbols;
- developing logical arguments;
- remembering generalised results (Kennard, 2001, p. 10).

The reader should note the twin prongs of analytical thinking (grasping the structure of a problem and logical argument) and synthetic thinking (generalizing patterns and approaches). The nature of mathematics itself ensures that both these kinds of thinking will be involved in any significant mathematical endeavour and, therefore, in any description of mathematical ability. The reader may also be surprised that none of the lists of characteristics of mathematically able pupils in primary schools makes reference to prodigious skill in numerical calculations. Krutetskii (1976) found that this was not a necessary component of high mathematical ability.

References in Krutetskii, Kennard and the DfEE documents to pupils showing flexibility in thinking indicate that in this subject also there are aspects of creativity, such as non-rigidity and non-reliance on stereotype procedures, that are significant in the identification of pupils who are really gifted. Exceptional ability in mathematics is not just high achievement in the standard elements of the curriculum. In my own research I have explored the relationship of mathematical creativity to mathematical attainment (Haylock, 1997). Pupils of equally high mathematical attainment can show vastly different performances on tests designed to reveal mathematical creativity (mathematical tasks requiring divergent thinking in problem-solving and problem-posing and breaking from established procedures). Conventional mathematical attainment limits the pupil's performance in terms of mathematical creativity, but does not determine it (Haylock, 1987). Low-attaining pupils do not have sufficient mathematical knowledge and skills to demonstrate creative thinking on the kinds of tasks used in the research. But the higher the level of attainment the more possible it becomes to discriminate between pupils in terms of the indicators of mathematical creativity. The pupils with the greatest facility for overcoming fixation and for thinking

divergently in mathematics are usually in the very highest attaining group –
but even in this group there are significant numbers of pupils who show very
low levels of these kinds of creative thinking in mathematics. Using this model
we might identify the mathematically gifted pupil as one who is both a high
attainer and highly creative (flexible, divergent, non-rigid, unconventional) in
their approach to mathematical tasks. These pupils are found to show low
levels of anxiety to mathematics, to have high self-concepts, to think in broad
categories (being able to see similarities between mathematical entities) and
to be willing to take reasonable risks in a mathematical context.

The guidance for teaching gifted and talented pupils provided by the QCA
provides a useful summary of this section:

> Pupils who are gifted in mathematics are likely to:
> * learn and understand mathematical ideas quickly;
> * work systematically and accurately;
> * be more analytical;
> * think logically and see mathematical relationships;
> * make connections between the concepts they have learned;
> * identify patterns easily;
> * apply their knowledge to new or unfamiliar contexts;
> * communicate their reasoning and justify their methods;
> * ask questions that show clear understanding of, and curiosity about, mathematics;
> * take a creative approach to solving mathematical problems;
> * sustain their concentration throughout longer tasks and persist in seeking solutions;
> * be more adept at posing their own questions and pursuing lines of enquiry.
>
> (National Curriculum website, Gifted and Talented Guidance)

High ability in science

In science, because of the nature of the subject, with its emphasis on drawing
conclusions from experiments, able pupils in primary schools are likely to get
most opportunity to demonstrate and develop such key generic cognitive
skills as planning, organizing, classifying, problem-solving, reflecting and evaluating. In addition, there is a huge amount of technical knowledge and terminology which pupils with an exceptional fascination for things scientific can
acquire, even at primary level. Primary teachers will tell you, for example, of
pupils with an extraordinary knowledge of astronomy, or an extensive understanding of electric motors or a comprehensive knowledge of fossils. But the
creative aspect that we usually look for in any discussion of giftedness is also
potentially there in primary science. It begins with pupils spotting patterns or
associations in their observations and in recognizing that a principle discovered in one scientific context can be applied in another. It is shown in the
process of hypothesizing, where the pupil draws on some experimental or
observational data to formulate a theory or principle that can then be checked
by further experimentation or observation. Creativity is shown further by the
pupil who is innovative in experimental design. These creative aspects of the
process of thinking scientifically feature in the description of pupils with high

scientific ability, provided by Coates and Wilson (in Eyre and McClure, 2001, p. 92). These authors assert that such pupils have a natural curiosity about the world and the way things work; that they enjoy hypothesizing and show an ability to express scientific knowledge and understanding logically and coherently; that they use scientific vocabulary accurately and appropriately; that they are able to transfer knowledge and understanding from one situation to another and can spot and describe patterns in results; and that they show innovation in experimental design and in the way they collect and record data.

The curiosity of the able young scientist about the world and the way things work can sometimes lead to an extraordinary persistence in researching some personal interest, with the pupil consuming reference books and lapping up more and more facts and scientific principles about the subject in question. It is not uncommon for the able scientist to 'show intense interest in one particular area of science (such as astrophysics), to the exclusion of other topics' (National Curriculum website, Gifted and Talented Guidance). They may have scientific hobbies, have an unusual interest in science books and science fiction, and enjoy talking to the teacher about new scientific information they have acquired.

The QCA, on the National Curriculum Gifted and Talented website, provides a detailed description of some further characteristics of pupils who are gifted in science. The guidance asserts that such pupils are likely to:

- be extremely interested in finding out more about themselves and things around them;
- enjoy researching obscure facts and applying scientific theories, ideas and models when explaining a range of phenomena;
- be able to sustain their interest and go beyond an obvious answer to underlying mechanisms and in greater depth;
- be inquisitive about how things work and why things happen;
- ask many questions, suggesting that they are willing to hypothesize and speculate;
- use different strategies for finding things out;
- think logically, providing plausible explanations for phenomena;
- put forward objective arguments, using combinations of evidence and creative ideas, and question other people's conclusions;
- decide quickly how to investigate fairly and how to manipulate variables;
- consider alternative suggestions and strategies for investigations;
- analyse data or observations and spot patterns easily;
- strive for maximum accuracy in measurements of all sorts, and take pleasure, for example, from reading gauges as accurately as possible;
- make connections quickly between facts and concepts they have learned, using more extensive vocabulary than their peers;
- think abstractly at an earlier age than usual;
- enjoy challenges and problem-solving, while often being self-critical; and
- be self-motivated, willingly putting in extra time (adapted from the National Curriculum website, Gifted and Talented Guidance).

However, teachers are alerted to the possibility that these pupils may approach undemanding work casually and carelessly, they can be easily bored by over-repetition of basic ideas, and that, although they may be methodical in their thinking, this may not be the case in the recording of their results and findings.

Acceleration or Enrichment

The trick in providing learning opportunities for all pupils in school is to ensure that they are sufficiently challenged but without experiencing too much failure. Just as low-attaining pupils can be easily demotivated by experiencing too much failure in the tasks they are given in schools, so can high-attaining pupils by too little challenge. However, challenge does not come simply from moving the more able pupils through the standard curriculum at a greater pace. This can be part of the answer, but such an approach (often called acceleration) is based on the false premise that the standard curriculum is appropriate and sufficient for all pupils. The discussion above about the characteristics of gifted and talented pupils indicates that these pupils are capable of engaging substantially with a much broader range of activity, with material that is not just 'harder' but qualitatively different (often called enrichment) with opportunities to foster aspects of their creativity. So, as well as stretching more able pupils vertically (acceleration), we should be looking for ways to stretch them sideways (enrichment).

Acceleration is sometimes understood as an organizational device, meaning the moving of the pupil to work with a class or set in an older year group, for those subjects in which special talent has been identified. There are obviously advantages to this in terms of moving through the standard curriculum more quickly, but often such an approach will still fail to provide the pupil with the sideways stretching that they need as well. Pupils will often be unhappy to be separated from their age-group peers and may experience greater social problems in integration with older pupils. There are also some very obvious practical difficulties of organization. For example, having reached the top set in the top year group in a primary school in, say, mathematics, ahead of their chronological age, where does the pupil go the following year? Most primary schools will therefore tend to keep their gifted and talented pupils working with their own year groups, but seek to ensure special provision within lessons where the material may be insufficiently challenging, and to supplement this with additional opportunities outside normal class lessons.

The special provisions within ordinary class lessons are likely to be a combination of acceleration (moving the pupil on to more advanced material) and enrichment. Particular knowledge and skills to be learnt by the majority of pupils later on can be selected to be taught to the more able pupils specifically because possession of this knowledge and these skills might open up possibilities for a broader range of experiences for them. For example, in mathematics, very able Year 4 pupils (ages 8 and 9) can begin to learn to use algebraic notation in mathematics, not just because it is more advanced mathematics, but specifically because it provides the pupils with a tool they can use to articulate the generalizations arising from their explorations of pattern in number.

Stretching them sideways

The descriptions of the characteristics of gifted and talented pupils provided above are the starting point for determining how to stretch these pupils sideways. The basic curriculum principle for the teacher planning to meet their special needs is to ensure that they are provided with experiences and opportunities that develop these exceptional qualities and characteristics.

For example, in English language a characteristic of the exceptionally able pupil is their ability to take on demanding tasks, researching, comparing and synthesizing information from a range of different sources. The QCA gives an example of how a unit of work for a Year 6 class based on the school information booklet might provide opportunities for the more able pupil to develop this kind of ability:

> Most pupils generate accounts of their own experiences to include in the booklet, or work together to write an introduction to the school for visitors. Pupils with special gifts in literacy could carry out a much more demanding 'review, research and rewrite' exercise. They could critically analyze the content and design of an existing booklet and generate alternative proposals for a new document, incorporating the contributions of their fellow pupils. This would allow the most able pupils to explore how the use of language can be effectively related to illustrations and other design features of texts.
>
> (National Curriculum website, Gifted and Talented Guidance)

For some further practical suggestions for challenging the more able language user, the reader is referred to Dean (1998).

In mathematics, the QCA proposes that activities for the exceptionally able should aim 'to increase pupils' ability to analyse and solve problems, stimulate originality and encourage initiative and self-direction'. Activities should challenge pupils 'to develop their thinking through, for example, observing, comparing, classifying, hypothesising, criticising, interpreting and summarising' (National Curriculum website, Gifted and Talented Guidance). Many such activities are provided in, for example, the National Numeracy Strategy mathematical challenges for able pupils (DfEE, 2000d). A particularly useful resource for teachers is the Internet-based material provided by NRICH (NRICH website), a project based at the University of Cambridge School of Education. This project aims to establish a permanent national centre in the UK for curriculum enrichment to provide mathematical learning support for very able children of all ages. The learning and enjoyment of mathematics is promoted through an Internet newsletter and the participation of university students as peer teachers providing an electronic answering service. The NRICH centre also offers support, advice and inservice training to teachers, and resources for mathematics clubs.

In science teachers can give pupils with exceptional scientific ability access to more ICT-based information for research, they can give pupils the chance to modify an investigation being undertaken by the whole class to make it more challenging, or they can expect these pupils to provide explanations and connections, when other pupils are reporting only information and observations. Individual science projects in an area of personal interest carried on both at school and at home are often one of the most effective ways of engaging the more able young scientist. For some practical suggestions for these kinds of activities in science for more able pupils the reader is referred to Coates and Wilson (in Eyre and McClure, 2001).

Activities outside the class lesson

A number of actions are taken by many primary schools to ensure proper support for their gifted and talented pupils. First would be the appointment of a member of staff with responsibility in this area. This member of staff would be expected to research resources, including useful and relevant websites, to consult LEA guidance and to develop contacts with relevant organizations, specialist teachers in the local high school, LEA advisers and experts in the field outside of the school. This 'gifted and talented co-ordinator' would take the lead in the development of a school policy, outlining the principles and provision in this area to which the school is committed. Governing bodies will often appoint one of their members to exercise oversight of this area.

Putting on musical and dramatic performances, participating in sporting competitions and producing school magazines and newsletters, for example, are all well-established opportunities for a range of particular gifts and talents to be fostered. But in addition to such public activities, many schools have found ingenious ways of providing additional challenge for more able pupils outside the normal class lessons. For example,

- a school arranges for their more able pupils to participate in a mathematics challenge event organized by the local university for mathematically able pupils in local primary schools;
- a school organizes a literary circle for more able language users, inviting pupils to read and discuss books, poetry and to share their own writing;
- a group of primary science and mathematics teachers, supported by two enthusiastic teachers from a high school, organize a series of termly events for able young scientists, including visits to local science laboratories and industrial sites;
- a school commissions a more able language user to visit a local author, to interview them and to write a piece for the local newspaper;
- a school arranges for a mathematics educator from the local university department of education to spend an hour a week working with a small group of very able mathematicians;
- in co-operation with the parents, a teacher puts together a collection of science experiments and challenges that can be performed at home by an exceptionally able pupil; or
- the parents of more able pupils are encouraged to arrange for their children to attend weekend events provided by subject organizations or summer schools designed to stretch the gifted and talented pupils.

Further support and guidance

In recent years curriculum provision for the gifted and talented pupils has been an area of increased activity. As has been noted above, the QCA through its

National Curriculum Gifted and Talented Pupils website, has provided guidance on teaching such pupils. This includes guidance on identification of the gifted and talented, school policies, roles and responsibilities, management of provision, how to match teaching to pupils' needs and on issues of transition. Very active in this field in the UK has been the National Association for Able Children in Education (NACE website), which is the professional association that promotes and supports the education of gifted and talented pupils. Members of this association have generated a substantial number of books in the last few years, reflecting the burgeoning interest in this field. Local education authorities, often prompted by OFSTED inspections, are also actively producing guidance for their schools in this area. It is encouraging to see that at last in Britain the special needs of the gifted and talented pupils in our primary schools are being addressed seriously by all who have a part to play in their education.

Issues for Reflection

- What, if anything, do the following terms contribute to your understanding and recognition of gifted and talented pupils in primary schools: precocity, attainment, underachievement, excellence, aptitude, promise, intelligence, creativity, exceptional performance, prodigy, genius?
- In your experience do gifted and talented children in primary schools have more problems in terms of personal and social development than other children, or not?
- What would be the arguments for or against moving an exceptionally able pupil to work with an older year group for one or more areas of the curriculum? In what circumstances might a primary school judge this to be an appropriate course of action?
- For a primary school year group with which you are familiar, for each of English, mathematics and science, identify some examples of activities for exceptionally able pupils that would foster their creativity.
- What would you want to see included in a primary school's policy for provision for gifted and talented pupils?

Summary of Key Points

- Exceptionally gifted or talented pupils in primary schools form a very varied group of highly individual children.
- These are pupils, therefore, who should demand of their teachers as much individual attention to their special needs as those at the other end of the spectrum of school achievement, if they are to develop their gifts and talents to their full potential.
- Gifted and talented pupils are likely to have no more problems in terms of personal and social development than other pupils of their age, although they may exhibit certain characteristic personal qualities, such as curiosity, independence, persistence and nonconformity.

- Gifted and talented pupils can be identified in terms of general cognitive abilities, or by using Gardner's theory of multiple intelligences, or by reference to subject-specific behaviours (particularly in English, mathematics and science).
- In all areas, exceptional ability combines high achievement in conventional terms with aspects of creativity.
- Curriculum provision for very able pupils should be a balance of some acceleration through the standard curriculum and a range of enrichment activities.
- Enrichment activities within class lessons should focus on the fostering of the particular characteristics that exceptionally able pupils show in that subject area.
- Schools should supplement their provision for their highly able pupils within class lessons with a range of opportunities outside the classroom.
- In recent years there has been a growth in the provision of guidance, resources and support for teachers to enable them to meet the needs of gifted and talented pupils.

Suggestions for Further Reading

Freeman, J. (1998) *Educating the Very Able: Current International Research.* London: The Stationery Office (for OFSTED). This is a key text, summarizing the implications of international research findings. Sections deal with ways of identifying very able pupils, their characteristics and how to educate them. The strength of the book is that assertions are based on evidence rather than opinion.

Eyre, D. and McClure, L. (eds) (2001) *Curriculum Provision for the Gifted and Talented in Primary School: English, Maths, Science and ICT.* London: David Fulton Publishers Ltd, in association with NACE. This very practical book has useful contributions dealing with provision for very able pupils in the core subjects of the primary curriculum. It would be a good first text for someone coming new to this field.

DfEE (2000) *National Literacy and Numeracy Strategies: Guidance on Teaching Able Children.* London: DfEE. This book is an important text for all primary schools and teachers, providing government guidance on how to ensure that the special needs of able children are catered for properly within the national strategies for numeracy and literacy.

Porter, L. (1999) *Gifted Young Children.* Buckingham: Open University Press. This is a gem of a book for all teachers of younger children, as well as for parents of gifted children. It provides a rationale for gifted education as well as comprehensive and practical guidance for working with able children from birth to about 8 years of age.

12

Gender Issues in Primary Schools

Jenifer Smith

The following topics and issues are covered in this chapter:

- gender and the child's sense of identity;
- the danger of generalizations about gender;
- stereotypical behaviour and young children;
- teachers' own attitudes and beliefs about appropriate behaviour for boys and girls;
- the issue of boys' underachievement;
- compliance and the achievement of girls and boys;
- reading, writing and talk in relation to gender issues in primary schools;
- the role of story;
- the teacher's role in developing the child's sense of identity;
- the importance of valuing each child as an individual;
- links with home;
- role models; and
- the central role of observation, reflection and talk in promoting the child's sense of identity.

Here are some familiar images from primary school life:

1. Two 4-year-olds wearing pink hair slides sit in the sand pit together.
2. A teacher runs up and down the touch-line, yelling encouragement to the school football team.
3. One child will only write and draw using pink pens.
4. Another child says that writing smells and the pencils always break.
5. One child wears shorts or trousers all the time.
6. Another wears a green lurex skirt while playing at vacuum-cleaning.
7. A 7-year-old wins the goalkeeping competition at the school fair.
8. A 10-year-old always carries a book and reads whenever possible.
9. A 4-year-old consistently wears a blue sweater and a police helmet.

10. A teacher is sitting quietly with a child who is crying.
11. A teacher is leading a class up a mountain.

Before you read this chapter, think about the individuals described above and whether you have ascribed them a male or female character. Then turn to the end of the chapter to find out who is what. Reflect on your own assumptions and expectations of masculinity and femininity and how these might have an impact on the classroom.

One of the major educational issues in the public domain is the concern in this country about the achievement of boys in school when compared to that of girls. Epstein et al. (1998, p. 4) suggest that:

- the discourses in which debates about the schooling of boys have been framed are both narrow through the ways in which terms of 'achievement' and 'education' have been understood and masculinist in style;
- they lack a historical perspective;
- it is unhelpful to set up a binary opposition between the schooling of girls and that of boys according to which, if one group wins, the other loses; and
- questions around equity and differences among boys and among girls as well as between boys and girls are the key to understanding what is happening in schools.

This chapter addresses such issues raised by current research as these. I propose a view of the nature of gender identities and the ways in which teachers in primary school might think about them. Rather than a notion of predetermined and polarized definitions of masculinity and femininity, I suggest that there are many ways to be masculine and feminine and that each individual adopts a number of different ways of being so. Simplistic models of gender-related behaviour and solutions to what is seen as a problem can be seductive. However, gender identity and its impact on success in school (however you may wish to define that) is complex, contradictory and often surprising. In particular, I argue that reflective talk is a major feature of schools where all pupils, girls or boys, can understand their own identities and flourish.

Gender and the Child's Sense of Identity

There are many ways of being male or female. School is one of many influences which contribute to a child's sense of self. Teachers should find ways of talking with children and with other adults about who we are and how we construct and reconstruct ourselves in terms of gender. It is important for schools to develop an awareness of the nature of gender and the issues which it raises alongside other questions of identity and learning. There is still much of interest to be discovered about gender-related behaviour in classrooms and about the ways in which girls and boys frame and reframe their gender identities. Once teachers begin to look closely at what happens in the classroom and, especially, begin to talk with children and each other about issues related to gender, the unhelpful distinctions between male and female become more blurred.

The danger of generalizations about gender

There is a danger that individuals can be ignored within generalizations. A Welsh primary school undertook research prompted by boys' failure to succeed in literacy (Maynard, 2002). The teachers found that boys' difficulties were less obvious than they had at first thought and that boys' and girls' perceptions of certain aspects of literacy such as story-writing and silent reading were very similar. Towards the end of the project teachers tended to focus on the strengths and difficulties of individual pupils rather than talk about boys and girls in generalized terms. They began to acknowledge that there may be more variance within groups of girls and boys (which may be related to a range of other factors, including class, race, religion and poverty) than between boys and girls as a whole.

The teachers in Maynard's study, however, did agree that understandings of what it means to be male and female have an impact on attitudes towards learning and attainment. They maintained that challenging boys' commitment to hegemonic masculinity would be likely to have a positive benefit on their attainment. However, they felt that girls, also, needed to develop a different view both of what it means to be female and of what it means to be male. The teachers' discussions highlighted the complexity and sensitivity of exploring, and possibly changing, boys' and girls' views of masculinity and femininity. Ultimately, they decided that it was not the role of the school to intervene. They saw their role essentially as preparing pupils for society 'as it was'.

Teachers may well be justified in feeling cautious about interfering with their pupils' sense of self, but perhaps we should see children as rather more robust, and as capable of making their own decisions about who they want to be and how they choose to act. It may not be a case of persuading children to take on attitudes and behaviours of our choosing, but rather that the school has a responsibility to help children articulate and explore how they might see themselves, and in so doing, to open up possibilities that might otherwise be denied. 'We need a contradictory, gender, gender-relations model of equal opportunities work that can speak directly and recognisably to both girls' and boys' messy, awkward, lived experiences. And we need that fresh model urgently' (Epstein et al., 1998, p. 91).

Gender behaviours are not predetermined

Gender – in the sense of defining male and female in terms of behaviours, attitudes and roles – is a cultural and social construction, not a biological given. It is something that individuals create while interacting with each other and in a variety of contexts throughout their daily lives. Although there are significant physiological differences between males and females, gender behaviours are not biologically fixed and immutable. To believe that gender behaviours are predetermined limits action and tends to oversimplify thinking about gender.

Children should be seen as agents of their own destiny, able to interact with experience. Models of childhood which do not see children in this way might lead teachers to be cautious about the kind of interventions with which they feel comfortable (Maynard, 2002; MacNaughton, 2000). It is disingenuous to believe that teachers remain neutral. Nor can we ignore the messages conveyed by the institution of school itself. So, however teachers choose to behave, whether they feel they are actively intervening or not, the school, the classroom and the playground will have an impact on how children see themselves in terms of gender.

The process of deciding who we are is internal and personal, but it is also social. But children receive many different messages about who they should be from the society in which they live. Children negotiate many different understandings and learn ways of resisting the contradictory expectations of others (Cherland, 1994; Lloyd and Duveen, 1992; MacNaughton, 2000). Children actively construct meaning through reading and interpreting their experiences of the world. However, they are not free to construct just any meaning or identity. They are limited by the alternatives made available to them. Some meanings are more powerful than others, because they are more available, desirable, pleasurable and more able to be recognized by others. It may well be that some of these meanings are precisely those about which teachers feel ambivalent. How children construct their social understandings, and how they make their choices about how to behave and how to resist, remain thoroughly interesting questions. When teachers observe children closely with such questions in mind, they can be surprised by what they learn. Sometimes they find things they want to challenge and sometimes they find themselves facing contradictions within their own sense of self.

Stereotypical behaviour and young children

MacNaughton (2000) worked with 12 kindergarten teachers in Australian schools who were interested in exploring gender equity in early years classrooms (children aged 4 to 5 years). They observed children's play patterns and found that girls and boys regularly chose to play in very different areas. Girls played in decorative, gentle, passive and domestic play areas. Boys' play was full of aggression, full of action and lots of movement in areas such as construction and the sandpit. Boys and girls controlled the space they used differently. Boys controlled their space through physical aggression, girls through language. Girls avoided confrontation at all costs. Boys were more expansive and were louder in their use of space. If boys moved into a space and girls suspected a confrontation they would leave, so that boys were able to move in and try to take over the space. However, girls were not happy if boys wished to take a major role in the home play area and cast them as babies or pets. As one boy explained, that was only fun if they were a bad pet.

Paley (1984), aware of these differences, spent a year in the kindergarten where she worked, observing children's play.

> Kindergarten is a triumph of sexual self-stereotyping. No amount of adult subterfuge or propaganda deflects the 5-year-old's passion for segregation by sex. They

think they have invented the differences between boys and girls and, as with any new invention, must prove that it works. The doll corner is often the best place to collect evidence. It is not simply a place to play; it is a stronghold against ambiguity.

(Paley, 1984, p. ix)

Paley recognizes her own bias towards the girls' patterns of play (though she is seriously disturbed by the girls' hushed application of silver nail polish) and her discomfort with superhero play. However, her close observations of boys at play have taught her that boys' play is serious drama and she tries to make sense of a style that is discordant to her. In the course of the year – in line with many other observers of children's gender-related behaviours – she discovered that, although there are sharp differences between boy' and girls' behaviours there is a real danger in making assumptions about either group. By the end of the year she saw play involving superheroes as the essential play of little boys, recognizing that everything about such fantasy play is make-believe except the obvious feelings of well-being that emerge from it.

Many studies of gender-related behaviour teach us not to jump to conclusions, nor to deny opportunity through generalized assumptions. Both Paley and the teachers in MacNaughton's study concerned themselves with areas of activity from which children seemed to be excluded because of the children's own ideas about gender. Paley, for example, worried that boys were not gaining sufficient experience of cutting and drawing because they did not choose those activities. She asked the boys why this was so and learned that the boys had so much playing to do that the table-top activities had been removed before they had time to get round to them. Once she made those activities available for longer the boys were happy to get involved in them. On the other hand, girls were seen to be missing out on the experience of building creatively with blocks. Both she and one of the teachers in MacNaughton's study spent some considerable time making these a part of girls' activity.

The strong ideas about gender-related behaviour that many children in the early years possess can challenge those children who do not share the dominant view. Boys, in particular, who do not display stereotypical male behaviour must learn ways of negotiating their sense of self. Teddy, a boy in the kindergarten described by Paley, took a long time to renegotiate his sense of self in that social context. She observed him discovering what is and is not allowed and finding a way of being himself. Quite often it is in the role-play area where such differences emerge. Sam, a boy who enjoyed a sparkly skirt and a pink teddy bear, was tolerated in his kindergarten setting, but his mother, despite her desire for him not to be sexist, was concerned for him to 'get it right' before he moved on to school (MacNaughton, 2000).

Gender and Achievement

Boys underachieving?

At the time of writing, the underachievement of boys dominates any discussion of gender in schools. In the last three years there has been a flurry of projects which focus on the achievement of boys. In the media it is boys' failure to achieve that is the focus of attention. The public debate is often alarmist and presents male and female, boys and girls, as inevitably and irredeemably different. The current preoccupation with targets and target-setting has particularly highlighted boys' achievement because the majority of pupils identified as needing to improve are boys. The picture of achievement in primary schools is based on national tests in English, mathematics and science. Little attention is paid either to achievement in the foundation subjects or in other areas of human endeavour. The 'kind of globalized moral panic' (Epstein et al., 1998, p. 3) with which the underachievement of boys has been met has generated a rush to come up with instant solutions to a problem, rather than a more reflective and equitable consideration of gender differences and the implications of these for teaching and learning.

A significant proportion of the most recent research focused on gender places its emphasis on the raising of boys' achievement and places girls in real or metaphorical brackets (Bleach,1998; Noble and Bradford, 2000; Wilson, 2003). Strategies proposed to improve boys' performance are justified by the claim that what is good for boys benefits girls also, even if that simply means that more focus for boys means less distraction for girls. However, there is no simple explanation for the gender gap in education. A closer look at statistics presents a more complex picture than much recent rhetoric suggests. In general, high- and low-ability boys perform on a par with equivalent girls, although there is a tail of underachieving boys. Boys tend to do both worse and better than the lowest- and highest-attaining girls and more boys than girls need special needs support.

Although girls aspire to and achieve jobs in professions such as law and medicine, they rarely appear at the top of those professions. To emphasize gender as the root of underachievement is to ignore other significant factors and it remains the case that for too many children the future is not equal or filled with opportunity. There is evidence, for example, that social class is a more significant factor in underachievement: 'Overall the underachievement of boys at school is a strongly classed and radicalised phenomenon. Indeed class and the associated level of education of parents (for both boys and girls) continue to be the most reliable predictors of a child's success in school examinations' (Epstein et al., 1998, p. 11).

Compliance and achievement of girls and boys

Historically, boys' and girls' successes and failures have been interpreted differently by commentators. There has been a tendency to attribute boys' achievement to something within – their innate brilliance or natural potential – whilst their failure is attributed to something external – teachers, teaching methods or texts. Likewise, girls' failures are attributed to something within – usually the nature of their intellect – and their success to something external – their teachers or the context – or devalued as being due to lower-order qualities such as neatness or diligence.

In the late nineteenth century, when the Schools' Inquiry Commission made the first systematic and public assessment of boys' and girls' performance, it was found, repeatedly, that girls outperformed boys (Cohen, 1998). Concern in response to this finding was not how boys would keep up with girls, but about the danger of overstrain for the girls! Cohen (ibid., p. 27) observes that 'the figure of the "morbidly" diligent girl and that of the "healthily" unconcerned boy became a commonplace in educational writing'. There is an uncanny reminder of such discourse in recent literature. Noble and Bradford (2000), for example, warn that the way in which girls succeed is perhaps damaging and has implications for their futures. They maintain that the National Curriculum tends to demand 'a well-organised, compliant, procedure-serving teacher and pupil. It tends not to encourage the radical, the lateral thinker, the bloody-minded, the intuitive. ... more girls than boys seem better equipped to slog through the curriculum quagmire' (ibid., p. 5).

The received wisdom is that most girls succeed at school because they are compliant and some boys underachieve because they are alienated. It may well be that, when the curriculum and the pedagogy adopted by teachers present difficulties, both boys and girls find ways of resisting their demands. Some boys' resistance tends to be more vocal and disruptive than that of girls, and draws more attention. Compliance is one strategy available to pupils for coping with the demands of school. But compliance is equally damaging to the achievement of both boys and girls in terms of higher-order thinking, such as problem-solving and creativity. By contrast, alienation is a short step from the risk-taking and independence of thought that lie at the heart of these higher-order cognitive skills. The key point to remember is that both compliance and alienation are learnt responses, reinforced by teachers, parents, peers and society.

Issues Related to Literacy

It is in the area of language that gender issues are most significant in primary schools. I make no apologies, therefore, for giving special attention to this area of the curriculum. My experience is that literacy plays a major part in the creation of gender-related identities. If we recognize children in primary schools as agents in constructing their own identities, then schools, and the teachers in them, have a part to play in entering into dialogue with them and in sharing stories which help them to make sense of who they are, who they might be, who they wish to be.

Reading, writing and gender

Within the area of literacy in primary schools, research on reading consistently reveals that girls read more than boys. Cherland (1994) characterizes girls' reading as a form of resistance and observes that boys read more non-fiction. But, whilst some boys may resist fiction in prose form, they enjoy stories in comics, in film and on television. These sources of narrative may not be acknowledged properly in school. Millard (1997) suggests that we should be aware of the more limited role that narrative fiction in book form now plays in children's lives. Ellis (in Barrs and Pidgeon, 1994) describes how reading aloud from a wide range of fiction, poetry and non-fiction challenges children's prejudices.

The reading resources chosen in school, particularly the choice of books, provide pupils with ways of thinking about themselves and how they wish to be in relation to the world. Involving pupils in analysing resources for gender and cultural bias is a way of helping them to think about these issues. Clearly, classroom resources should aim for inclusiveness, but we should certainly not ghettoize any one kind of text. Just as some teachers are ambivalent about the heroes from cartoons which boys enjoy, so they might be concerned about the popular fiction that girls read. One answer is not to ban the reading of such material, but to engage openly with them and discuss them, whilst at the same time offering a very wide diet of reading resources.

Recognition of children's preferences may be particularly important when responding to writing. Girls' stories tend to have an emphasis on relationships and they are inclined to write in the third person. Boys often write in the first person, placing themselves at the centre of their own heroic stories, or they engage in a quirky, comedic writing which sometimes runs counter to school culture and is consequently less well appreciated.

When reading, it is a male tendency to place oneself in the text, projecting onto central characters, whilst female readers tend to find the texts in themselves, relating it to their own experience of life and relationships. Boys seem reluctant to engage with the self in relationship, but girls tend not to engage with the world beyond themselves. This may mean that their ability to engage with certain kinds of learning is less well developed and their approach to tasks in science, for example, may be misunderstood. These ways of knowing and learning should not be seen as being in opposition, but as part of the same process. The boy who considered writing to be 'smelly' later considered writing as a favourite activity in a classroom where the teacher's attitude makes all kinds of writing possible, and where it was a girl who set the trend for a spate of non-fiction writing.

The youngest boys in school like to be on the move, and nursery teachers have found that materials for reading and writing placed outside the school building attract plenty of use. One nursery teacher observed that boys chose to write outside on the very same whiteboard that they had ignored indoors. This teacher found that there were girls who had benefited from plans that she had instigated with boys in mind. She concluded therefore that there would be boys who would benefit from rethinking literacy from a girls' point of view. Rather than thinking in terms of girls and boys working in different ways, it is more productive to plan for varieties of learning preferences, in the knowledge that it will benefit all pupils to have experience of and to become comfortable with a range of ways of thinking and acting.

Talk and gender

Whether we are thinking about gender-related identities or about how gender may or may not have an impact on achievement, reflection and talk seem central to awareness and self-knowledge. MacNaughton (2000) identifies two metaphors for thinking about ways in which adults can engage with children about issues of identity. The first of these is the metaphor of dialogue, promoted by Gilligan (1988). Gilligan proposes that the self is defined by gaining voice and perspective, and is known through the active process of talking with others, listening to them and being listened to by them. We need to learn to respond to others without losing who we are as we do this. In dialogue with others we learn who will attend to us and who will care for us and under what conditions. We learn who we can and should be, as we learn from others what kind of values and behaviours they believe to be important. Children are engaged in the task of learning what makes them distinct from others and also, particularly as they enter the world of school, what ways of being will show others that they are normal within the social setting.

Plans which depend on the use of talk need to take into account different ways of using talk and to recognize that all pupils need to learn how to negotiate pair and group conversations. The quality of interactions is highly important and teachers are key role models. Talk in the classroom can be a powerful vehicle for raising self-esteem and for understanding oneself as a person and specifically as a learner. Time within the day for reflection and review, for pupils to receive positive and explicit feedback, and to learn how to reflect on their progress and their behaviour helps to create a thoughtful and inclusive classroom. This requires a context where pupils can speak without fear, where each individual girl and boy is valued. Talk which communicates the idea of equal opportunities should be seen in every aspect of the school. The ways in which male and female staff communicate is crucial in modelling the kinds of behaviour to which a school might positively aspire.

Story and gender

The second of MacNaughton's metaphors for adults engaging with children about identity is identity formation as narrative (Gherhardi, 1996). This characterization of identity formation imagines us as actors who role-play and construct images of ourselves in relation to others: 'Actors tell stories, while spectators evaluate them and participate in their construction within a repertoire accessible in situated time and space ... The telling of one's own story ... is inherently a creative process by which a situated narrative of identity is constructed' (Gherhardi, 1996, p. 32).

Narrative has long been recognized as central to our developing sense of self and our understanding of others and the world around us (Britton, 1992; Bruner, 1986; 1996). In the social setting of school we all tell stories about ourselves, we play different roles, critique the performances of others and are critiqued ourselves. Often, this process is hidden. In terms of an equal opportunities classroom, a consciousness of the stories that we and children tell and the roles we play is particularly important. Stories, both personal and public, both oral and written, are woven into the fabric of primary school classrooms. Thinking about who tells stories and how they are responded to is not simply a question of political correctness, but an opportunity to explore the ways individuals and the community make sense of the world.

Part of the process of using stories in the classroom is responding to and critiquing them. As teachers we have to think about the ways in which we can make the classroom an open safe space for children to explore a whole range of ideas. Maynard (2002), in reflecting on the teachers' adoption of a genre-based approach to reading and writing, concludes as follows:

> What, then, might be the future of story writing in primary schools? Given that this form tends to be related to personal expression (and child-centred education?), has story writing become irrelevant in the functional (adult-centred) world of twenty-first century education? And, if so what might we be at risk of losing? … Stories are often essentially concerned with moral questions about good and evil, weak and strong. But within our society these bipolar categories are also gendered: reading and writing stories provide a means through which children work out and develop their developing sense of what it means to be male or female … . While we may not be at ease with the nature of these gendered understandings, are we right to deny children this space to make sense of this important (primary) aspect of their sense of self?
>
> (Maynard, 2002, p. 136)

Paley (1984) describes how she used fairy stories as a vehicle for discussion and shows how she experienced and reflected upon boys' and girls' different ways of reading those stories. Paley developed a way of working with stories and drama in nursery and reception classes which gives children, and teachers, a real opportunity to use stories to tackle important issues and to explore them together. Put simply, children dictate stories to their teachers throughout the day. At a given time there is the opportunity for them to direct the enactment of their story. They choose the actors and their roles and perform the stories in front of their peers. Sometimes the stories are no more than one line long, and sometimes children want to perform the same story several times as they savour it and explore its implications. In this way young children practise being spectators, commentators and narrators and, in so doing, develop their own understanding of what it means for them to be female or male.

The School's Contribution

In another nursery (Lloyd and Duveen, 1992) Seth dresses himself in a pink nightie and tries to put on a tutu that is far too small for him. He is undeterred by the girl who tells him the tutu is not for him, because he is a boy. The teacher, however, helps him to select a skirt that will fit, but then – in a compromise that reveals her own sense of what is appropriate gender-related behaviour – encourages him to wear a waistcoat as part of the ensemble. As Duveen comments: 'Teachers are highly trained professional workers, but in a domain as important to social life as gender they encounter a struggle between competing representations. Authorities may identify approved attitudes but they cannot prevent teachers from holding other beliefs' (Lloyd and Duveen, 1992, p. 3).

The teacher's role

Whether they like it or not, teachers have a strong interactive role in the child's sense of identity. The whole-school community should be aware of the issues which relate to gender and to reflect on the values that are presented through their teaching, in the environments where they teach, and in the ways they respond to children. Individual teachers can begin by thinking about their own sense of self and how they experience themselves as masculine or feminine. They can then ask others to observe their behaviour in classrooms in terms of gender-related issues. They may discover that they act in ways that they are not aware of, despite their best intentions.

As children interact with the world about them, their relationships with other people can protect or transform their identities. The teacher's task of negotiating children's understandings is one that needs careful thought. As in the example above, stories of adult ambivalence about a boy's preference for things regarded as feminine are commonplace in accounts of early years settings. We need to be aware of how this limits opportunities for young males. Girls would seem to have a relatively wide variety of options open to them, but often many options are denied to boys because they are deemed to be effeminate (Millard, 1997). Teachers should work to counter any tendency in boys to resist the mere thought of engaging with female experience in fiction, for example. This attitude narrows the range of literary and virtual experiences open to them. In the primary school, certainly amongst younger children, the nature of gender-related identity is likely to be pronounced. But teachers have the choice as to whether their expectations and the opportunities offered to pupils reinforce sexual stereotypes or challenge them; whether they open up the range of experiences for girls and boys, or limit them.

Valuing the individual

A DfES project based at the University of Cambridge (Raising Boys' Achievement) has found that primary schools where boys and girls are equally successful are characterized by:

- a clearly articulated ethos with a focus on the individual;
- a friendly caring environment;
- a culture of equality where no one is allowed to dominate and all are equally valued; and
- an emphasis on self-esteem and confidence (Raising Boys' Achievement website).

How these characteristics are manifest may vary from school to school. What they seem to have in common is a cohesive sense of community where differences are perceived as being between individuals rather than between categories of pupils, such as boys and girls. Invariably, there is a strong staff community which involves all adults in the school and where discussion of professional issues is a matter of course.

Links with home

When raising awareness of gender issues, contact with home is crucial, both in terms of sharing the teacher's thinking with parents and involving them with the school and child. Schools can learn from parents about their attitudes towards gender issues, whilst parents welcome ideas about how to help their children achieve their full potential in school. A study by Rundell (2001) of boys who are able writers from a variety of backgrounds gives a hint as to how parents can encourage boys to overcome any reluctance to engage with reading and writing. Rundell found that the boys saw their families involved in literacy as part of home and work, and that their parents had high expectations but did not exert too much pressure. Fathers supported play-based literacy experiences, playing alongside boys on the computer, for example. Mothers supported school-based literacy work, helping with homework and spelling. Both parents supported ICT use. The reader is referred to Chapter 7 for further discussion of the role of parents in primary school education.

Role models

Some two-thirds of primary teachers in England are women, yet more than 50 per cent of headteachers at the same schools are men. Men form 1 per cent of the teaching staff in nurseries and only 12 per cent of graduates on primary PGCE courses. The Teacher Training Agency in England has made it a priority to increase this proportion, recognizing the importance of primary school children getting positive role models from both female and male adults.

David Williams (*Guardian*, 18 May 2002) suggests that one reason that men fail at the interview stage is that they fail to demonstrate their interest in working with young children or have not thought about the nature of a male role model. A school which is serious about equal opportunities may wish to ensure that all adults, both teaching and non-teaching staff, are involved in thinking about what this means. Noble (1998) cites the importance of male role models to a large number of boys who do not come across an authoritative male figure until secondary school, but warns against a model which reinforces 'laddish' behaviour.

One thing a school policy could ensure is that pupils meet and visit a range of men and women who fulfil a variety of adult roles in the community and beyond. Such an entitlement goes beyond gender, to an awareness of opportunities and varieties of experience.

Pupils themselves can become strong role models. Older pupils, both boys and girls, can learn and value the importance of taking care of younger pupils. A buddy system for reading benefits both teacher and learner, where an older child undertakes to share books with a younger child. In some schools a weekly Circle Time for groups of pupils across the age range of the school promotes the thoughtfulness, understanding and sense of responsibility, which are necessary to address gender issues in the classroom context. (See Chapters 8, 14 and 15.)

The way forward

Schools where all children and adults are respected and valued as individuals, whatever the nature of the community they serve, do not emerge without hard work. The activity at the core of that work is reflective talk. Teachers must work hard to listen to what children have to say, to discuss their behaviour with them, to explain and to share different points of view, to discuss expectations and to share feelings and responses. They must also talk to each other about their beliefs, about the pupils, and about issues which have an impact on their teaching, such as their attitudes to girls' and boys' behaviour and achievements.

Early childhood practitioners (Francis, 1998; MacNaughton, 2000) suggest that, through their words, images, storylines, movements and songs, teachers can raise the awareness of young children of how they make and remake meanings. They suggest that we can talk with children about how they know things, how they express these things and how they make sense of new experiences. We can show them in what ways daily experiences influence what meanings they give to different aspects of their lives. My contention is that such raising of awareness and deepening of understanding is possible throughout the primary years – and that this, in the end, is the key to developing the child's sense of identity as an individual boy or girl interacting with others and the world around.

Gender and equal opportunities for girls and boys in the primary school are, in many ways, still uncharted territory. This chapter cannot provide easy answers about how to work with our prejudices and the bias which can limit pupils' success at school. But it does propose that observation, reflection and talk amongst every individual involved in a school can be an engaging and challenging way to begin.

Issues for Reflection

- Think about the stories that are told in a primary classroom. These may be oral stories: anecdotes, role-play, personal stories; stories in words or pictures. They may be created by individuals in the classroom, or appear in different media, video, print or sound. Who tells the stories and how do they tell them? How would engagement with these story-telling experiences help to develop a child's sense of identity as an individual girl or boy?
- In a classroom observe how many times girls or boys ask questions and answer questions? How many times does the teacher respond to girls or boys? Are there differences in the ways that the teacher speaks to girls and to boys? Discuss your observations with some friends.
- What stories do you tell about yourself? Think of two or three stories about your childhood and one which concerns your identity as an adult in school. How do they inform how you see yourself as masculine and/or feminine?
- Reflect on your own attitudes to stereotypical and non-stereotypical gender-related behaviour in children. How would you as a teacher respond

to this in the classroom?

● In what ways might primary teachers have different expectations for boys and girls in terms of achievement and behaviour? Do such preconceptions make it difficult for the teacher to value and encourage the development of each child as an individual?

Summary of Key Points

● Gender behaviours are not predetermined, but socially constructed.
● Each child needs to develop their own sense of identity and what it means to them to be female or male.
● Generalizations about gender-related achievement and behaviour are unhelpful for a teacher committed to valuing each child as an individual.
● Teachers' own attitudes and beliefs about appropriate behaviour for boys and girls influence the ways in which they respond to stereotypical and non-stereotypical behaviour in children.
● Children in primary schools need positive male and female role models.
● Story and narrative are central to developing a child's understanding of self and how they function in the world as a boy or a girl.
● Reflective talk is a key feature of schools where all pupils, girls or boys, can understand their own identities and flourish.

Who is What?

(See the beginning of this chapter.)

1. One girl and one boy
2. Female teacher, all-male football team
3. Female
4. Male
5. Female
6. Male
7. Female
8. Male
9. Male (he of the green lurex skirt)
10. Teacher and crying child, both male
11. Female

Suggestions for Further Reading

Epstein, D., Elwood, J., Hey, V. and May, J. (1998) *Failing Boys?* Buckingham: Open University Press. This is a thought-provoking collection of essays which explore the issues surrounding boys' 'underachievement' from a critical perspective. Together the essays offer a complex and challenging view of gender and achievement which provides a number of ways of helping the reader to think constructively and adventurously about gender and schooling.

Barrs, M. and Pidgeon, S. (eds) (1994) *Reading the Difference: Gender and Reading in Elementary Classrooms.* Ontario: Pembroke. This is a very readable and even-handed collection of essays which addresses issues of gender in literacy through case study and which offers useful suggestions for action.

Maynard, T. (2002) *Boys and Literacy: Exploring the Issues.* London and New York: Routledge Falmer. The focus of this book is one primary school in Wales where the staff explored the issues surrounding their concerns about boys and literacy. The book is one of very few that focus on gender and primary practice. It provides an interesting insight into staff perceptions and practices and the changes that occur as teachers engage with the relationship that exists between gender, school and literacy.

Paley, V.G. (1984) *Boys and Girls: Superheroes in the Doll Corner.* Chicago, IL and London: University of Chicago Press. This very readable book explores the differences in the ways children play and how that relates to self-definition. It is filled with vignettes of children at play and snatches of their dialogue as Paley attempts to alter stereotyped play and to uncover her own biases and values.

13
Education for a Multicultural Society

Fiona Thangata

The following topics and issues are covered in this chapter:

- the difficulties of terminology;
- the notion of multicultural education in a multicultural society;
- multiculturalism as opposed to assimilation and integration;
- teaching children with English as an additional language;
- Traveller children;
- a culturally responsive curriculum;
- tokenism;
- school life and home links;
- antiracist education;
- characteristics of successful multiethnic schools; and
- children's awareness of differences.

Overheard at home time at a primary school:

> Child A: Is that your Dad?
> Child B: Yes.
> Child A: But he's brown and your mum is white.
> *Child B remains quiet.*
> Child C: So. It doesn't matter.

The school is often said to be a microcosm of society. However, visits to schools in different parts of the country are likely to provide widely varying impressions of the society in which we live. Visit a primary school in Greater Manchester and one may find a school population composed of 70–80 per cent Bangladeshi children, most of whom are second- or third-generation British citizens and whose accents are indistinguishable from their white classmates. Visit a primary school in rural Norfolk and one may find a population that is 100 per cent white, many of whom may never have met anyone from another country or culture. Another primary school might have two or three Traveller children who are at school for only part of the year and leave over the summer months to travel to fairs around the country. Visit a primary school in a town where there are many refugees and the school is likely to have a very diverse mix of children, speaking a number of different languages and from a variety of different cultures. You can undoubtedly add further examples from your own experiences. However, the teaching staff in any of these locations is likely to be quite similar – mainly female, white and middle class, and often with little intercultural experience. Despite the growing diversity of the pupil population, the teaching force has not changed in the same way.

This chapter looks at some of the issues involved when we consider the role of primary school education in a multicultural society, and indeed the meaning of multicultural education. It is not a list of things to do or not do, nor is it a recipe for working with children from different backgrounds. There is no easy checklist leading to success. There are more questions than answers, but probably the most important aspect is to raise awareness and encourage reflection and debate about the issues. We all have our own sets of values, assumptions, expectations and even prejudices. To say, 'I'm not racist, I treat all my children the same, whether they are white, black, or purple' is to miss the point. In the same way, the same type of argument falls short of providing equal opportunity for all when considering children with special educational needs. Effective teachers do not 'treat everyone exactly the same' because they recognize that different children have different strengths, interests, learning styles and needs that must be considered in order for them to develop to their full potential.

Many of the issues raised here should be placed in the more general context of the aims of personal and social education and citizenship discussed in Chapters 14 and 15.

Terminology

As the Parekh Committee report (2000) discusses, the language used to describe and define race relations in Britain is problematic. Terms such as *minority* and *majority* signify fixed groups of people. In any one school or setting, the use of the term *minority* to describe a particular group of pupils may be quite inaccurate. The term *ethnic group* often leads to stereotyping and obscures individuality within a group. The term *integration* implies a one-way process in which minorities are to be absorbed into the cultural structure of the majority. The term *minority* suggests less important or marginal. The popular use of *ethnic* often implies non-Western or non-British, as in ethnic food, dress or music. The use of the term *race* often emphasizes physical appearance. Although this is an important word, because it is linked to *racism*, it often has to be used in the context of other terms, such as *racial equality* and *cultural diversity*, to highlight the need for equity but also the recognition of similarities and differences.

Multicultural Education

A multicultural society

It can be argued that Britain has been a multicultural society for many centuries. For example, African troops were based in Britain during the Roman Empire (Gundara, 2000). Many Africans came to Europe during the slave trade in the seventeenth and eighteenth centuries. The increase in the numbers of people coming to Britain after the Second World War was largely as a result of the breakup of the British Empire and the need for unskilled labour in Britain. This brought many people from the Caribbean, who were welcomed as a labour force but who met with social hostility. Later, people came from the Indian subcontinent (India, Pakistan and Bangladesh); some became shopkeepers, opened restaurants or flourished in business. As a way of resisting discrimination and racism, many tended to maintain strong family ties and insulate themselves from the wider community (Gundara, 2000). The Chinese community also grew in the period following the Second World War and remains one of the most marginalized of immigrant communities (Gundara, 2000). Refugees have entered Britain from various parts of the world for many centuries, although today's news media might lead one to believe that immigration and asylum seekers are recent phenomena.

Assimilation and integration

The education policies of the 1950s and 1960s took an *assimilationist* or *integrationist* stance. This was based on the conviction that the most important issues were for all children to be competent in English, and that, by leaving aside their own culture and background and being assimilated into British culture, they would be able to succeed on an equal footing. From the mid-1960s, assimilationist policies were criticized. Many migrants fully intended to maintain their home language and culture. Research suggested that bilingual children performed better in schools that valued their home language and culture, and which provided bilingual teaching and/or resources (Rutter, 1994). The assimilation/integration model gave way to multiculturalism.

Multiculturalism

A multiculturalist approach to education is concerned with developing programmes and practices that equip all students with the knowledge, skills and values needed to participate successfully in a culturally diverse society. Multicultural education aims to celebrate diversity, to improve provision for children from ethnic minority groups and to prepare all children for life in a pluralistic society. The Swann Report (Swann, 1985) was an important landmark in the attention given to multicultural education and in highlighting racism in schools and in society. Officially called *Education for All*, the Swann Report advocated a multicultural education system for all schools, regardless of location, age-range or ethnic composition. The report included in its vision the need to:

> look ahead to educating all children, from whatever ethnic group, to an under-standing of the shared values of our society as a whole as well to an appreciation of the diversity of lifestyles and cultural, religious, linguistic backgrounds which make up this society and the wider world. In so doing, all pupils should be given the knowledge and skills needed not only to contribute positively to shaping the future nature of British society but also to determine their own individual identities, free from preconceived or imposed stereotypes of their 'place' in that society.
>
> (Swann, 1985, pp. 316–17)

The report provided clear data on ethnicity and educational attainment, iden-tifying racism as a major factor in the educational experiences of black chil-dren in the UK. Although criticized for not taking a strong enough stance on institutionalized racism (Gardner, 2001), the report did provide a forum for debate and conferences on multicultural issues. Its major achievement was to move the focus away from assimilation and integration towards an acceptance of cultural diversity.

Critics of multicultural education (Dhondy, 1986; Stone, 1986) argued that it was no more than a superficial, liberal response and did not tackle the real issue of racism in society. Multicultural education did not address under-achievement by certain groups, notably Afro-Caribbean pupils who were more likely to be excluded from classrooms than any other group of pupils. The practice of multicultural education in schools was also criticized for trivi-alizing the goal of multicultural education, which was to transform schooling to include the needs and perspectives of many cultures in shaping the ways in which children are educated and, thus, to transform society. Multicultural edu-cation was often an add-on rather than a real change in the curriculum. Troyna (1984), for example, made disparaging references to the 3 Ss interpretation of multicultural education: saris, samosas and steel bands. Styles of dress, cooking and types of music, whilst of interest, were not seen as the most important aspects of the curriculum, and therefore were marginal topics that did not really change anything.

English as an Additional Language

Lack of familiarity with the English language can hinder pupils' progress in many subject areas. Suitable support for pupils with English as an additional language (EAL) may include having concrete objects or pictures when intro-ducing new terms, visual clues on worksheets and clearly labelled wall displays. It may be possible to use dual- or multi-language labels around the classroom. Teachers can learn some vocabulary in a child's first language, including names of familiar objects as well as useful words or phrases. For example, I found this strategy was helpful when teaching Bangladeshi children who were still begin-ners in speaking English. Helping their teacher to correctly pronounce words in Bengali not only demonstrated to them that their first language was being valued, but also gave them confidence to try out new words in English.

Whole-class sessions are beneficial to EAL pupils and they do not necessarily need to be withdrawn for most of their lessons. Differentiated questioning can include them in discussions, and chanting (of key words or number sequences, for example) can build confidence within a group setting. These EAL children can also be asked to respond in a non-verbal way, for example, by an action or picture, pointing to an object or word. They need not be rushed into responding in English before they are confident.

Approaches to teaching numeracy

The National Numeracy Strategy (DfEE, 1999a) makes several useful recommendations for working with EAL pupils, most of which apply equally well to other subject areas. I will take this, therefore, as an example of approaches to teaching children with EAL.

The strategy advises: 'Take care not to underestimate what children can do mathematically simply because they are new learners of the English language. The expectation should be that they progress in their mathematical learning at the same rate as other pupils of their age' (DfEE, 1999a, p. 22). It may be that EAL pupils are familiar with the numbers or concepts in their first language and so any apparent lack of understanding is due only to unfamiliarity with the English language. If they are not familiar with the concept in their first language then their understanding of the concept needs to be developed through appropriate means. This could include use of concrete objects, pictures and discussion with an adult or peer in the first language. Bilingual classroom assistants can also be of tremendous help in the classroom, not only for language help, but also because of the cultural understanding they offer. 'It helps if English language beginners can converse with other children or adults who speak the same home language' (DfEE, 1999a, p. 22).

It is important for teachers to ascertain what level of knowledge a child has in their first language as well as in English, and not to assume the same level of understanding or lack of understanding for different children. It is also essential not to automatically place children with EAL with children with learning difficulties, since their learning needs will probably be different.

New or specialized vocabulary should be introduced carefully to avoid confusion. Mathematics, for example, has a lot of technical vocabulary and so there is a need to emphasize understanding of meaning. Particular emphasis should be placed, for example, on:

- the language associated with the symbols for the four operations $(+, -, \times, \div)$;
- words that may have a different meaning in mathematics than in everyday use (for example, product, difference, volume);
- words that sound similar to other commonly used words (for example, sum/some; whole/hole).

It may be useful to develop a class dictionary with children's explanations and illustrations or examples of commonly met words. The National Numeracy Strategy also provides vocabulary lists for the various Key Stages.

Valuing first languages

The first languages of children, and the number systems, songs and games from their countries, can be used in the primary classroom. This gives value to the other cultures, acknowledges differences and highlights similarities. Teachers can ask children how to say greetings and common words in other languages, and to share popular songs and games from their own culture. A few simple words of greeting can be used for calling the register or for giving simple instructions. I have found that all children are fascinated to see, for example, the 100-square written using Chinese or Bengali numbers. The African board game of Boa/Mancala is popular with many children and is worth learning as a game of strategy. Examples such as these promote the idea that all peoples do mathematics, science, art and design, play games and make music. It places the emphasis on common sharing, and not just on highlighting differences.

Communicating with EAL pupils

Obviously, it is important to pronounce a child's name correctly. It is insensitive to try to Anglicize or shorten a name from another culture to make it easy for the teacher to pronounce. It is also important to find out as much as possible about the culture, first language and, if relevant, country of birth of an EAL pupil. It is also essential not to assume that one's own cultural norms apply to everyone else. For example, in some cultures it is considered important for a child to make eye contact with an adult who is speaking with them. In other cultures, children are expected to avert their eyes in the same situation. In some cultures, pointing at an individual is an unacceptable gesture. As teachers, we need to be aware of these differences and not blame a pupil for inappropriate behaviour or responses without understanding the reasons behind it.

Traveller Children

Reports (OFSTED, 1999b; Swann, 1985) have identified Traveller children as the ethnic group most at risk in Britain's schools. The Swann Report (Swann, 1985), for example, included a section on 'the educational needs of Travellers' children', and talked of the 'extreme hostility' which the travelling community faces from the settled community. At school the children are often subjected to name-calling, discrimination, stereotyping, social exclusion, low teacher expectations and interrupted learning. A survey in Sheffield found that racist name calling was what Traveller children most hated about going to school (Kenrick, 1998). Official figures show that Traveller children are more likely to be expelled from school than black or white children. The cause is nearly always retaliation to name-calling or bullying (Kenrick, 1998). There are now several hundred teachers specifically appointed to work with Traveller children, many of whom belong to the National Association of Teachers of Travellers. Traveller Education Services across the country are endeavouring to provide school–home links and support for Traveller children. In Norfolk, for example, some of the services offered include:

- assisting schools in meeting the particular needs of Traveller children that result from their nomadic or semi-nomadic lifestyle, with the aim of increasing access and attendance, and enhancing pupil performance;
- individual Traveller pupil support, where appropriate, to address gaps in teaching experienced and/or a delayed start to formal education, resulting from client mobility patterns;
- advice for school staff regarding appropriate teaching strategies and materials to meet individual pupils' preferred learning styles;
- development and loan of materials to support individual Traveller pupils' learning and full inclusion;
- consultation with the various Traveller communities and individual families; and
- assistance with home/school liaison where appropriate (Norfolk Traveller Education Service website).

To facilitate continued attendance at school, a government regulation made in 1997 allows Travellers' children to be registered at more than one school at the same time. It is important to note, however, that not all Traveller children travel. Attendance by Traveller children living in houses or on permanent caravan sites is, for obvious reasons, more regular than that of the children of families who are still travelling. About 5,000 Traveller children are still nomadic – often because their caravans are regularly moved on by police and local council officials (Kenrick, 1998). Most Traveller parents welcome the chance of basic education at the primary school level. Literacy and numeracy are viewed as relevant life skills. However, as children get older, the school subjects on offer seem less relevant to real life (life within their community and earning one's living), and attendance drops off.

Traveller children and their families do not necessarily want their lifestyle singled out in the classroom. If, for example, the class teacher knows that a Traveller child knows a lot about horses and might wish to share that information with the class, it would be helpful to give the child time to ask at home if that would be acceptable. This shows sensitivity and allows the family to be involved in the decision-making process. Traveller families often do not welcome teachers or other officials turning up at the place they are staying. This is often better done by members of the Traveller Education Service who have built up contacts amongst the Traveller community.

If children are going to enrol at more than one school, it is important for links to be made between the schools, to support continued learning. A portfolio of work could be made available for the child to take to the next school, along with detailed reports of learning achievements and areas for development. Traveller children may not be familiar with some of the school conventions, especially as they may have to adjust to different schools' policies and rules. It is important, therefore, for the class teacher to be sensitive to this and to provide time and opportunity for these conventions to be learned.

Culturally Responsive Curricula

A multicultural curriculum should reflect the diversity of Britain and the wider world. It should promote the notion that within that diversity there are many shared values, similarities and common goals as well as differences. It should also provide well chosen and positive examples from all cultures that avoid reinforcing negative images and stereotyping. Among the aims of a multicultural curriculum are the empowerment of all individuals and raising the academic achievement of all pupils.

Resources

Texts and resources should be checked for bias and stereotyping. Here are some questions to aid in this process:

- Do the texts present people from a variety of community groups?
- Are those people in a range of jobs and activities or is there evidence of stereotyping, such as portraying a black person only doing sport or playing music?
- Are a variety of names used in the text?
- Are photos and illustrations of developing countries positive or negative? (For example, showing only pictures of disasters, such as floods or famine, or photos of scantily or shabbily dressed children, creates or reinforces images of underdevelopment and dependency.)
- Are examples of stories from other cultures included (such as the *Tales of Anansi* from the Caribbean), as well as examples of texts that address the experiences of a variety of peoples living in Britain?
- In art and music are global examples and artefacts included, such as musical instruments, music from other countries, sculptures, masks, carvings, textiles and basketry?

Examples need to be carefully chosen, otherwise negative attitudes can be reinforced. Well-chosen examples can highlight similarities between peoples (all cultures make music, create art work and use locally available materials to create objects) as well as provide opportunities to explore and celebrate differences and to learn about other cultures.

History

Including examples from history can help to illustrate how different cultures have contributed to global knowledge. For example, in mathematics the symbol for zero developed independently in India and in South America (Mayas). The place-value system of digits that we use now, including the concept of zero, reached Europe from Indian mathematics through Arabia, and replaced the Roman numeral system. However, as Gardner (2001) points out, unless high-quality materials are available, teachers are unlikely to spend hours researching new areas in order to include a multicultural dimension, when commercially produced packs without this dimension are readily available on familiar topics.

Avoiding tokenism

One of the criticisms of multicultural education is that is tends to be an 'add-on' and does not fundamentally change anything in school or in society. The mention of the religious festival of Diwali or colouring Rangoli patterns in an attempt to be 'multicultural' is tokenistic if these examples are used in isolation, without consideration of how they fit into the overall curriculum. Rangoli, for example, is a traditional Indian decorative art form and could be incorporated into art lessons or into mathematics within the study of geometric shapes, symmetrical designs and geometric transformations. There should be a sound educational reason for including any particular topic or example. The examples and topics need to be integrated, and related to the children's experiences so that meaningful learning can take place. If the examples chosen are educationally worthwhile, then they are appropriate for all pupils. Good quality materials for teachers will help them to know about the educational reasons for incorporating various topics into the curriculum.

School Life and Home Links

Awareness on the part of teachers of individual children's home culture and strong school–home links can help to make school a comfortable environment for all children. Examples include the following:

- Do not assume that all children, or their parents, want to be included in a Christmas nativity play. Consultation with parents is essential. Is it possible to have other aspects to an end-of-term play that are not solely Christian?
- Although the school lunch menu may not be suitable for every child every day, it is possible to avoid, for example, making ham sandwiches in class if it is likely to cause offence to some religious groups. Other fillings can be made available.
- Do not assume that all parents will feel comfortable coming to the school to discuss their child's progress. Other ways of communicating with home may be necessary.

The parents of some EAL children may not be confident users of English. If this is the case, the school will have to consider the best way of communicating with the parents. In some instances, a bilingual teaching assistant may be able to help, or an older sibling, a relative or neighbour. Sometimes the EAL child may be able to assist with translating information for his or her parents.

Anti-racist Education

Dissatisfaction with multicultural education gave rise in the 1980s to the promotion of anti-racist education. Some schools and LEAs, particularly in and around London, began to develop policies aimed at confronting racism and providing equity of opportunity to learn for all pupils. Issues considered included the following:

- Is the curriculum multicultural or are minority groups represented in a stereotyped way?
- Are school resources free from bias?
- Do school resources show positive images of all sectors of society?
- How do teachers and the school administration deal with racist incidents?
- What assumptions and expectations do teachers have about various pupils?
- Are some groups of pupils more likely than others to be excluded from school?

Racism

Racism can take many forms. It can be overt, such as in name-calling, or much more subtle as in making assumptions or having expectations of certain children or groups of children. It can often be unintentional or even well intentioned, but that does not make it any more excusable. The Swann Report (Swann, 1985) and the Macpherson Report (Macpherson, 1999) both highlighted institutionalized racism. For those who had been at the receiving end of racism in any form, the reports came as no surprise. Racist remarks or attitudes often arise through ignorance or general stereotypical assumptions. One of the most powerful ways, therefore, to overcome our own ignorance and prejudices is to become better informed about different cultures and communities and not to assume that what is true for one child from a particular community will necessarily apply to other children from the same community.

Characteristics of successful multiethnic schools

What are the characteristics that make a multiethnic school successful? Blair and Bourne (1998) identified several aspects that contributed to a school's success. Most importantly, the school staff took the time to listen to and understand the perspectives of pupils and parents. They used feedback to evaluate institutional policies and practices and to develop an inclusive curriculum. The school recognized the importance of learning together with the local community. Other important features were:

- strong leadership on equality issues;
- good links with parents and the local community;
- high expectations of teachers and pupils;
- ethnic monitoring to ensure equality of opportunity;
- clear systems to monitor progress and target resources;

- strategies to avoid exclusions; and
- clear guidelines for dealing with racist incidents.

Policies for tackling racism

Successful schools, whether multiethnic or not, have a clear policy on tackling racism. Allegations and incidents are followed up promptly, using clearly understood whole-school procedures to ensure fair and consistent treatment of all pupils (Blair and Bourne, 1998; Cline et al., 2002). Successful strategies include:

- noting racist remarks or incidents in a logbook;
- having a bullying box where children can write notes about any incidents without having to speak to their teachers; and
- informing parents about action taken.

(See also the discussion of bullying in Chapter 8.)

However, Cline et al. (2002) also found that many children do not report racist name-calling to their teachers, who then remain unaware of the situation. Reasons for this included thinking that teachers were unable to stop the name-calling from happening, not wanting to make the situation worse or not wanting to draw attention to the fact it was happening at all. Some parents also played down the incidents, feeling powerless to do anything about it. Strong leadership and prompt action by the headteacher were seen to be effective and encouraged trust on the part of parents. Some parents dealt with the matter themselves or encouraged older siblings to protect younger ones.

Children's awareness

It is sometimes suggested that young children are 'colour-blind' in the sense of being unaware of difference in skin colour, hair type and so on. However, children as young as 3 or 4 years of age are very aware of themselves and of how they are similar to or different from others in looks (Kendall, 1996). My own daughter, for example, who is of dual black African and white British heritage, is all too aware at 5 years old of how her curly brown hair is different from that of her classmates, all of whom have straight hair. She draws pictures of herself with long, straight hair and openly voices her desire to have straight, blonde hair, to be 'like her friends'.

Young children growing up in a multicultural community experience cultural diversity as part of their everyday world, whereas for children living in a monocultural community, it may be more difficult to perceive that there may be communities different to theirs. Books and television programmes can help to broaden their perspective. Children are not colour-blind, but are naturally curious about differences between themselves and their friends. It is the way that adults respond to their questions and observations that encourages either a tolerant, accepting attitude to differences, or the beginnings of a racist attitude. As James and Jeffcoate (1986) argue, schools are concerned with the formation of attitudes and cannot escape responsibility for hostility towards ethnic minorities. Teachers must remember that their own attitudes and expectations, however subtle, will be picked up by children and can influence the attitudes which they in turn will develop.

Issues for Reflection

- Examine your own schooling and background. How have these experiences shaped your opinions and attitudes towards racial and cultural diversity?
- We all have our own beliefs, prejudices and expectations. How can we ensure these do not adversely affect the way we treat children from diverse backgrounds in the primary classroom or school?
- How might you make use of Circle Time/PSHE/citizenship to address issues of racism and to promote respect and tolerance towards others?
- How can a school prepare children for life in a culturally diverse society?

Summary of Key Points

- Teachers should have high expectations of *all* children.
- All community groups are composed of individuals, with different interests, views, school needs. Teachers need to know their pupils as individuals.
- Multicultural and anti-racist education is important for everyone, not just for pupils in multiethnic schools.
- A multicultural curriculum is not an add-on, and should not be trivialized or tokenistic.
- All children have an entitlement to access to the full curriculum.
- Teachers should not treat all pupils the same, but should make a distinction between equality of provision and equality of opportunity.
- Effective schools deal openly and consistently with racist incidents, informing parents of action taken.
- Young children are not 'colour-blind'; they notice and are curious about differences.
- Texts, stories, posters and audiovisual materials should be chosen to portray a multicultural society.
- Multicultural/antiracist education is about similarities and common themes between cultures as well as about differences between them.

Suggestions for Further Reading

Books

Runnymede Trust (2003) *Complementing Teachers: A Practical Guide to Promoting Race Equality in Schools.* Manchester: Granada Learning. This report offers practical guidance on the promotion of 'race' equality and cultural diversity within the classroom. It aims to support teachers and other professionals in the implementation of changes to education and classroom practice brought about through the Race Relations (Amendment) Act 2000 and wider educational reform. It includes a CD-ROM with downloadable lesson plans and activities.

Meek, M. (ed.) (1996) *Developing Pedagogies in the Multilingual Classroom: The Writings of Josie Levine, Selected and Edited by Margaret Meek.* Stoke-on-Trent: Trentham Books. A very readable collection of anecdotes and pedagogical theories concerning pupils with English as an additional language.

Kenrick, D. and Bakewell, S. (1995) *On the Verge: The Gypsies of England.* Hatfield: University of Hertfordshire Press. Donald Kenrick has written extensively about the Travelling community. This is a very informative book.

DfES (2003e) *Aiming High: Raising the Achievement of Gypsy Traveller Pupils.* London: DfES. This report offers advice and practical guidance on action that can be taken to raise the achievement of Traveller pupils.

Websites

Times Educational Supplement website, EAL section, http://www.tes.co.uk/your_subject The EAL material can be accessed through this URL. It offers practical classroom strategies, plus common misconceptions about EAL pupils, and suggestions for further reading.

DfES website, Ethnic Minority Achievement section, http://www.standards.dfes.gov.uk/ethnicminorities This site aims to provide support to LEAs and schools. It includes links to recent publications.

Runnymede Trust website, http://www.runnymedetrust.org This site has a wealth of information and useful links on many aspects of race equality and cultural diversity, including schools and the curriculum.

Multicultural Pavilion website, http://www.edchange.org/multicultural This site from the University of Virginia offers a wide range of dialogues, resources and links on equity in education.

McGraw Hill website, Multicultural Supersite, http://www.mhhe.com/socscience/education/multi This site provides a broad range of information and links.

Britkid website, http://www.britkid.org Britkid is a website about race, racism, and growing up in Britain. It is aimed at young people, but contains much useful information for anyone, including factual information on immigration, asylum and a teacher's section.

14
Personal, Social and Health Education

Rob Barnes

The following topics and issues are covered in this chapter:

- the wide-ranging themes that contribute to PSHE;
- developing relationships and learning to see things from other people's points of view;
- a positive and democratic classroom ethos;
- person-centred responsibility in PSHE;
- class and group discussion in PSHE lessons, Circle Time;
- PSHE across the curriculum;
- emotional growth;
- resources for PSHE;
- teachers raising questions about the children's PSHE; and
- assessment of PSHE.

This chapter looks at personal, social and health education. It draws on the programmes of study provided in the National Curriculum for England (DfEE/QCA, 1999), the Internet and material provided by practising primary school teachers. It also relates to the useful guidance for schools found in documents from the QCA (QCA, 2000a). The chapter does not deal with citizenship education as this is discussed in Chapter 15. In many primary schools PSHE is currently taught with citizenship, so some of the points made here are also relevant to issues discussed in Chapter 15. The material here also relates to the primary school teacher's responsibility for pastoral care, discussed in Chapter 8. Clearly, one of the most significant ways in which teachers can show practical care for the personal needs of their pupils (their pastoral care role) is by having a commitment to their individual development in the areas of personal, social and health education (their role as a teacher of PSHE).

Wide-ranging Themes in PSHE

What a puzzling mix of topics there is within a PSHE curriculum. One moment it seems that a teacher's job is to develop pupils' confidence and the next it is to talk about the dangers of playing on railway lines. One lesson in PSHE might involve learning about how to deal with accidents and medical emergencies. Another lesson might look at ways to resolve arguments and conflicts by using role-play exercises or group discussion. Yet another might concentrate on healthy eating. Personal, social and health education includes such matters as personal responsibility, health, awareness of safety, drug education, emotional growth, the influence of media and advertising, making choices and developing good relationships. It is therefore not surprising that examples provided in official guidelines range from being a playground mediator to communicating with children in other countries by satellite or email. A trawl of the Internet also reveals that resource materials involve quite simply 'learning about life'. A common thread is that of pupils becoming aware of themselves in relation to others within a civilized society.

Is PSHE really a subject? Certainly it is not just about doing a set number of lessons in prescribed topics, because it needs to encompass much more than this. It is a whole-school philosophy and an attitude to relationships and responsibilities. Without considering its power and impact on school and home life, teaching PSHE becomes meaningless. No wonder it is so wide-ranging in its remit and its variety of themes. Personal, social and health education is more a responsibility that is shared by everyone in school than a subject. Responsibility is the engine of pupils' personal development and it is PSHE lessons that fuel it.

Making PSHE effective requires a positive and democratic classroom ethos at the outset. As one primary school teacher puts it:

> You'll get nowhere without first creating a positive attitude and environment to talk about PSHE. If children can't discuss and come to some conclusions themselves, then all you have is a set of empty rules, information and platitudes. I see PSHE as a way to turn negative attitudes to positive ones and it's from there children really listen instead of just hear. If you want PSHE to be dynamic and useful, then it can't be delivered like a pep-talk or a lecture. It needs to lead to responsible action in daily life and a classroom 'can-do' culture where everyone is valued.
>
> (Primary school teacher)

Unfortunately, not all children arrive at school with good social skills or a developed sense of responsibility. If nothing needed to be brought to the attention of pupils in school, then there would be no incidences of bullying, intolerance or anti-social behaviour. There would be no need to deal with risks and their consequences, drug misuse or issues of right and wrong. Actively implementing a PSHE school policy is the difficult part. It is one of those curiosities of society that we do not need to go far back in the history of education to find classrooms where teaching of right and wrong was backed by the use of corporal punishment. Of course, even then many pupils still co-operated because they wanted to, but the tradition of discipline instilled through drill was a far cry from encouraging pupils to make responsible personal choices. Obedience was considered a paramount trait and the term 'social skill' was not in common use. Now we have moved in a different educational direction and we need a more democratic classroom culture in which to promote PSHE. Teaching this area of the curriculum is not going to be achieved by giving children information and telling them what to do. Successful PSHE actively involves pupils in arriving at constructive conclusions for themselves and as a social group.

Just how democratic some classrooms are can be seen in the growth of peer-support groups (Cowie and Wallace, 2000). These are designed for pupils to alleviate distress in their peer group. Bullying and conflict are just two areas in which peer-support groups can help. Cowie and Wallace point out in their introduction that working in this way requires a shift towards a more democratic, participatory style of classroom teaching. They also point out that pupils make wonderful mediators, so there are pay-offs for any classroom ethos which goes in this direction. Some teachers would find a participatory style difficult to contemplate if their style has been autocratic and their teaching didactic. At the other end of the scale are teachers who indulge in participatory discussion which results in fruitless guessing. This is often participation for its own sake, so somewhere between these extremes lies a combination of discussion, clear explanation and independent learning.

A checklist of key topics in PSHE (not including citizenship) is:

- self-esteem;
- being positive;
- safety;
- hygiene;
- diet and exercise;
- person-centred responsibility;
- emotional growth;
- decision-making;
- right and wrong (see Chapter 15);
- sex education;
- drug education;
- race, ethnicity and culture (see Chapter 13);
- gender (see Chapter 12);
- bullying (see Chapter 8);
- care for the environment.

It is impossible within the space of this chapter to deal with all these topics, and several of them, as indicated, are discussed elsewhere in the book. Within this chapter I will discuss specifically the areas of person-centred responsibility and emotional growth, as well as suggesting some general strategies that can be used for many of the other aspects of PSHE listed here.

It is also helpful to observe that much of the checklist above could be absorbed into the dual themes of teaching pupils about relationships and teaching them to appreciate things from the point of view of other people.

These are high on the PHSE agenda and present a major educational goal for those teachers who have the responsibility of initiating egocentric young children into the idea that the world does not revolve around them as individuals. Like many other topics in PSHE (such as to become confident or to understand what it means to be independent), learning to relate and to recognize other people's feelings are not so much taught as arrived at. The National Curriculum for England requires children to be introduced to these topics: 'KS2 Pupils should be taught: a) that their actions affect themselves and others, to care about other people's feelings and to try to see things from their point of view' (DfEE/QCA, 1999, p. 140). Who could disagree? This is just one aspect of PSHE but like the rest of the suggested content, it needs turning into practical activities.

Person-centred Responsibility in PSHE

Children are likely to find it difficult to untangle a concept such as responsibility because it can mean different things. Being a responsible person can be perceived as 'something adults make you do', often connected with rules. From a child's viewpoint adults may appear to do anything they like, yet impose rules on children about bedtime, homework and where and when to play. What is thought fair and responsible in an adult's eyes is not necessarily viewed the same way by a child. The rules of a school or a society are sometimes hard for children to understand, and PSHE can be helpful in unravelling these. Taking self and group responsibility may be something rarely explained or experienced at home. Responsibility can obviously involve trust, as in 'taking responsibility for checking your own correct answers' or looking after money and property. By contrast, some children might think responsibility means 'looking out for myself' – regardless of the effect my behaviour has on other people.

Becoming responsible in a person-centred, rather than a self-centred way is one of the better characteristics of adulthood. Adults who can only focus on their own needs and desires are likely to find it difficult to empathize with anyone else, let alone feel responsible. At the heart of effective PSHE is the development of person-centred responsibility. This regards other people's needs, rights and responsibilities just as importantly as our own. Developing person-centred responsibility is perhaps a grandiose aim in PSHE because it requires a growing awareness of self in relation to others. It also requires a realistic degree of understanding of self in relation to events that happen. As Carl Rogers put it in his classic book *Freedom to Learn*: 'The individual who sees himself and his situation clearly and freely takes responsibility for that self and for that situation is a very different person from the one who is simply in the grip of outside circumstances. This difference shows up clearly in important aspects of his behaviour' (Rogers, 1983, p. 278).

As teachers we are inevitably in a position of power and that includes the power to influence for the common good. It is worth remembering that some children arrive at school strongly influenced by a disadvantaged home background or having a deep-seated need for lots of attention. Personal, social and health education is not a compensation for any of these factors, but it can be a force for generating a much stronger consciousness of social and group values. This is reason enough for taking the time to teach topics in PSHE, because the rest of the curriculum focuses on other concerns. Teaching children the value of sharing, co-operating, caring and learning life skills provides reference points for the rest of the curriculum. Students may be learning mathematics or science, but they also need to learn about how to cope with the world in which these areas exist.

Ways in which PSHE is Taught

Primary school children will learn best through activities within the school context as well as through using experiences they bring to the classroom. This is as true within PSHE as with any other area of the curriculum. There is a wide variety of ways of engaging children with PHSE learning. For example, to promote 'listening and concentrating' they might play games such as clapping to music, or hear a whispered message and pass it round the circle. Another means of encouraging children to consult and participate is to gather views about an issue. Surveys can include questionnaires and interviews so that pupils can focus on what they already know and ask what they want to know about. Sometimes this needs to be done anonymously through a questions box. One class of Year 5 pupils, for example, had a 'help-slip' tin with a slot. Pupils used this for voting on a number of choices, for responding with comments on an issue or as a means for raising their own questions.

Class and group discussion

Many teachers equate the teaching of PSHE with Circle Time. Circle Time is an activity where pupils sit in a circle and each in turn has a chance to speak and be heard, or miss a turn if they do not feel confident enough. Circle Time normally has a rule that only one person at a time speaks. There may be other rules such as agreeing on a signal to speak, or not criticizing what anyone has said. Usually there is an object such as a teddy bear, shell or significant talisman which is held by the person to indicate that it is their turn to speak. The talisman is passed from person to person. Circle Time is a particularly useful way of discussing issues such as fairness, honesty, compassion, relationships and responsibilities. One of its obvious attractions is that individual views have an airing in a whole-class setting. This can generate a positive peer-group consensus about issues and can be a positive forum for talking about problems arising during the week within the class. There are, of course, many other ways to run discussion groups. In fact, learning to discuss within both small and large groups is actually a PSHE objective in itself.

Here is what one teacher of 9-year-olds says about Circle Time and working in groups:

PSHE provides a designated time in the week when you talk about issues. Sometimes we have a suggestion box, but the important thing is they are confident enough to tell you what's bothering them. Personally I start with Circle Time, especially if there's something specific that's happened in the week I want us to talk about. They'll otherwise go off in threes or fours to brainstorm using big sheets of sugar-paper. For example, this week it's class elections and they're discussing what makes a good class representative. Or we might brainstorm in groups 'What makes a good friend', or 'What makes a good parent?'. I want lots of input for discussion. If we were brainstorming something to do with safety, I might send off one group to do 'safety on the railways', another 'safety on building sites' and another 'safety on rivers'. And I'd get the groups to report back. I might top up with some whole-class teaching to make sure the information is all there.

(Primary school teacher)

Lower down the age range, independent discussion groups are less common and Circle Time is a better way to handle issues such as friendships and safety. A group of 5-year-olds, for example, might be passing a smile around the whole circle as a starting point for discussion about resolving arguments. This exercise and other Circle Time games can be impressive in their effect. They promote group awareness and rituals that can form positive discussion habits.

PSHE across the Curriculum

Integrating PSHE into other lessons and activities widens its scope. One of the advantages of working with primary school children is that links can be made across the curriculum and issues raised can be followed up elsewhere.

I would teach something about healthy eating in a science session. PSHE isn't just a lesson in itself. As PSHE co-ordinator, I look for areas of the curriculum where it can also be taught. A lot of things, like the effect of physical activity, would be done in science. In geography we would compare our lives with those of people living in other countries. Some of it is done in RE, some in history, like comparing your own life with people in a different situation. In some countries there is child labour and we might compare that with what happened in England in Victorian times down the mines. We'd discuss the rights and wrongs of children working. If you look at the PSHE syllabus, things like children's rights come up. But rather than teaching this in isolation, if we're doing the Victorians, that's where we'll look at the issues. Then we might make our weekly PSHE lesson an extension of the children's rights issues.

(PSHE co-ordinator in a primary school)

Emotional Growth

An important aspect of how PSHE is taught concerns its emotional context. This picks up the earlier point made about whole-school attitudes and responsibilities. School-wide issues about relationships, self-esteem, bullying, work and play involve people's feelings. So do issues which involve whole-school behaviour policies, school councils and school rules. As part of their PSHE, pupils need to develop in terms of understanding their own and other people's feelings and emotions. Not all children have a vocabulary that distinguishes feelings. Even pupils in Year 6 can still have a very limited range of language to talk about how they and other people might feel or respond emotionally. Some teachers who deal particularly well with this encourage the development of emotional learning within both PSHE and literacy lessons. Mosley (1996) suggests, for example, that Circle Time can have activities which promote emotional growth, such as 'Getting to know you'. In this application of Circle Time, children might choose a positive adjective to describe themselves, such as 'I am happy Sam' or 'I am brave Lucy'.

One teacher of 9-year-olds explains how she tackles the pupils' development in the area of emotional growth as follows:

> They often have poor emotional literacy. If we can improve their vocabulary about feelings it's a good start. For instance, I've found they tend to reduce discussion of people's emotional response to 'upset', 'bored' and 'happy'. They even resist the word 'angry' which is really surprising. They'll say someone is 'a bit upset' for anyone who is really distressed, disappointed or even angry. They might say 'They're mad', meaning angry, but their most frequently used word seems to be 'bored' or 'boring' which seems to cover a huge range of emotions. What I'd really hope to achieve is that they learn to make distinctions both in their own feelings and in interpreting what they read and see. They can distinguish between 'bored' and 'day-dreaming', 'bored' and 'distracted through distress', and 'bored' and 'unhappy because your parents are splitting up'. If you can get them to use words with greater precision, then from a personal development point of view they're getting closer to understanding their own feelings. I can use this vocabulary in PSHE to put them in touch with their emotions.
>
> (Primary school teacher)

This teacher brainstorms several emotional words as part of her teaching. An example would be for a group to brainstorm words on a sheet of paper for the word 'upset'. The group would chart a range of emotions from 'mildly upset' to 'distraught' and 'enraged'. The emotions associated with 'happy' might range from 'pleased' to 'ecstatic'. This can also encourage the use of feelings as currency in the classroom. Not every teacher would want this, but it can be a powerful means to set a safe emotional context for discussion. Many of these words have implications for yet further discussion. The same teacher comments:

> You can't necessarily hang all these words along a clothes-line, but it does help to tease them out. For example, we ended up discussing 'joyful' and whether this was something you shared with others, or a feeling you kept just for yourself, or a feeling that was transient or one that was deep and profound. That was really well worth doing because of what children volunteered about themselves along the way.
>
> (Primary school teacher)

The connection this emotional context has with literacy is that PSHE can be taught very effectively through stories. Stories with an emotional message are as old as humanity. Parables such as that of the biblical story of the good Samaritan (Luke 25: 25–37) go way back in history. Some children's stories trade on fear, such as the old German *Strewwelpeter* story where Augustus, a 'chubby lad', dies of starvation after refusing his soup for five days (Hoffmann, 1903). There are cautionary tales which include cruel examples of children losing a thumb because they sucked it, fidgeting and coming to a bad end through playing with matches. This might seem a negative way to encourage responsibility and positive values. The reality is that describing the consequences of drug abuse will inevitably involve similarly appalling and perhaps exaggerated case histories. Tales of what happens if substances are misused are bound to be fearsome, as are tales of violence or death as a result of ignoring safety issues. Alternatives to cautionary tales of poor eating habits are more positive books such as *D.W. The Picky Eater* (Brown, 1998), suitable for younger children. Still in a positive vein would be a book such as *Harvey Angell* (Hendry, 1991), suitable for older children in a primary school.

Resources for PSHE

We do not need to look very far to find examples of PSHE-specific activities because there are plenty of resource books and Internet sites available. There is actually so much material that it is difficult to know what to emphasize. Resources for PSHE are most likely to take the form of information, suggestions for activities and data gathered by pupils themselves. Tacade, a charity providing information for teachers on alcohol and drugs education, is a useful source of resources for teachers in these areas. Discussion to develop understanding requires reliable resources like these, not just uninformed opinions or prejudiced data. For example, developing a healthy lifestyle relies on what is currently known about diet and exercise. Personal safety relies on being reliably informed of the need to avoid dangerous play areas, potentially dangerous situations and road safety issues.

One of the best ways to understand what balance of topics is necessary for PSHE is to look at resources both through publishers' catalogues and local education authority schemes or guidelines. Some of these map out lessons for each year group. Even so, as we have noted above, central themes in all PSHE policies and programmes are those of living fulfilling relationships and recognizing the rights of other people, however different they may seem. The resources available do not in themselves provide a PSHE programme of teaching and learning. These have to be devised across a school and year group.

The Ride Foundation website is a resource for life skills and drug education. It provides low-cost students' workbooks, samples of which are often free to UK schools. Programmes are written to meet the English National Curriculum (DfEE/QCA, 1999) guidelines and endorsed by OFSTED. Looking at Lesson 3 of Ride 1000, for 9-year-olds, for example, shows that it deals with nicotine and solvents. It discusses reasons for not smoking, pollution and abuse by solvent inhalation. The Kids' Health website provides children with the opportunity to access a substantial package of resources designed to tackle PHSE issues in living a healthy life. A summary of its contents can be found by looking at the web-button titles, which include 'Dealing with Feelings', 'Staying Healthy', 'Everyday Illnesses and Injuries', 'My Body', 'Growing up', 'Kids' Talk', 'People and Places', 'Things That Help me', 'Watch Out', 'Kids' Health Problems', and 'Health Problems of Grown-ups'. Sometimes there is a topic for the week, which may be anything from National Alcohol Awareness Week to a focus on coping with nightmares.

The *Guardian*, a UK newspaper, also has an Internet site providing a range of resources for teachers (The Guardian Education website). The *Guardian* does not offer lessons and resources, but it does provide links to UK projects in PSHE. For example, there are relevant links to the Centre for Alternative Technology and The Marine Conservation websites. Some caution needs to be exercised if children access these sites as they are actually resources for teachers and parents. At the time of writing they include links to sites worldwide, such as worksheets provided by the Hong Kong Institute of Education, and links to the Samaritans. Neither of these sites is designed specifically for children and the content is at a tangent to school-based PSHE in the UK.

Random House website provides an excellent catalogue of books about topics such as developing confidence, respecting differences, developing a healthy safer lifestyle, responsibility and relationships with others. Of the local education authority sites, the Birmingham Grid for Learning website offers interactive web-based activities and worksheets for PSHE. This site is just one of many local authority sites, but it is a particularly useful one for both teachers and children. Some of the online games are remarkable for their interactive high-quality learning. Topics include teachers' documents about using the site and programmes for children such as 'Stop the Bullying', 'Tidy the Classroom', 'Safe Places', 'Teddy's Day Out', 'The Green Cross Code', 'Road Safety Crossword', 'Walk to School', and 'Fire Safety Day'. In many of the games, children click the mouse-button on pictures and images to win the game.

Raising Questions and Assessing PSHE

In planning PSHE activities for children, based on the National Curriculum requirements, some questions that teachers might ask themselves would be:

- How can we agree class discussion rules?
- How can I encourage self-responsibility in children?
- How can we start to care more about the environment of the school?
- How can I improve the way pupils look after school visitors?
- How could we make links with a local farm, garden centre or conservation unit?
- How could we improve recycling?
- How can I minimize bullying?
- Why are behaviour codes important?
- How can we improve awareness of the safe use of medicines?

There is nothing to stop children devising questions like these themselves as a way of engaging them with PSHE issues. The resulting actions might be as basic as providing a better wet-playtime resource such as a play box, or developing a playground watch scheme to care for the environment. Some questions, for example, will lead to extensive plans to promote healthy eating, rather than just agreeing that it is a good thing. In several schools, for example, the habit-forming snack machines, which made money for the school, have been abandoned in favour of a fruit diet at break times.

Teachers' reflections on their own practice, by asking questions such as these, are the basis of evaluation of PSHE. For example, a key question would be: 'How do we know that we do what we say we do in PSHE?' This is a policy evaluation question that could prompt a whole-school review. Part of the evidence to inform such an evaluation will be the teachers' assessment of the children's learning in PSHE. This, however, is difficult, because in the classroom, no checklist of items to assess is going to do much to reveal how well PSHE has been taught. There are some aspects of PSHE which defy objective assessment because they are not to do with improved understanding or remembering information. Pupils' self-esteem is one of these, particularly since it rises and falls depending on situations. Assessing self-esteem could anyway be unhelpful because it could actually lead to labelling some pupils in their own eyes as failures. Self-assessment of personal qualities can be implemented so long as the pupils themselves pose the questions and make judgements. Even so, some children have a natural tendency to assess themselves negatively and do not see the value of assessing their strengths. Assessment needs to be done in such a way that it produces plans and targets for the future, rather than a list of past failings. In some cases a teacher will agree a positive assessment with a pupil as part of that pupil's plan to improve behaviour and learning. Well-handled, personal assessments can be a boost to self-esteem, because qualities such as reliability, tenacity, resilience and good performance are highlighted instead of just being taken for granted.

Factual knowledge and understanding of PSHE can be assessed through quizzes and games. Examples would be the safe use of medicines, or the effect of drugs. Quizzes and word searches are a non-threatening way to assess information and they are popular with children. Some teachers use role-play to assess knowledge of health and safety. An advantage of this is that the peer group can also assess the role-play of things like dealing with a road accident victim or handling food in a hygienic way. Involving the peer group in assessment can lead to discussions of fairness and responsibility, so in itself assessment relates to PSHE. Assessment of factual information can also be done one to one between pupils and lead to discussion or peer-group support.

Assessment can, of course, be documented and recorded in the form of certificates of achievement presented in class or school assemblies. Schools are required to keep records on all aspects of pupils' development, so there has to be some means of reporting PSHE even if it is not strictly assessable. Informal quizzes and word searches can still provide some means of assessing knowledge and understanding. A short-cut for recording what has been learnt is to design assessment sheets in a form which can be used later for reporting achievements. Some schools have developed their own award schemes for accrediting competencies and skills. Nationally in the UK there are schemes such as the Duke of Edinburgh Award Scheme and the Award Scheme Development and Accreditation Network youth award. Although the easiest aspect of PSHE to assess is factual knowledge, some personal qualities such as the ability to share and co-operate can still be assessed. We might, for example, want to create a certificate of achievement based on assessment of a pupil's 'ability to discuss effectively'. This could include a checklist for assessing how thoroughly a pupil searched for evidence and how well they presented their arguments to peers. There would also be some assessment of how well they coped with opposing views and how well they respected diverse opinions.

Whether teachers should use some kind of grading system, such as a five-point scale or levels of achievement, is an important issue. Teachers are unlikely to want their pupils to make comparisons of their grades in an area of learning that is so closely tied to the individual as a person. Grades and marks almost always create stress, so it is healthier for a pupil to be told that they have achieved a level of competence in discussion than for them to receive, say, a grade C or lower. The whole issue of assessment in this area of the curriculum involving grading is controversial because it often flies in the face of trying to promote a positive ethos for PSHE. As PSHE is something that permeates the school day, many teachers prefer to provide a descriptive report on progress in PSHE rather than to grade those aspects of it that will submit to grading. That way they avoid limiting assessment to a narrow perception of PSHE.

This chapter has focused on PSHE examples and attitudes to its practice in the classroom. The final content of a school's programme will usually be decided through a whole-school policy, based on local authority guidelines. Inevitably, teachers become concerned with what they have to cover through topics in PSHE but this can be to miss the point. Teaching and learning through PSHE is more a matter of attitude and responsibility than a set of topics. The hit list of topics will be decided by policy and curriculum design, whereas attitude and responsibility are states of mind.

Issues for Reflection

- How do we ensure that PSHE teaching is effective?
- What governs a teacher's choice of topics in PSHE?
- What subjects in the National Curriculum are most likely to promote PSHE?
- What is the relationship between PSHE and citizenship (see Chapter 15)?
- How can pupils be encouraged to explore PSHE topics independently?
- What aspects of PSHE can be assessed?

Summary of Key Points

- PSHE in the primary school is wide-ranging in its topics and purpose.
- Two overarching themes in PHSE are developing relationships and learning to see things from other people's points of view.

- Making PSHE effective requires a positive and democratic classroom ethos.
- Not all children arrive at school with well-developed social skills.
- One of the better aspects of becoming an adult is to develop person-centred responsibility; PHSE activities in a primary school can begin to develop this.
- Teachers are in a position of power to influence for the common good.
- PHSE can be taught as a separate subject, but it is also promoted in teaching across the curriculum.
- Circle Time is a useful strategy for teaching some aspects of PHSE in a primary school, but teachers should not limit PSHE activities to this.
- Primary school pupils need help in emotional growth; this can be developed in PHSE activities and also in literacy through exploration of the language of feelings.
- Resources for PSHE are extensive and include Internet sites.
- Planning for PSHE can be done by the teacher raising questions.
- Assessment of PSHE is possible, but may be limited and requires reporting rather than grading.
- PSHE is more a matter of attitude and responsibility than a set of compulsory topics.

Suggestions for Further Reading

Brown, M. (1998) *D.W. The Picky Eater.* London: Red Fox. A story about positive reasons not to be a picky eater; suitable for reading to younger children in the primary school.

Cole, B. (1996) *Drop Dead.* London: Jonathan Cape. These and many other stories by this author can be a safe way to introduce difficult topics to children from about the age of seven years upward. She uses outrageous humour to tackle sensitive issues such as mortality.

Hendry, D. (1991) *Harvey Angell.* London: Red Fox. This Whitbread-Award-winning story for older primary school children mixes mystery with allegory. It features an orphan called Henry and an electrician called Harvey Angell. Henry gradually works out that Harvey Angell's job is more concerned with mending people's lives than electrical goods.

Hoffmann, H. (1903) *Strewwelpeter.* London: Blackie and Son. Some children adore these old cautionary tales.

Mosley, J. (1996) *Quality Circle Time.* Cambridge: LDA. This book has become a much used classic for teachers in primary schools and has been influential in shaping the content and focus of PHSE lessons.

QCA (2000) *Personal, Social and Health Education at Key Stages 1 and 2: Initial Guidance for Schools.* London: QCA. Essential guidance for primary school teachers in England, but relevant to those teaching elsewhere as well.

Rogers, C. (1983) *Freedom to Learn*. Columbus, OH: Bell and Howell. Essentially for educators who regard therapy as an important aspect of learning. This is an established thought-provoking text.

Strauss, G. and Browne, A. (1991) *The Night Shimmy*. London: Jonathan Cape. Eric breaks through a self-imposed silence and opens doors into his unhappy mind. This is a story with potential for promoting emotional growth, suitable for children aged 7 years and upwards.

15
Spiritual Development, Moral Development and Citizenship Education

Barbara Vanlint and Jacqueline Watson

The following topics and issues are covered in this chapter:

- the broad-ranging interpretations of spiritual development;
- moral development and the values that underpin it;
- citizenship education;
- pressure on these areas of the curriculum in a content-laden curriculum;
- a whole-school approach to spiritual and moral development and citizenship;
- classroom activities for promoting spiritual and moral development and citizenship;
- the use of Circle Time;
- citizenship across the curriculum;
- the contribution of school councils; and
- spiritual education and RE.

The central importance of primary school education in relation to a child's development as an individual is underlined in the following assertion from the Norwegian Core Curriculum, which will resonate with the aspirations of teachers in many countries: 'When children start school they start upon a great adventure which with luck and care can last them a lifetime' (Royal Ministry of Education, Research and Church Affairs, 1997, p. 11). All teachers and parents recognize that education is for life. By the time the pupils in our schools have completed their compulsory education we will want them to have a real understanding of life in all its dimensions and how to live it. Primary schools should therefore begin the work of developing and encouraging in children the sensitivity and skills needed to take an active and responsible role in society, to get on with each other and to live their lives to the full. For these reasons spiritual development, moral development and citizenship education (CE) have great importance for children's lives – and for the future of the world in which they are growing up. These are challenging aspects of the school curriculum. They include ambiguous terms, confusing concepts and much controversy. However, they can also be empowering for both the teacher and the children, involving imagination, creativity and initiative.

Spiritual development and moral development are often placed in the context of the spiritual, moral, social and cultural development of pupils. This is a huge area which cannot be discussed adequately in a single chapter. So this chapter says nothing specifically about social or cultural development other than to the extent that social development is embedded in citizenship education. Cultural development partly relates to the need for children to have access to cultural activities, for example, music, theatre and dance, but also includes multicultural awareness, which is an important issue in its own right. This is discussed in Chapter 13. In the Primary School National Curriculum for England (DfEE/QCA, 1999), CE is linked with PSHE. Personal Social and Health Education is discussed in detail in its own right in Chapter 14. Spiritual and moral development are also clearly linked with RE which is discussed in detail in Chapter 16.

What is Meant by Spiritual, Moral and Citizenship Education?

In Britain it has always been understood that education involves more than just pupils learning information and acquiring skills. It also has to do with enabling children to develop as people who can contribute to society. Since 1944, various Education Acts for England and Wales have placed education in the context of the spiritual, moral, social, cultural (and mental and physical) development of pupils. Currently, in England, OFSTED includes these aspects of the teaching and learning context in its brief for inspection of schools.

Schools, then, are concerned with the development of the child as an individual person but they are also concerned with the development of the child within and for society. The introduction of citizenship education to the English National Curriculum (DfEE/QCA, 1999) took forward the notion of the education of the child as a member of society and therefore in need of education for democracy.

Spiritual development

The word 'spiritual' appeared in the context of the English school curriculum for the first time in the 1944 Education Act. It was probably used because it had a wider scope and was more inclusive than the word 'religious'. Spirituality is a difficult concept to define. Various government bodies have put forward a number of descriptions of spiritual development. It is assumed in these that everyone has a spiritual nature and, consequently, much of the discussion of spirituality in education is concerned with inclusiveness. Spiritual development is seen as being important for all pupils, whether or not they are religious. Official publications stress, therefore, that spiritual development is not just another term for the development of religious belief or a personal faith. The National Curriculum Council for England, for example, in a discussion paper on spiritual and moral development, asserted:

> The potential for spiritual development is open to everyone and is not confined to the development of religious beliefs or conversion to a particular faith. To limit spiritual development in this way would be to exclude from its scope the majority of pupils in our schools who do not come from overtly religious backgrounds.
>
> (NCC, 1993, p. 2)

This point was reinforced by the School Curriculum and Assessment Authority and by OFSTED:

> Some people believe that they need not concern themselves with promoting pupils' spiritual development ... because they believe that spiritual development depends on religious faith. Those who believe in God will understand spiritual development differently from those who do not. But spiritual development is independent of religious belief. It is the entitlement of all pupils and the responsibility of all adults.
>
> (SCAA, 1997, para. 2.1, p. 20)

> 'Spiritual' is not synonymous with 'religious'; all areas of the curriculum may contribute to pupils' spiritual development.
>
> (OFSTED, 1994, p. 8)

This leads to the second major point of agreement about spiritual development. It is an aspect of education which impacts on all areas of the curriculum:

> Spiritual development is an important element of a child's education and fundamental to other areas of learning. Without curiosity, without the inclination to question, and without the exercise of imagination, insight and intuition, young people would lack the motivation to learn, and their intellectual development would be impaired ... . The knowledge and understanding essential to both spiritual and moral development, and the ability to make responsible and reasoned judgements should be developed through all subjects of the curriculum.
>
> (NCC, 1993, pp. 3 and 6)

It is accepted that it would be inappropriate and impossible for teachers to assess a pupil's spiritual development. So rather than checking on standards of achievement, as they would for other areas of the curriculum, OFSTED inspectors look for evidence that a school provides opportunities for spiritual development. Such opportunities should be available not just in religious education lessons and in collective worship, but across the whole-school curriculum. But what exactly is spiritual development? Here are two attempts to describe this broad-ranging concept in official publications:

> Spiritual development relates to that aspect of inner life through which pupils acquire insights into their personal existence which are of enduring worth. It is characterised by reflection, the attribution of meaning to experience, valuing a non-material dimension to life and intimations of an enduring reality.
>
> (OFSTED, 1994, p. 8)

> To promote pupils' spiritual development is actively to try to ensure that pupils' experiences, at least in school, are conducive to the development of a healthy spirit and that experiences of the sort that shrink the spirit are minimised. Schools should try to encourage in pupils a healthy inner life, a solid sense of self ... . Spiritual development is also concerned with the development of intellectual curiosity, the energising desire to explore, to find answers and to understand.
>
> (SCAA, 1997, para. 2.1, p. 20)

The significance of spiritual development is seen in terms of its contribution to social, aesthetic and personal growth, in other words, the essence of being human:

> Deprived of self-understanding and, potentially of the ability to understand others, they may experience difficulty in co-existing with neighbours and colleagues to the detriment of their social development. Were they not able to be moved by feelings of awe and wonder at the beauty of the world we live in, or the power of artists, musicians and writers ... they would live in an inner spiritual and cultural desert.
>
> (NCC, 1993, p. 3)

> Spiritual development is concerned with the vital animating essence of human beings, as human beings and as unique individuals. This essence is fundamental to human nature ... Most of us will also have experienced ... the feeling of being at ease and happy with ourselves and life generally, the feeling of being full of goodwill and energy, ready to take on anything ... if one feels like this often enough, especially in childhood, one will be developing in spirit. Such people will be increasingly: open and responsive, aware of themselves and of life's challenges; trusting, in themselves and in others (and, for some, in God); willing to engage, to take responsibility and to do what is right with courage and hope; able to love others, be generous in spirit and respond well to life's challenges.
>
> (SCAA, 1997, para. 2.1, p. 20)

Moral development and citizenship education

Whereas spiritual development is about the inner person, feelings and awareness, moral development and citizenship education focus more on the fostering of attitudes and values that underpin an individual's behaviour in relation to others. In a pluralist Britain – multi-faith, multicultural and with a high tolerance of individualism – reaching consensus on moral values is clearly problematic. Since the 1980s, however, there has been growing concern in Britain (and in the West generally) that society is spiralling out of moral control, particularly in relation to the behaviour of young people. In 1996 the British government asked SCAA to bring together representatives from religious traditions, education, government and society generally to agree a set of common values. They produced a Statement of Values which is now included in the National Curriculum handbooks for both primary and secondary school teachers. The headline points in this statement cover the self, relationships, society and the environment:

- We value ourselves as unique human beings capable of spiritual, moral, intellectual and physical growth and development.
- We value others for themselves, not only for what they have or what they can do for us. We value relationships as fundamental to the development and fulfilment of ourselves and to the good of the community.
- We value truth, freedom, justice, human rights, the rule of law and collective effort for the common good. In particular, we value families as sources for support for all their members, and as the basis of a society in which people care for others.
- We value the environment, both natural and shaped by humanity, as the basis of life and a source of wonder and inspiration (DfEE/QCA, 1999, pp. 147–9).

From these headlines follow sets of practical implications, such as respecting the privacy and property of others, supporting the institution of marriage, respecting the rule of law, understanding our responsibilities for other species, and so on. The statement does not include religious beliefs, principles or teachings, although the introduction recognizes that these are often the source from which commonly held values derive.

Citizenship was introduced as a cross-curricular theme in 1990 but it was sidelined after the introduction of other educational initiatives, particularly the literacy and numeracy strategies. Concerned to tackle problems of anti-social behaviour in young people and the declining commitment to the notion of being a good citizen, in the late 1990s the government called together an Advisory Group on Citizenship. Their final report put forward a rationale and framework for citizenship education (QCA, 1998). Citizenship education was then included in the National Curriculum for Primary Schools in England in 2000, with similar developments in other parts of the UK. In this context citizenship is linked with PSHE, where the second out of five elements of PHSE and citizenship is called 'Preparing to play an active role as citizens' (DfEE/QCA, 1999). The teaching objectives under this heading reflect a number of values in the Statement of Values referred to above. For Key Stage 1 pupils (ages 5–7 years), for example, the curriculum for citizenship includes such things as:

- taking part in discussions and debates about topical issues;
- recognizing right and wrong choices;
- understanding and willingness to accept class rules;
- taking responsibility for the needs of other people and other living things;
- awareness of belonging to families and communities;
- contributing to the life of the class and the school;
- looking after the environment; and
- learning about the sources and uses of money (DfEE/QCA, 1999, p.137).

For Key Stage 2 pupils (ages 7–11 years) these expectations are extended and toughened up significantly, including such things as:

- understanding the reasons for rules and laws, and learning how to take part in making and changing rules;
- recognizing the consequences of anti-social and aggressive behaviour, such as bullying and racism;
- recognizing conflicts between expectations at school and at home;
- understanding other people's spiritual, moral, social and cultural experiences;
- learning to resolve differences;
- understanding democracy, locally and nationally;
- learning about the roles of voluntary, community and pressure groups;
- appreciating the range of national, regional, religious and ethnic identities in the UK;
- exploring issues related to allocation of resources and sustainability; and
- exploring how the media present information (DfEE/QCA, 1999, p. 139).

Some reflections on these areas of the curriculum

Government documents and most educational authors appear to assume that spirituality is part of human nature and that morality is dependent on spirituality. What is less clear is whether spirituality and morality could be nurtured independent of some kind of 'world view', whether this be religious or secular. David Hay argues that spirituality is biologically based and has evolved in human beings because it has survival value. In Hay's terms it is about an individual reflecting on his or her own awareness of reality, independently of any formal religious context.

> I have ... presented a notion of spirituality as something biologically built into the human species, an holistic awareness of reality which is potentially to be found in every human being. Although historically it has very close links with religion, it is logically prior to religion ... . The awareness ... refers to a more reflexive process – being attentive towards one's attention or 'being aware of one's awareness'.
>
> (Hay, with Nye, 1998, pp. 59–60)

Hay looked closely at children's spirituality in his research with Rebecca Nye. Nye concluded that spirituality includes 'a compound property' which she calls *relational consciousness*. This has two complex properties: 'An unusual level of consciousness or perceptiveness' and an awareness of relationship 'to things, other people, him/herself, and God' (ibid., p. 113). In other words, increased spiritual awareness involves our being more aware of our relationship with everyone else and everything else, thus increasing our moral sensitivity to others and to our environment. Hay and Nye argue that certain kinds of exercises can encourage and develop this spiritual and moral awareness or relational consciousness. 'The teacher has four major responsibilities: (a) helping children to keep an open mind; (b) exploring ways of seeing; (c) encouraging personal awareness; and (d) becoming personally aware of the social and political dimensions of spirituality' (ibid., p. 163).

Hay's influential ideas were first developed in relation to RE, arguing that RE should place greater emphasis on awareness-raising, reflection and contemplation. However, Hay recognized that this kind of awareness could be encouraged more generally, such as in music and poetry, and, along with Nye, he has argued that relational consciousness must be promoted throughout the whole school to increase children's sensitivity towards others. He is particularly concerned that the spiritual and moral dimension to education is essential to counter social disintegration and to achieve a real sense of social responsibility.

Hay's work is in opposition to an approach to spiritual and moral development through RE which would conventionally rely on the transmission of a body of religious truth embodied in other people's stories. Clive and Jane Erricker take a similar child-centred approach to that of Hay, which leads them to emphasize the child's own experience as the starting point for spiritual and moral development (Erricker and Erricker, 2000). They argue that to develop their spiritual and moral awareness, children do not need to be told what to think by adults. Rather, they need space to talk and to be listened to, so that they can construct meaning for themselves from their own experience. If they are to become sensitive to the narratives of others, children need the opportunity to develop their own stories derived first from their own experience of life. The Errickers see the type of classroom that is conducive to this spiritual process, therefore, as 'a place of conversational activity within the disorderliness of everyday social life; a place of unfolding thought and performance' (Erricker and Erricker, 2000, p. 73).

Clive and Jane Erricker, like many other commentators, believe that teachers do not sufficiently recognize and value children's spiritual capabilities, and that schools often crush rather than develop children's spirituality through the imposition of a body of spiritual ideas and moral values.

> There is an agenda, devised through curriculum circumscription and desirable outcomes ... [which] seeks to produce certain types of citizen, valuing certain religious constructions of human purpose, even if not subscribing to them, and agreeing a consensus of normative morality. The problem is not whether these are good aims, but that they are imposed aims. Pupils and students know that they are expected to buy into them.
>
> (Erricker and Erricker, 2000, p. 123)

David Hay's and the Errickers' approaches to spiritual and moral development independent of a religious context have been criticized, in particular by Andrew Wright and Adrian Thatcher. Wright believes that children need to be nurtured spiritually and morally within the context of the religious tradition of their culture and/or family. He argues that religious knowledge – what he calls 'spiritual literacy' – is vital to spiritual development and that children cannot be nurtured in a 'vacuum', drawing merely on their own experience or narratives (Wright, 1999). Adrian Thatcher, arguing from a theological and strongly

Christian perspective, says that spiritual development must be grounded in Christian teaching, particularly if it is to be sufficiently robust to critique contemporary ethical issues (Thatcher, 1999). At present, these views are not shared by most educators and are not reflected in government documents. However, some religious groups in this country would like to see a greater number of religious schools, arguing that such schools enable a child's spiritual and moral development to take place within the religious tradition of their family.

Other educators have talked about spiritual and moral development in terms of pupil and teacher well-being or mental health, encouraging virtue or love, or even about a spirituality of dissent which questions some of the 'values' of western democracy. So spiritual and moral development covers a wide area of understandings (Watson, 2003a). Perhaps it includes something of them all.

Citizenship is a new subject in the curriculum in this country, but it is being welcomed cautiously by educational authors and teachers alike (Watson, 2003, cited the Farmington Institute for Christian Studies website). The caution is prompted by questions about the nature of citizenship and what an education for democracy should look like. For instance, should we be educating our children as citizens of the nation, Europe, the world, or all three? Should citizenship teach children how to be 'good' citizens, in which case who determines what is a good citizen? Should citizenship and an education for democracy encourage children to accept or question the political and social status quo. Should it encourage children to value or question the electoral system of democracy? Although there are questions to address and debate here, CE is an exciting new opportunity, particularly because the curriculum is not actually tightly prescribed by central government and its future development will largely depend on what *teachers* choose to do.

A Whole-School Approach to Spiritual and Moral Development and Citizenship

A school's policy on spiritual and moral development and citizenship should include a commitment to encourage children to take a more active role in all aspects of school life, recognizing the pupil's place within this secure community as an opportunity to develop the skills and attitudes required to contribute to communities more generally. These areas of the curriculum also give teachers greater choice in what they teach. A chance for the spirit to be explored and encouraged should be the right of every child and primary school teachers should ensure that there are opportunities for this, particularly since, for many children, school may be the only place where this is likely to happen. As we have noted above, spiritual, moral and citizenship education should not be limited to any one subject or one slot on the timetable, because the child's development in these respects spans the whole curriculum.

The class teacher in a primary school has a key role to play in this process but unfortunately a great deal of pressure is put on these teachers at present. The primary school curriculum is content laden and prescriptive, and is driven by an emphasis on achievement and standards. National test results and positions in league tables are given unjustified priority in curriculum planning. Instead of beginning with a child's experience, capturing their imagination and exploring learning with them, teachers are asked to teach things which often seem to have little relevance to the child and to teach in such a way that links between subjects do not readily occur. In such a context real spiritual and moral growth can be stifled. Yet children learn best when they become fascinated by the world and have the values and attitudes that lead them to explore it. In this respect the development of the human spirit is a prerequisite for learning across the curriculum.

> Children will learn better if their minds are captured by the magic of phenomena, the beauty of nature and the awesome qualities of the world around then … . A curriculum underpinned with an active spiritual basis will lead to reduced peer pressure (caused by low self-esteem) and children believing and trusting in their ability to make their own choices and taking responsibility for their own rational actions.
>
> (Torrington, 1998, p. 35)

This is the kind of principle that begins to sound like genuine education, rather than mere transmission of knowledge and skills. Developing this approach, Brown and Furlong (1996, p. 9) suggest that spiritual development might be achieved by:

- recognizing the existence of others as independent from oneself;
- becoming aware of and reflecting on experience;
- questioning and exploring the meaning of experience;
- understanding and evaluating a range of possible responses and interpretations;
- developing personal views and insights; and
- applying insights gained with increasing degrees of perception to one's own life.

The ethos of the school is vital to the spiritual and moral development of children as well as for education for citizenship. In the most effective schools one senses a spiritual and moral climate, and pupils and teachers alike demonstrate qualities of good citizenship as each one takes their part in the school community. For true success, the school must have a clear vision of the value of this aspect of the education process and this vision should be shared by all staff, teaching and non-teaching, as well as governors, in a written and agreed school policy. But more than that, a commitment to these aspects of genuine education must be fundamental to the beliefs of the school and will therefore underpin all its policies and strategies, from those for individual subjects to such policies as special educational needs, pupils' behaviour and bullying. It should form the basis of life in and out of the classroom, concerned not just with lessons but with how adults and children relate to one another.

Teachers change children's lives by imparting not just knowledge and skills but also values and attitudes. Teaching cannot be value-free. To develop a child spiritually a teacher must be spiritually 'alive' and aware of themselves and their own values. 'What the teacher is, is as important as what the teacher knows' (Priestley, 1985, p. 115). It is not just what is taught or how it is delivered; the spiritual health of the teacher also plays a part in a child's spiritual development. Primary school pupils will flourish in the care of a teacher who is more often than not in good spirits, who communicates positive attitudes to life and to learning. In the same way, a teacher's sense of justice can reflect on a child's moral development. So, teachers need to be able to take control of their activities in the classroom, to slow down, to listen and to reflect, and to allow *themselves* (that is, their own personalities, enthusiasms, attitudes and values) back into the classroom. As teachers we still have some control over how we teach and this can greatly affect the spiritual and moral development of the child. One teacher put this succinctly as follows: 'The morale and self-esteem of the teacher leading the class probably has the most to do with the spiritual climate of the classroom. To be spacious a teacher needs to be confident' (quoted in Vanlint, 1999, cited on the Farmington Institute for Christian Studies website).

If a teacher is inspired by what he or she teaches, then the children are more readily inspired also. Teachers must be sensitive to 'the strangeness and wonder lying just below the surface even in the commonest things of daily life' (Webster, 1982, p. 69, quoting Bertrand Russell). In order to foster the development of children, we should try, wherever possible, to begin from where the children are, from their experience, so that they then become absorbed with a desire to broaden their experience and understanding. More use can be made of the pupil's own experience through art and drama, and their awareness of spiritual and moral concepts is enhanced through literature and through sharing the life experiences of other people. Teachers should not be afraid to share their own personal thoughts and feelings with children so that spiritual and moral growth is seen as important to everyone in the community.

This all seems very obvious but it is so often lost under the pressures of the present system of schooling in this country. It is important for the spiritual and moral well-being of their pupils that teachers feel good about themselves and what they are doing. They will also feel more fulfilled themselves in their daily work. Teachers should have an attitude of wanting to learn alongside children, to discover with them and to make mistakes. In this way teachers can empower children to make decisions and, ultimately, to have ownership of what they undertake in school. Just as teachers need to feel good about themselves, so do children. Far too many do not. The way that we as teachers relate to children, both in and out of the classroom, therefore, has much to do with the spiritual and moral development of the child and their development as future citizens. Pupils who experience large doses of tolerance, encouragement, praise, fairness, security, approval, acceptance and friendship are more likely to develop positively as spiritual and moral individuals and as good citizens than those whose experience is dominated by criticism, hostility, ridicule and shame (see Nolte and Harris, 1998).

Classroom Activities for Promoting Spiritual and Moral Development and Citizenship

The initial response from many teachers to spiritual and moral development and citizenship education is, 'Where can we find the time to fit these in?' In reality there are many ways in which teachers can develop a sense of spirituality and morality in children and open their eyes to the wider sense of what it means to be a citizen. These can range from ongoing activities such as adopting a school charity and following its work for a year, to specific class-based activities such as Circle Time.

Circle Time

We have already seen in Chapters 8 and 14 how Circle Time is used in primary schools to engage pupils with personal and social issues. Circle Time is a wonderful method for developing self-esteem and thus promoting spiritual and moral education. Generally children enjoy participating in Circle Time and, consequently, it provides a secure context for raising issues about how we live our lives and what we value and care about as individuals. One of the key factors in Circle Time is that the physical arrangement of the teacher and pupils puts everyone on an equal footing, so that each one is more likely to feel that their views and contributions are of value. Here are some suggestions for using Circle Time in relation to the themes of this chapter:

- discuss ethical, moral or social issues that have arisen within the curriculum or school, where it is felt that a more in-depth discussion could give each child the time to further their thoughts;
- deal with problems that have arisen within the classroom, giving children the chance to air their feelings in a secure environment and to listen to the views of others;
- further engage children with their own learning by getting them to discuss how a particular lesson works (or does not work) for them and how it could be bettered;
- discuss conflicts at school, at home and in the wider society and develop the skills they need to resolve these; and
- explore ongoing spiritual, moral and citizenship issues, such as alcohol and drug abuse, smoking, stealing, vandalism, age issues, vegetarianism, relationships, racism, bullying and topical news items.

Citizenship across the curriculum

Citizenship can be introduced into the timetable on its own, if the timetable allows, but it can also be linked to other curriculum areas. The school curriculum provides many opportunities for discussion and work on areas associated with citizenship education. For instance, the Qualifications and Curriculum

Authority suggested scheme of work for geography in Key Stage 2 includes 'What's in the news?' as well as units about the local and global environment. History provides topics linked to human rights. Many areas in religious education can be used to develop awareness of issues associated with being an active and sensitive member of society. Looking at the beliefs of others can open children's eyes and bring greater tolerance. This could be something as simple as looking at vegetarianism or as complex as exploring views on death. Literacy can provide in-depth discussion based on texts which raise issues about the contribution of the individual to a community. Carefully selected topics for persuasive writing and arguments – such as writing a newspaper article about environmental issues or preparing an anti-racist poster – can contribute a great deal.

Many primary schools will devote a week to focusing on one particular curriculum area. Following this model, schools could run a citizenship week which could provide opportunities for more in-depth work on relevant topics within each curriculum subject on the timetable. It could also include contributions by outside speakers from, for instance, Oxfam, Amnesty, Friends of the Earth, the Police, or the local Member of Parliament.

School councils

As with those aspects of the child's development explored in Chapters 8 and 14, school councils have an important role to play in the context of this chapter, particularly in citizenship education. School councils provide an excellent way to develop the notion in children of contributing actively to the community in which they work, a key feature of citizenship education. The school council offers children the chance to see democracy at work. They can begin in a small way, just giving children the chance to air their views and to organize some fund-raising events. But, if developed fully and taken to their logical conclusion, they can lead to the children having a great deal of influence and say in the running of their school. This occurred in Highfield Junior School, Plymouth, a school run by Lorna Farrington, whose book (Highfield Junior School, 1996) makes for an interesting read (see the suggested reading at the end of the chapter).

School life

There are other opportunities within school life that can be explored and developed.

- Assemblies offer the chance to bring in outside speakers from a variety of areas who can open children's eyes to the lives of others, providing opportunities for spiritual and moral development and education for citizenship.
- A house system which offers children a chance to represent their house and to organize events and competitions, to encourage others and to take on

roles of responsibility within school, can foster citizenship.
- Citizenship, a moral sense and personal responsibility can also be encouraged through developing in children the ability to solve disagreements themselves either face to face or by training children to act as mediators. Similarly, older children can be trained to act as 'buddies', to look after or to act as confidants to younger children (see Chapter 8).

Spiritual education and RE

As we have stressed throughout this chapter, spiritual development should occur across the curriculum because it concerns the very essence of humanity. It is not only to do with things religious. But, of course, RE teaching must address fundamental issues to do with humanity and so it should make a key contribution to spiritual and moral development. Unfortunately, policy often dictates that spiritual development is pushed aside in RE in favour of knowledge acquisition, in other words, learning about religion. Religious education teaching can fall into the same trap as the rest of the curriculum and get caught up in the process of justifying its position as a compulsory subject by offering content-led, assessable syllabuses that seem at times to have little to do with spiritual development. It can become overly concerned with facts about the different religions rather than the spirit of the individual, who may, of course, have no defined religious feelings (Rudge, 1998), and can be reduced to just giving knowledge without real understanding or ownership or concern for the development of the spirit. 'Religious educators should develop a programme which would provide inner space, so that children can permit themselves to become aware of and give a proper sense of validity to their religious intuitions' (Hay, 1982, p. 46).

Religions are a response to life and the world. They are a way that a group of people have found to establish values and a way of living, to get the most out of life and to put something back in. Religious education can be a way of developing in human beings a degree of insight into their own and other people's experiences and thus deepening their understanding of their place in the world. To really begin to develop children's understanding and their spirituality we need truly to engage them in what they are doing, not just through activity but subjectively through questioning and thought. We must excite their interest so that they will want to explore further and to deepen their awareness. As with other areas of the curriculum, the way to achieve this is to begin with the child's own experience so that they know that they are involved and that they have an understanding on which to build. We conclude with some examples of how such an approach could be developed around a number of RE themes.

Sharing
Look at the children's views on sharing; how they feel about sharing; what they share and do not share. Examine sharing in relation to almsgiving and world resources and how sharing is symbolized in, for instance, a Christian Communion or the Sikh Langar.

Food
Look at the children's likes and dislikes. Examine religious and non-religious views on vegetarianism and how food is used on special religious occasions such as Muslim Ramadan.

Journeys
Look at journeys that are special to the children. Examine religious pilgrimages and religious stories about journeys, such as the Israelites' flight from Egypt or the Hindu story of Rama and Sita.

Symbols
Ask children to design a symbol that represents them as individuals and what is important to them. Examine the meanings of symbols used by the major religions.

Death
Ask children to think about how they would like to be remembered and what they believe about life after death. Examine the beliefs and practices of different religions, such as those associated with reincarnation or resurrection.

Values
Look at the values the children themselves hold and then look at the values common to all religions, and their meaning for individuals and for society.

Religion and life
Look at rules and why we have them in school, in families and in society. Examine some of the laws of this country and look at their basis in Christianity. Examine other religious rules, such as the Buddhist Eightfold Path.

Special books
Look at a book that is special to each child and reflect upon what their choice of book says about them. Examine the importance and message of religious texts, such as the Bible, the Qur'an and the Torah.

Issues for Reflection

- If you are currently teaching or training to teach, ask yourself: does my teaching allow space for reflection and wonder? Do I encourage pupils to reflect on difficult moral situations? Do I encourage pupils' self-esteem? Do I listen to pupils?
- Do you think it is possible to make provision for spiritual and moral development in every curriculum subject? Will some subjects lend themselves more naturally? Are any subjects value-free and devoid of spiritual and moral issues?
- Do you agree that spiritual development is independent of religion or personal faith? What, in your view, is the relationship between RE and spiritual

and moral development?

- What do you understand by 'citizenship'? Do you consider yourself to be a citizen of a country, of Europe, the world, or all three? What are the implications of your answer for the teaching of primary school children?
- What do you understand by 'democracy'? Should a commitment to democracy be a shared value in education?
- How could a primary school give pupils more opportunities for taking responsibility within the school community?

Summary of Key Points

- The notion of spiritual development is subject to broad-ranging interpretations, a number of which have been explored in this chapter. Most authors and government agencies identify spiritual and moral development as an educational endeavour independent of religion or personal faith; others, however, argue that spirituality and morality should be nurtured in the context of the religious tradition of the child's family or culture.
- An agreed statement of values underpins the current English school curriculum for moral development and citizenship. These values refer to the self, relationships, society and the environment.
- Citizenship education is now a component of the primary school curriculum in England and includes things such as: topical issues; recognizing right and wrong choices; rules and laws; personal responsibility; families and communities; the environment; money, resources and sustainability; anti-social and aggressive behaviour, bullying and racism; dealing with conflicts; democracy; voluntary, community and pressure groups; national, regional, religious and ethnic identities; and the media.
- There should be a whole-school approach to spiritual and moral development and citizenship, written down in agreed school policies and underpinning teaching across the curriculum, teacher–pupil interactions, school councils and all aspects of school life.
- Children need to be listened to and to feel they are valued. Spiritual, moral and citizenship education provide opportunities for children and teachers to share their opinions and beliefs. These aspects of the curriculum are about self-awareness, aesthetic response, attitudes and values, and consequently are under pressure in a content-laden curriculum with an emphasis on testing, standards and achievement.

Suggestions for Further Reading

Hay, D., with Nye, R. (1998) *The Spirit of the Child*. London: HarperCollins. This book gives the results of a study by David Hay and Rebecca Nye into young children's spirituality and includes the children's voices. It argues for greater attention to be given to nurturing the spirituality of the child both for the child's sake and for social and moral cohesion.

Erricker, C. and Erricker, J. (2000) *Reconstructing Religious, Spiritual and Moral Education.* London: Routledge Falmer. This book includes a detailed discussion of what might be meant by spiritual and moral education. The first part of the book, the authors admit, may be unhelpful to some readers, but the book is invaluable as an overview of this field. The second part of the book gives practical ideas for classroom activities.

Highfield Junior School (1996) *Changing our School: Promoting Positive Behaviour.* Plymouth: Loxley Enterprises Ltd. This book is about the experiences at Highfield Junior School when it was run by innovative head teacher, Lorna Farrington. This is an inspiring read and also gives plenty of ideas for school activities related to spiritual, moral and citizenship education.

Nolte, D.L. and Harris, R. (1998) *Children Learn What They Live: Parenting to Inspire Values.* New York: Workman. This book works section by section through Dorothy Law Nolte's famous poem, 'If a child lives with criticism, he learns to condemn'. It deals with the effects on children of criticism, hostility, ridicule and shame, contrasted with tolerance, encouragement, praise, fairness, security, approval, acceptance and friendship.

16
Religion in the Primary School Context

Linda Rudge

The following topics and issues are covered in this chapter:

- the complexity of defining religion;
- the distinction between religion as an inclusive concept and religions;
- who is religious?
- what is learnt from the 2001 census?
- the nature and place of secularism;
- the role of education in relation to religion;
- the marginalization of religion in school and education policies;
- the teacher's personal position in relation to religion in schools;
- primary pupils' engagement with religion;
- the place of religion in the primary curriculum;
- collective worship;
- the notion of religious literacy as a requirement for all primary teachers.

Primary schools in England are required to teach religious education, although the syllabus is locally determined and it is not a subject in the National Curriculum. However, religion is not just encountered in RE lessons in primary schools. It is a professional consideration for teachers:

- in classrooms, in planned teaching of various curriculum components and in unplanned responses to questions arising during the teaching of any subject;
- in playgrounds, in supporting pupils through a disagreement or in a developing friendship;
- in school halls, during collective worship, during a lunchtime discussion or at a parents' open evening; and
- in staffrooms, in discussion with colleagues about RE, school worship or a particular child's background.

Not surprisingly, religion remains a live and controversial professional issue in all schools. This chapter explores professional issues arising from the relationship between religion and education, and assumes that the starting point for development in this area has to be the teacher's knowledge and understanding of their pupils. Knowledge and understanding of religions is the second stage of development. The chapter begins by exploring the concepts of religion and of secularism, and embraces the principle of inclusivity. The chapter concludes with the argument that all primary teachers need access to a religious literacy in order to contribute to a religiously inclusive education.

Religion and Religions

The substance of this chapter is shot through with controversy, raising professional issues that should stimulate debate and reflection. The problem with the concept of religion in schools, and elsewhere, is that it can promote a sense of 'us and them', or 'those that do and those that do not'. This exclusivity can run counter to the principle of inclusivity in schools.

Definitions of religion

So, what is religion? There are many different answers to this question. The selection of definitions below might provoke some helpful immediate reaction. Religion is:

- 'belief in a superhuman controlling power, especially in a personal God or gods entitled to obedience and worship; the expression of this in worship; particular system of faith and worship; a thing that one is devoted to' (Thompson, 1992, p. 765);
- 'a system of beliefs and practices that are relative to superhuman beings' and that such beings are specifically related to 'beliefs and practices, myths and rituals' (Smith, 1995, p. 893);
- an expression of human relationships with the numinous (Otto, 1950) or the holy, bound up with direct experience, internal emotional energy and external expression in community;
- the working out of ultimate questions that cover meaning and purpose such as: Who am I? Where did I come from? Where am I going? What is important? How should I live? (In this definition, everyday settings, and normal experience can provide access to religious truth and the expression of it);
- a framework for living;
- a phenomenon that encompasses various systems of beliefs and values;
- an expression of human spirituality that makes specific reference to the numinous, the holy, the divine and/or to superhuman beings (Rudge, 2000; Teece, 2001).

Wilfred Cantwell Smith (1979) has brought another perspective on religion to those concerned with its role and position in society and education. His ideas suggest the centrality of faith in human development, as opposed to the concept of religion. Clearly, education has an influence on the formation of an individual's faith. The questions then are, what kind of education? What kind of influence? What kind of faith?

Religions

There is also a view that there is no such thing as religion, only *religions* as systematized expressions of humanity's concern with appropriate ways of living, and as forms of social control. This view has affected the history of religion in schools and the way it is encountered and explored. The phenomenological approach to the study of religion (Smart, 1989) and the systematized study of religions (Hick, 1989) provided ways in which religions have been often described in school settings and curriculum materials.

Teece (2001) records Smith's theory that religions as they are perceived today are in any case constructs of the modern world. These matters are of importance because education has developed a tradition of presenting all religions as static and homogenous, when they are in fact dynamic and diverse (Jackson, 1997; 2000; Nesbitt, 1998).

Whatever the merits of these different ways of defining religion and religions in academic terms, religion, as a broader and all-encompassing concept, is arguably more important in school settings than religions. Schools are inclusive communities that define their own systems of beliefs, values and codes of behaviour within certain parameters. They draw on the predominant culture of the time or place, and accommodate and celebrate the diversity of cultures and subcultures that make up society and the local school community. The essence of humanity and of human endeavour can be seen in the primary school context. Some would argue that the real work of the primary school, with its emphasis on human values, virtues and personal development in its broadest sense, is the essence of religion.

In practical terms, this means that in situations where teachers are talking about religion and religions phrases such as, 'People who are Christian/Jewish/Buddhist do this and believe that ... ' should be used, rather than 'Christians/Jews/Buddhists do this and believe that ... '. Placing the human being first in the sentence alerts children to the humanity of religious believers. Asking children 'and what do you do or think ... ?' also includes them in the dialogue and alerts them to their own developing humanity (Grimmitt, 2000).

Who is religious?

The expression of world views based on religious traditions or major world faiths, as they are sometimes known, are most likely to be drawn from Buddhism, Christianity, Hinduism, Islam, Judaism and Sikhism. Most primary school teachers recognize that they need a basic knowledge of these faiths, at least. However, there are important local variations. The growth of new religious movements, the re-emergence of ancient forms of worship such as paganism, and the growth of individualized spiritualities must also be taken into consideration when religious issues are considered in schools.

The majority of adults in Britain today are not so firmly affiliated to a religion that they attend regular worship, use God-centred or sacred language in their everyday lives or actively participate in faith community events and practices, yet there is a diffuse, residual religiosity amongst the majority of the adult population. Most teachers in primary schools would describe most pupils in their schools as 'not religious', and would describe themselves in the same way. 'I'm not religious but ... ' is a popular way of opening a discussion on RE for many teachers. But an interest in the spiritual, if not in structured religion, is still very much part of school life, and of wider UK society.

The 2001 census

The 2001 census evidence is that the majority of people in the UK label themselves and/or dependent members of their family with a religion or an identifiable spirituality. A high percentage of the population returned an answer to an optional question which identified themselves or members of their family as 'Christian'. Over 42 million people responded in this way, out of a population of nearly 66 million (National Statistics Online website).

Of course, surveying religious attitudes and affiliations is an inexact science. The census question was optional, and it was the first time in the UK census that such a question had been posed. The figures raise questions about how and why people responded as they did. Is it a case of actual Christian predominance or a religious revival? Was it a case of people 'playing safe'? Do many people calling themselves 'Christian' actually mean 'not something else'? Would the churches accept the description of all of these people as Christian, at a time when regular attendance at church services is falling?

An analysis of the other responses to this question also raises some interesting points for primary schools and their communities. Islam is the second largest religion (about 1.6 million) from amongst those chosen by respondents, then Hinduism (559,000), Sikhism (336,000), Judaism (272,000) and Buddhism (152,000). According to the government website about 16 per cent of the population stated that they had no religion and about 6.5 per cent chose not to respond.

For the purposes of this chapter then, the word 'religion' is used in two ways:

- as an inclusive concept, to discuss the faith, beliefs and values of all pupils, and
- as a term to include 'the religions' as systems that inform those beliefs and values.

Some academic studies of religion describe these as world views (Smart, 1989) and they therefore include atheistic, humanist or secular stances. When addressing professional issues about the position and role of religion in education, these views have to be included in the debate.

Secularism

Secularism should therefore be subject to the same kind of scrutiny, analysis and acceptance in school settings as religiosity, and world views associated with the divine or sacred. The word secularism generally signals attitudes, values, institutions or communities not concerned with the sacred. Dictionary definitions give us 'secular: not concerned with religion' (Thompson, 1992, p. 823) and 'secularism: term that ascribes to human actions, thoughts or institutions the properties of worldliness' (Smith, 1995, p. 970). Secularism is not concerned with 'superhuman beings', but secularized people can still be interested in spirituality and in ultimate questions. Essentially, secularity does not draw its authority from a notion of the divine, but it may recognize faith as a human virtue and as an expression of something that is 'good'. This is the basis of secular humanism.

Secularization has grown in Britain during the last 150 years as participation in public worship has declined and many places of worship have closed (Wolffe, 1993). However, none of the countries within Britain is an entirely secular state, and set alongside the increase in secularization has been a religious revival in certain contexts.

Secularism is often viewed by both religious people and secular people as anti-religious, or as irreligious. The term secular is often used in a pejorative sense. Religious educators sometimes point to the good that RE can do in countering secularism (Cooling, 2000; Watson, 1993). In equating secularism with materialism, hedonism or immorality, they have sometimes presented a negative view of the secularized worlds in which the majority of people live. These views promote a sense of exclusivity as if any definition of religion and sometimes, by extension, RE naturally precludes positive consideration of secular attitudes and values.

The Place of Religion in Primary Schools

The role of education

Primary school education should not be viewed merely as human instruction but as human encounter. Learning in the primary school context takes place through the everyday life of the school community, through children's relationships with each other and with their teachers and other adults, as well as through the teaching and learning within curriculum subjects. This is an essential consideration in any discussion about world views, beliefs and values religious or otherwise. The child's own experiences, views and commitments are a valid and vital part of that encounter.

Religious and secular world views and their values are promoted and sustained through complex and powerful forms of communication and expression. Education and the mass communications media are two of these forms. If secular means concern with worldliness – this world as opposed to any other – it is hard to argue with the assertion that schools, teachers and their pupils are mostly concerned with the 'here and now' and the more immediate future. This is not to say that they have no concern or interest in spiritual or sacred matters but, the dominant culture in which they work is one more directly concerned with the temporal or secular than the sacred or divine. If community schools are to be really inclusive places, it is difficult to justify the view that religious values and attitudes should be held up as the ideal to which secularized communities and individuals should aspire. Open to debate is the role in this respect of religiously affiliated schools (voluntary controlled or voluntary aided – see Chapter 1).

A religious education, or an education in religion, should enable children to:

- consider their own individual and developing patterns of belief;
- think about shared human experiences; and
- learn about the teachings and traditions that support spiritual experience, belief and practice (Read et al., 1992; Rudge, 2000; Teece, 2001).

Individual religions might not always appear to do these things, especially when viewed from the outside, but then neither, it might appear, does secularism. It is the professional role of the teacher as interpreter that mediates and accommodates competing agendas and truth claims for the benefit of all the pupils in their care.

Recognition of the complexity of individual and social human development is the first step towards inclusivity, in schools and elsewhere, and an important part of reflection on professional issues linked to religion and education.

The formal relationship with religion

The position and role of religion in primary education arise from the relationship between organized religion, especially the Anglican Church, and the state. The complexities are apparent in the legislation and guidance that govern schools in England today, and in the different types of schools that exist (Wright, 2003).

Teachers work in settings that use different normative cultures. Aided schools, for example, are more likely to use the beliefs and values of a particular religion to set the tone, ethos and codes of behaviour for the school. An LEA community primary school is more likely to draw on secularized systems for its ethos or 'mission statement'. These same teachers may be living their personal lives in settings that use alternative cultures and value systems to the normative one used in their school. Some teachers are teaching in settings that are highly charged and vibrant with the live religious issues emerging from cultural diversity; others are teaching in apparently monocultural contexts, where religious and cultural diversity exists, but in less obvious ways. However, all teachers have to deal with situations in which beliefs and values will raise questions, and in which professional issues about handling these will arise.

Most teachers work in schools that are governed by secular institutions such as LEAs and school governing bodies. But even LEAs and governing bodies have representatives who are affiliated to religions, simply because they are religious by upbringing or choice and commitment. In some cases they have been appointed to represent a specific religious point of view.

Schools exist under government legislation formed through debate and statute ordered by a religious monarchy. The royal succession and coronation of the monarch demonstrate clearly the central and vivid role of Anglican Christian religious symbolism in state affairs (Rudge, 2002). There are those (Bocking, 1995; Bolton, 1997; Hull, 1989; 1991; Rudge, 1998; 2000) who have argued that the historical development of the religious components of the curriculum have become illustrative of an attempt to make secularized political and cultural literacy dominant over religious literacy. This view is contentious, but it is something teachers are aware of and is often raised in initial and continuing education programmes.

The marginalization of religions

While these connections with religion and religions remain important in terms of controlling structures, the recent emphasis on citizenship education in the curriculum is an interesting illustration of the dominance of secularized political and cultural literacy over religious literacy (Jackson, 2003; Watson, 2003b). Religious values and religious language often now take a subordinate role in the formation of school aims and ethos. Religions are marginalized, or at least usually hidden within words like 'culture', in all curriculum documents other than those related directly to RE. The word 'spiritual' also seems to be more acceptable in official advice even if its definitions are just as elusive (see Chapter 15 in this book).

If social surveys and other research demonstrate that most of the adult population is at least loosely affiliated to a religious tradition or to a broader spirituality, then teachers and most children are likely to be of a similar background. What is clear is that open and regular commitment to a religious tradition in a traditional sense, involving obedience or reverence to a deity, rituals, worship and festivals, is not the way of most people in the teaching profession, or of most of the pupils in the classrooms of England.

The teacher's own position

For teachers, their own world views, religious or otherwise, are often played down when teaching about, or even encountering, religion and religions in school. They feel this is the safest approach to a thorny issue. Teachers in community schools are trained not to proselytize for a religion within the context of RE. They should not try to convert pupils to their faith or world view; this would be in contravention of legal regulations governing RE. If, however, a child asks a teacher what they believe or have faith in, the teacher is free to respond, within certain boundaries.

How far does this apply to other curriculum contexts, or to those of an atheistic or humanist persuasion? In science, for example, if a pupil expresses an opinion about the theory of natural selection based on a religious commitment, and the teacher dismisses it as inappropriate or untrue, is this good practice? The short answer is 'no'. Such a response runs counter to the principle of inclusivity. By imposing their own view on an issue, a secular-humanist teacher can be just as guilty of proselytizing. Teachers are in a position of authority and pupils will look to them for answers. But the key principle to remember is that the relationship between teacher and pupil depends on trust and mutual respect.

In a context of mutual respect, should a teacher be willing to offer their own world view for examination and scrutiny by the pupils? Only the teacher will know how far they are willing to go in sharing their innermost and often deeply held convictions with a lively class of 7-year-olds. Teachers often employ distancing techniques when handling controversial questions of a religious nature by asking: 'What do you think?', 'Why did you ask that?', 'What do other people think?' The QCA has produced useful advice on handling religious questions to which the reader is referred (QCA, 2000b).

Pupils and religion

When pupils enter the Foundation Stage, they have already had experiences of watching adult beliefs and values in action, and have started to develop their own. They may have been actively nurtured in a religious faith in homes where religious language is commonplace. For the families of these children there will be certain expectations of the education system. They will expect teachers to address and to be sensitive to particular needs of their children and to be aware of their sensitivities.

These needs might be related to food laws, dress and symbols, festivals and religious observances, the use, or not, of particular images, and behaviour in places of worship. Many of these emerge from cultural influences rather than religious orthodoxy or authority. Six major religions in Britain were mentioned earlier. Others could be added. First, within those major religions there are many denominations or separate movements. Some do not recognize or acknowledge one another. Within these separate movements there are sects that some other groups within the mainstream tradition would not recognize. Next, there are those religions that were labelled 'other' in the census including Jainism, Zoroastrianism, Rastafarianism, the Church of Latter Day Saints, Paganism and new religious movements.

Each of these religions, movements and sects is composed of individuals. Some will be orthodox and traditional practitioners of community-based religions, others will be those for whom religion is less active but it is still important. The first and best source is the teacher's local knowledge of their pupils, and the school's local knowledge of the communities it serves. Parents and carers are usually very willing to alert a school to the needs of their children. There are, however, other helpful starting points and they are listed in the suggestions for further reading given at the end of this chapter.

Then there are those world views that might, according to the census, be labelled 'no religion'. Do children from these backgrounds have specific needs and sensitivities related to these issues? Teachers should be sensitive to the positions of parents whose commitment to a non-religious or secular-human-ist stance is as important to them as the commitment of, say, a practising Christian, Jew or Muslim.

For the majority of pupils across Britain religious concepts and words are at best a peripheral part of their language in infancy. For many, the first time they hear, for example, the word 'God' used in a religious context (as opposed to its use as an interjection in everyday speech) will be in the school assembly, during a taught classroom experience covering a festival or when listening to their teacher reading them a story.

Teachers of young children, therefore, have to think carefully about how they use religious concepts and terminology, at what level and why. Religious concepts can crop up in any subject or school situation. For example, the following conversation was overheard in a reception classroom during playtime:

> First child: *Where did the rabbit go?*
> Second child: *It went to heaven.*
> First child: *How do you know?*
> Second child: *I saw the angels come and get it.*
> (The teacher has a sharp intake of breath.)
> First child (in a matter of fact way): *Oh.*

Older children in primary schools have a lively interest in beliefs and values, not just their own but also those of anyone who is distinctively different from them. This is where the interface between religion and education can become most exciting. Primary schools today are emerging as places where inter-faith (or inter-world view) dialogue is high on the daily agenda (Ipgrave, 1999; 2003), sometimes with extremely positive results in terms of community-building. Hughes (1994, p.132), commenting on the future of RE and religion in schools, asserted that primary RE 'missed the mark' if it did not celebrate the 'inner worlds of pupils', and prepare them to cope with competing ideologies and commitments.

A useful and thought-provoking collection of data on British children's attitudes to religion and religious/spiritual questions, appears on the Professional Council for Religious Education (PCfRE) website, collected as part of the RE Festival in 1997 and added to since. Children and young people's responses to questions about life, living and death appear as anonymized quotes with indicators of age, gender and world view/religious background if provided. It is a useful tool for teacher education, as well as an interesting website for children.

Religion in the Curriculum

Religion in the National Curriculum

Whatever their affiliation or main source of authority and funding (religious or secularized), state-funded primary schools in England today are required to follow the National Curriculum (DfEE/QCA, 1999). Although RE is not a nationally prescribed subject, it is part of the basic curriculum that schools have to provide, which has two aims for education that have an arguably religious dimension:

- to promote pupils' spiritual, moral, social and cultural development; and
- to prepare all pupils for the opportunities, responsibilities and experiences of life (DfEE/QCA, 1999, p. 11).

All schools have to make sure that these legal and educational entitlements for all pupils are addressed. Two obvious areas in which schools can partially achieve these aims are through RE and school collective worship . But if these aims are prominent in the whole ethos of the school, then religion – in so far as it relates to spiritual and moral development, to the individual's place in society, to individual responsibility and how we make sense of our life experiences – is likely to be encountered in all curriculum contexts, This may be directly, or indirectly, either through the curriculum content itself, through questions asked by pupils, or through the responses they give. How these encounters are handled depends on the skill and confidence of the teacher.

The National Curriculum Handbook (DfEE/QCA, 1999) also provides guidance on the values that schools should be promoting. These values (discussed in detail in Chapter 15) are related to oneself, to relationships, to society and to the environment. Teachers have to be alert to the interactions between their own values, the school's shared values and the faith-based values that pupils may bring into the classroom. Between each primary school and even between classrooms there will be a range of difference in how these values or others are interpreted.

The RE syllabus

The RE syllabus is locally agreed. Parents have the right to withdraw their children from all or part of RE. The numbers of parents doing so varies from year to year, but anecdotal evidence and evidence from inspection reports indicate that the national rate of withdrawal from RE is very low. Teachers also have the right to withdraw actively from the teaching of RE, but this is also unusual in primary settings. Not all primary school teachers are asked to teach RE, since some schools make use of a specialist RE to teach the subject across a number of classes.

Teacher training Standard S2.1b (DfES/TTA, 2002) requires those awarded QTS to have sufficient understanding to be able to teach RE with advice from an experienced colleague where necessary. Trainees can sometimes achieve QTS without having taught RE at all, because of the constraints of teaching practice arrangements. Probably because of concerns about the rights of withdrawal, the TTA excluded RE from the list of subjects that have to be taught and assessed during training.

In most primary schools in England and Wales, the locally agreed syllabuses for RE are determined by an Agreed Syllabus Conference, convened by the

LEA. Elected or invited representatives of local faith communities, local government and the teaching profession, agree on the subject's aims and content for their local area. These areas are demographically, geographically and economically very different, and debates continue about just how different RE should be in each one (QCA, 2003). In addition, the subject is monitored and supported by the local Standing Advisory Council for Religious Education (SACRE) in each LEA, made up of four committees representing the interests highlighted above. This council also has a particular remit in respect of collective worship.

Voluntary-aided schools are able to determine the content and teaching of RE according to their foundation and religious affiliation, and by approval of their governing body with the headteacher. However, some aided schools, mainly Church of England foundations, follow LEA syllabuses, on the advice of their Diocesan Education Board. Other aided schools use highly specified programmes for the study of religion that cover only those aspects that fit comfortably with the aims of the school and the wishes of the parent community and governing body.

Debates about the local status of RE versus its inclusion in a national curriculum, its aims and content, and its methods of assessment have pursued the subject since the 1988 Education Reform Act. Although it is locally agreed, RE and its teachers are supported by advice from central government, usually through the QCA, and are subject to inspection through OFSTED like any other subject. The exception is in aided schools, where inspection is carried out by specially trained members of the faith community, or by inspectors sympathetic to the faith.

The distinctive contribution that RE makes to the curriculum and to the development of pupils is summarized as follows:

> by developing pupils' knowledge and understanding of religion, religious beliefs, practices, languages and traditions and their influence on individuals, communities, societies and cultures. It enables pupils to consider and respond to a range of important questions related to their own spiritual development, the development of values and attitudes and fundamental questions concerning the meaning and purpose of life.
>
> (DfEE/QCA, 1999, p. 19)

This shows that RE is more than learning about religions. It is intended to be a transforming subject in which children learn through and from religion (Grimmitt, 2000). Religious education's content varies, but not as much as might be expected bearing in mind the local determination of syllabuses. In the year 2000, QCA brought out Schemes of Work for RE (QCA, 2000c) and these are followed in some primary schools alongside the agreed syllabus. Most teachers in primary settings rely on the training and confidence of the RE co-ordinator to produce long- and medium-term plans to help them with their short-term planning

Pupils' learning and progress in RE is assessed according to the requirements of the agreed syllabus, if relevant, and is reported to parents each year. It is often at parents' evenings that comments about the changing nature of the subject, and the position of religion in society, present teachers with sharp professional challenges.

Collective Worship

In addition to RE, and other aspects of the taught curriculum covering religion, schools are required by law to provide a daily act of collective worship. Most schools try to agree on a policy of school worship that is as inclusive as possible in order to ensure that this potentially rewarding part of the school day does not become divisive or irrelevant to pupil needs and backgrounds. However, this requirement for worship to take place does present teachers, and school governors, with dilemmas that many of them would prefer to avoid.

This is not surprising, as school collective worship, as interpreted by government guidance and through some inspection reports, does appear in some respects to be legally, educationally and philosophically opposed to the aims of RE and to other aspects of the curriculum. The majority of acts of worship during a term are required to be 'wholly or mainly' of a 'broadly Christian character' (DfE, 1994, p. 21). This emphasis on Christianity has caused considerable anxiety in the profession and amongst some parents. Interestingly, much of the anxiety has been expressed by Christians and Christian groups, concerned, for example, about the inappropriateness of Christian worship being conducted by teachers with no personal Christian conviction. Many teachers, professional associations and others involved in education would like to see the current requirements removed or radically altered (Dainton, 1995; Religious Education Council of England and Wales, 1996) but the government has never been persuaded that this is what parents want as well. Indeed, there is some evidence that the majority of parents like schools to provide worship, on the basis either that it does not do any harm or because they feel that the worship of God is an important part of the daily lives of children. Nationally the numbers of withdrawals are low compared with school population size, and governments take this as an indicator of parental support for this part of the school day. However, some school communities have been affected by the intense and justified annoyance felt by faith communities apparently marginalized and offended by the perceived attempts to impose Christian worship on all schools.

In any case, even as it stands, the area of school worship is open to a much wider interpretation than some schools are willing to employ (Cheetham, 2000; 2001; Webster, 2000). Schools are also able to apply to their LEA through the SACRE for a determination to provide worship of a different kind, although numbers of applications nationally are low. The important professional consideration is whether or not asking highly secularized institutions to provide collective worship is appropriate and, if so, how can teachers ensure that what is provided is educationally valid and appropriate to the backgrounds of the pupils and the staff who are participating in the event.

Religious Literacy

In summary, these different curriculum contexts and interpretations, and the variety of school settings, mean that school pupils all over England are encountering religion, and religious beliefs and values, in a diverse way. Some would argue that this is appropriate and something to be celebrated. However, diversity can sometimes degenerate into disparity and, in this case, pupils might not receive their entitlement to an education that really promotes spiritual, moral, social and cultural development. Diversity in the relationships between religion and education is not only engendered by the systems governing education, but through the professional and personal beliefs, values and attitudes of teachers themselves. This is an issue that needs to be examined further by anyone entering the teaching profession, and by those within it. Every teacher will encounter religion in primary school settings whether they want to or not; the degree of confidence with which they embrace the opportunity will have been affected by their personal lives, their initial training and their continuing professional development. Each primary school teacher needs, therefore, what we might call 'religious literacy' (Wright, 2000).

Religious literacy consists of:

- a familiarity with religious terminology, concepts, beliefs and values;
- a skill in using the language of religion;
- an ability to recognize where and how that language resonates with the lives people live every day;
- an ability to consider where and how personal and professional values have been developed and how they sit alongside those being promoted in schools.

Religious literacy requires a reflective approach to education and to teaching and an open-mindedness in relation to religious questions. While most writers exploring this theme have seen it as an essential part of a child's education, it is just as important for their teachers.

Issues for Reflection

- What do you personally understand by the terms *religion, religions* and *secularism* as they are used in educational debates today?
- Can you identify the sources of your own identity in terms of your own world view?
- Do you recognize any areas of professional development that might help you to develop a religious literacy for your own professional context?
- Should pupils have an entitlement to an education in religion and through religion? Are the current arrangements appropriate, or would you change things?

Summary of Key Points

- Religions play an important part in education but defining religion is complex.
- Religion is an active and vibrant part of society in Britain and so is secularism.
- The majority of adults identified themselves with a religion in the 2001 census, and especially with Christianity.
- Pupils have an entitlement to an effective education in religion.
- Parents expect schools to respond positively to their faith/world view backgrounds.
- Teachers in primary schools need religious literacy.

Suggestions for Further Reading

Books

Copley, T. (1997) *Teaching Religion – Fifty Years of Religious Education in England and Wales*. Exeter: University of Exeter Press. This is an engaging account of the position of religion in education since the 1944 Act; includes reflections from teachers of different generations.

Erricker, C. (ed.) et al (1993) *Teaching World Religions: A Teacher's Handbook produced by the SMAP Working Party on World Religions in Education*. Oxford: Heinemann. This book is a classic; a well-used and often quoted summary of the main things any teacher needs to know about religions, and more.

Gates, B.E. (ed.) (1996) *Freedom and Authority in Religions and Religious Education*. London: Cassell. The last section of this book is especially helpful on the experiences and needs of pupils of different religious backgrounds, but the whole book is full of gems from leading writers in the field of religion and education.

Grimmitt, M. (ed.) (2000) *Pedagogies of Religious Education: Case Studies in the Research and Development of Good Pedagogic Practice in RE*. Great Wakering, Essex: McCrimmon. A very useful book for RE specialists, excellent on the development of RE, and of interest to anyone wanting to know more about theories of religious education and pedagogical debates.

Teece, G. (2001) *A Primary Teacher's Guide to RE and Collective Worship*. Oxford: Nash Pollock. This is *the* guide; good-humoured, brilliantly written and underpinned with years of professional practice.

Websites

The following websites provide useful resources and discussion of issues in RE.

Professional Council for Religious Education website, www.pcfre/org.uk

Religious Exchange Service website, www.re-xs.ucsm.ac.uk

University of East Anglia Keswick Hall Centre for RE website, www.uea.ac.uk/edu/religion

17
Induction into the Profession

Sue Lawes

The following topics and issues are covered in this chapter:

- the statutory arrangements for the induction period;
- preparing for a first teaching post;
- planning for the first week of teaching;
- getting to know colleagues;
- professional development in the induction period;
- being observed;
- additional duties;
- getting the best out of meetings;
- managing time;
- sources of support and information for newly qualified teachers.

This chapter discusses a number of issues specific to newly qualified teachers (NQTs) in primary schools. It is addressed specifically to readers about to enter the profession or recently embarked on their primary school teaching career. It includes some information, some practical tips and some more general points relevant to the first year of teaching, based on my own recent experience of beginning as a teacher. Although many of the issues will be common to all those in their first year of teaching and those responsible for overseeing the induction of new colleagues into the profession, the government guidance referred to in this chapter was produced to support those who take up a teaching post in a primary school in England.

One of the key points in this chapter is that when you take up your first teaching post you are not just a class teacher (if 'just' is the right word). You are a member of a school staff. This is different to your experience on teaching practice. Of course, the teaching of your class will be of prime importance to you, and rightly so. But you will now be expected to fulfil a number of different roles, not only by the children that you teach, but also by other children and adults in the school, particularly your work colleagues, and parents.

Main Elements of the Induction Year

This section is a brief summary of the key elements of the induction year. A comprehensive guide to the induction period is provided by the TTA in a number of publications for NQTs about the induction period (TTA, 2003a; 2003b).

The purpose of the induction period

The induction period is intended to support NQTs during their first year of teaching. It has two main aspects:

- to provide NQTs with an individual programme of professional development and monitoring; and
- to help NQTs meet the National Induction Standards by the end of the induction period.

Induction should help NQTs build on what they achieved during their ITT programme as well as forming the basis of their longer-term professional and career development. Crucial in this respect is the Career Entry and Development Profile (CEDP) (TTA, 2003c), issued when trainees successfully complete their ITT course (discussed later in this chapter).

The induction standards

In order to complete the induction period satisfactorily, an NQT must:

- continue to meet the standards for the award of QTS (DfES/TTA, 2002), consistently and with increasing professional competence; and
- successfully pass six induction standards related to professional values and practice, knowledge and understanding and teaching.

The first of these requirements is to demonstrate the attributes and capabilities of the standards for QTS (DfES/TTA, 2002) consistently and independently, across a range of contexts and over an extended period of time. This represents a more demanding level of professional action than that needed to meet the standards for QTS at the end of an ITT course when trainees may have support and when teaching practices may be shorter than one half-term.

There are six induction standards. These are related to and build on the three key areas that are assessed at the end of ITT. The first is concerned with professional values and practice. To meet this standard NQTs have to 'seek and use opportunities to work collaboratively with colleagues to raise standards by sharing effective practice in the school' (TTA, 2003a, p. 7). The second standard is concerned with knowledge and understanding. To pass this standard NQTs have to 'show a commitment to their professional development by: identifying areas in which they need to improve their professional knowledge, understanding and practice in order to teach more effectively in their current post; and with support, taking steps to address these needs' (TTA, 2003a, p. 9).

The next four induction standards are all related to teaching. The first of these is about teaching children with SEN. Specifically, NQTs need to show that they can 'plan effectively to meet the needs of pupils in their classes with special educational needs, with or without statements, and in consultation with the special educational needs coordinator (SENCO) contribute to the preparation, implementation, monitoring and review of Individual Education Plans (IEPs) or the equivalent' (TTA, 2003a, p. 11). The second involves liaising with parents and carers on pupils' progress and achievements. To meet the third teaching standard NQTs have to show that they can 'work effectively as part of a team and ... liaise with, deploy, and guide the work of other adults who support pupils' learning' (TTA, 2003a, p. 15). The final teaching standard is concerned with managing children's behaviour. NQTs have to be able to 'secure a standard of behaviour that enables pupils to learn, and act to pre-empt and deal with inappropriate behaviour in the context of the behaviour policy of the school' (TTA, 2003a, p. 17).

Duration

The duration of the statutory induction period is three school terms. This is lengthened pro rata for part-time teachers. You do not have to start your induction immediately after you qualify. However, once begun you are normally expected to complete the induction period within five years of starting it.

The importance of the induction year

Satisfactory completion of the induction period is essential. Failure means that you will not be able to teach in a maintained school or a non-maintained special school. You only have one chance at induction, although if you fail you can appeal to the GTCE and they may agree to extend your induction. However, take heart. Very few NQTs fail their induction period, which means that the vast majority are successful.

Entitlement to non-contact time

This is time when you are not in contact with children. It amounts to 10 per cent of your teaching time and should be taken at regular intervals during the induction period. This time should be used predominantly for development activities that form part of a targeted and coherent programme of professional development.

Observation and assessment

One observation of your teaching is undertaken every six to eight weeks for a full-time NQT, to give a total of six in the induction period. Each observation is followed up with a discussion and feedback about your progress.

Towards the end of each term there is a formal assessment of your progress which takes account of the observations and the reviews of progress (see below). Following the assessment discussion with your induction tutor or headteacher, a report is sent to the LEA or the Independent Schools Council Teacher Induction Panel (ISCTIP). After the third of these formal assessment meetings your headteacher will make a recommendation to the LEA or ISCTIP about whether you have successfully met the induction standards.

Reviews of progress

These should occur once every six to eight weeks and should be a detailed review not only of your performance against your personal targets but also of your overall performance against the induction standards. You and your induction tutor should maintain a written record of these meetings.

Hitting the Ground Running

Even before the first term begins you start to face all the demands made on experienced teachers. But as an NQT you have additional pressures. The school, the children and your colleagues are all new to you and the experience of teaching for most NQTs is limited to periods of teaching practice. It is important to use the time between completion of your teacher training course and your first day in post to plan and prepare as much as possible. Aim to make the first day and week of teaching as focused as possible on getting to know the children and making sure that your classroom delivery is effective. Teaching is tiring, and the first week particularly so. The better prepared you are, the more at ease and confident you will feel.

The transition from trainee teacher to working teacher can be daunting, but also positively challenging and exciting. The NQT has to consider a broader range of matters than those encountered on teaching practice. Although you can refer to your induction tutor and other staff for advice – and it is important to do this – this is the first time that the class is 'yours'. Within the constraints of the school's culture and community, you now have some scope to establish routines and procedures that suit your philosophy and style of teaching.

It is always a good idea to visit the school and if possible the class to be taught, before you take up a teaching post. This helps you to start to build relationships with the children and staff, and to begin to become familiar with the school ethos and the physical environment.

Preparation for your first post can be undertaken in five main areas:

- practical matters;
- administration;
- fact-finding;
- planning; and
- grouping the children.

Practical matters

Practical points include thinking about and deciding on class layout and wall displays. The objective is to make the classroom welcoming and for you to mould the environment to your own teaching approach. When thinking about layout, consider the use of space and the sensible location of resources so that the children can access them easily. You need to think about the storage of children's books and resources, and about systems, such as where the children will put both finished work and work in progress. (Chapter 2 provides further discussion of the physical environment of the classroom.) Before you start teaching you can label such things as books, drawers and coat-pegs. Think also about the kinds of resources you will need to gather or make, such as key-word cards, posters or materials for practical activities.

Administration

Administrative points to remember include obtaining class lists and preparing various records such as pro forma and tick lists for recording children's progress and your assessments of their learning.

Fact-finding

Fact-finding covers not only becoming familiar with the children's names, but also gathering relevant facts about their family backgrounds, any welfare issues or matters of performance and behaviour. The information can come from written records or from talking to staff. (Read Chapter 8 on pastoral care for more detailed advice.) It is also important to find out what resources are available for you to use, their location and the school system for using them. You will also need to familiarize yourself with school policies and procedures. Most schools will have a school handbook which contains this information. If not, ask your induction tutor.

Things you need to know about before term begins include:

- the behaviour management policy and how this is applied in the classroom;
- resources and schemes of work, including the school reading scheme;
- the structure of the school day and how it is managed – in particular, playtime arrangements and duties, school bells and signals and assembly procedures;

- registration procedures, including how to complete the register and how school dinner money is collected;
- medical procedures, including what to do if a child is ill in your class;
- who's who among your colleagues, both teachers and support staff, especially subject co-ordinators, members of the management team and the SENCO;
- miscellaneous rules such as those about school uniform, the wearing of jewellery, snacks and other sweets and drinks, and toys;
- arrangements for when it is raining;
- procedures for receiving and letting children go at the beginning and end of the school day;
- procedures for school assemblies; and
- procedures to be followed during a fire drill.

Asking questions about these systems and being fully equipped with the answers will impress colleagues and help you to make a good first impression. It will also make your first few days at school less stressful.

Planning

You will be familiar with planning schemes of work and lessons from your teaching practices. Most teachers have termly and weekly plans and may have a brief daily overview of what they are teaching but they do not write detailed daily or session plans. If there is more than one teacher in your year group try to meet them in the holidays to learn about and, where appropriate, to agree the approach to planning.

Grouping the children

A key point to consider is the groups in which the children will work for different types of task. You may have to decide whether to take on existing groupings from the previous teacher, with the possibility of changing these in the light of experience, or drawing up new ones. You need to consider how you are going to organize the class for different activities, for example, by using random mixed-ability groups, ability groups or social groupings.

Baptism of Fire – the First Week

In your planning for the first week try to make sure that you have allocated time for activities that allow you to get to know the children, the children to get to know you and, in some cases, for the children to get to know each other. Depending on the age of the children, these could include drawing, writing and talking about themselves, their likes and dislikes at school and favourite toys, books or photographs that they bring from home. Aim for plenty of speaking and listening in school, as this is a key way of finding out about others. Circle Time, especially, provides just such opportunities. Speaking and listening, as well as writing activities, provide good opportunities for assessment of academic and social skills, which will inform your decisions about how you group the children.

Rules and routines

The first week is crucial for establishing classroom rules, routines and expectations, such as using quiet voices, no shouting, putting your hand up when you want to say something, sharing and taking turns. It is important that the children are involved in the rule-making process. This encourages a sense of ownership and therefore acceptance by the children, as well as consistency in the application of the rules by the teacher! The associated discussion will also help the children to understand why such rules are necessary.

Rules should be displayed clearly on the wall in words that the children understand, preferably using the children's own words. This acts as a reminder to which the teacher can refer the children regularly, particularly in the first term. The children could make their own displays for this purpose, a good opportunity for collaborative work.

You will need to establish a number of routines during the school day. These will be needed for such things as registration, lining up before leaving the classroom, assembly, returning from playtime, lunchtimes, the end of the day and tidying away after activities. Here are some tips:

1. Be firm from the outset. On returning to school, especially after the summer break, the children's attitude to school discipline is likely to have lapsed. It is easier to relax discipline later than it is to tighten up after a relaxed start. Children need to know and clearly understand the boundaries from the outset.
2. Expectations can be reinforced by repetition such as practising lining up until the teacher is satisfied it is being done safely, and with sufficient speed and lack of noise.
3. With so much for the NQT to take in, a notebook (or even a Dictaphone) is very useful for noting your own queries, points to raise with colleagues and informal assessments or information you want to retain about children.

New Kid on the Block

Having established your credibility with the children, you still need to establish good working and professional relationships with colleagues and parents. A recent commercial had the punchline, 'You don't have a second chance to make your first impression'. This first impression has to be a balance between projecting an appropriate degree of self-assurance and confidence, particularly with parents, and sensitivity to the greater experience and knowledge of senior colleagues. And remember you do not have to knock before going into the staff room!

Other teachers

No doubt you will start your job full of enthusiasm, with your own ideas as to how things might be done. By definition, this may mean doing things differently from how they have been done before in the school or the class, which may seem to established staff to carry an implied criticism of current practice. This is not to say that you should suppress your own ideas; simply be diplomatic in your methods of introducing them.

Establishing working relationships may require more effort than you might think, as teaching can be quite an isolating profession. You may have a teaching assistant, but you will be leading the class on your own, and it is easy to spend all your non-teaching time in the classroom by yourself, preparing, marking, putting up displays and on other classroom maintenance.

When you finally tear yourself away from your classroom and go into the staff room, it is important not to get your own impression of the whole school from the first colleague who speaks to you, or speaks to you at any length. Holmes (2003) describes the staff room as 'your refuge' and she offers the following tips for finding your place in it.

- Do not be daunted by other teacher's approaches to their jobs.
- Do not judge your fellow teachers too harshly.
- Remove yourself from any situation or conversation that makes you feel uncomfortable. Teachers always have a plethora of excuses they can employ to excuse themselves, e.g. an arrangement to see a pupil, photocopying to do ...
- Be discreet when others confide in you.
- Try not to use the staff room as an extension of your working space. Not only is it hard to concentrate in a room full of chattering people, but your mess could annoy your colleagues (Holmes, 2003, p. 104).

In addition to staff meetings and other compulsory get-togethers, staff may organize other events such as social gatherings. It is a good idea to join in as many of these as you comfortably can. You may well be the only new person in the school. It is to be hoped that your colleagues will make you feel welcome but this should not be taken for granted and you may need to be prepared to make the first move.

Do not forget that your colleagues are a useful resource. They will have ideas about how to deal with difficult children and about classroom activities, what works and what does not. You will be able to benefit from their experience and knowledge. As well as listening to colleagues in this way, you can also benefit from them listening to you, for example, to you sounding off if you have had a difficult morning. Ideally, a staff room is a place for dialogue and a degree of relaxation and fun. One word of warning though: be aware of who is listening to your comments. Parents and visitors may be using the staff room.

Teaching assistants

Teaching assistants may be undervalued as colleagues. They often have a wealth of experience, particularly in working through practical problems. You will probably spend more time with your TA than with any other colleague. Your teacher training course may not have covered person-management skills, but these are needed for your relationship with your TA. As with all supervisory relationships, it involves maintaining a balance between leading, consulting, sometimes recognizing their greater experience of the school and the age group, not demanding too much and also giving them autonomy. Above all, show them appreciation!

Headteacher

The headteacher has a responsibility to ensure that a suitable induction pro- gramme is provided for NQTs and to make the final recommendation to the appropriate body, generally the LEA, that the required induction standards have been achieved.

Induction tutor

Your induction tutor is a key person in your first year of teaching, so it is important to build a good relationship with him or her. The induction tutor will have day-to-day responsibility for making sure that you are provided with an appropriate induction programme and will be responsible for providing professional support and guidance, monitoring your progress and for under- taking your assessments.

Parents

It is important that parents and carers have confidence in you. While the staff room can be a refuge, even when colleagues are present, you are always on show with parents. This is true even in the relatively informal context of the playground when taking younger children in from and out to the playground at the beginning and end of the day. Remember that parents are entrusting their beloved offspring to you, so it is important not only that they have con- fidence in your ability, but also in your commitment to teaching and to their children. You should try not to look fed up and miserable even after the worst day at school! While you, as an NQT, may understandably feel less than con- fident in your own ability, you can at least give parents the confidence that you are well organized and efficient. For example, make an effort to learn quickly which children belong to which parents. You can initiate contacts with the parents by sending a letter home introducing yourself. In this letter, advise them of academic and practical arrangements, such as the topic for the half-term, days when the children require PE equipment, the days when library and reading books are changed, and arrangements for homework. Above all parents like to be kept informed!

Given that part of your remit as a teacher is to encourage the development of social skills in the children, parents are entitled to expect that you display appropriate social skills with them, even at the simple level of passing the time of day with them when children are entering or leaving the school. This makes life easier when the more formal parent consultations take place.

Governors

Governors are important and influential stakeholders in the school. You may have been interviewed by a member of the governing body as they have a strategic responsibility to see that the school is appropriately staffed. For this reason they may also take an interest in your progress during your induction year. You will normally have far less contact with external governors than with parents, apart from the obvious cases of parent-governors. However, it is worthwhile finding out who they are in case they appear in your classroom or you bump into them in the school corridor. The comments made earlier in relation to parents about self-confidence, commitment and sociability, apply equally to your relations with external governors. (Chapter 6 contains more information about the roles and responsibilities of school governors.)

Advisers

The LEA adviser (or a representative from ISCTIP) is kept informed about the arrangements for your induction and your progress throughout the induction period. They will be responsible for endorsing the headteacher's recommendation made at the end. As part of this they may observe you teaching.

That was only *Initial Training*

An ITT course is only the first major step in the continuing professional development that will go on throughout your career as a teacher. You should look on the induction year as the second major step. The link between the two is the CEDP.

Career Entry and Development Profile

All trainee teachers are given a CEDP at the end of their ITT programme. It should summarize the discussion they have had with their ITT providers about their strengths and professional development priorities. Newly qualified teachers are then required to share their CEDP with their school when they start teaching so that it can inform and support discussions about professional development priorities during the induction period.

The CEDP is intended to:

- help you make connections between ITT, induction and the later stages of your development as a teacher;
- focus your reflection on your achievements and goals in the earliest stages of your teaching career;
- guide the processes of reflection and collaborative discussion about your professional development needs which take place as part of your ITT and induction programmes;
- build on your achievements and identify your professional development needs;
- help you to prepare for meetings with your tutors and induction tutor; and
- help you to set your current priorities in the wider context of career and professional development.

It helps your school to:
- understand the strengths you developed and the experiences you had during your ITT;
- support your professional development;
- support constructive dialogue between you and your induction tutor; and
- make links between induction, continuing professional development and performance management (adapted from TTA, 2003c).

Towards the end of ITT you discuss your progress and achievements, as well as areas of your teaching that could be developed further, with your ITT tutor. This discussion and reflection form the basis for the first entry in your CEDP. From this starting point, at the beginning of your induction period, you and your induction tutor in school set your professional development objectives and plan your induction support programme. The agreed action plan is the second entry in the CEDP. The final entry in the CEDP occurs at the end of the induction period, when you and your induction tutor look back at your induction period and reflect on your progress, your support programme and your aspirations for continuing professional development.

Non-contact time

Full-time NQTs are entitled to the equivalent of half a day non-contact time each week. This may be taken as a day every two weeks or in blocks. The primary purpose of non-contact time is for you to make progress towards meeting the targets in your CEDP. You might want to use your time to observe other teachers in the school, visit other schools or attend courses. The use of the time will be planned in conjunction with your induction tutor so that your professional development needs are supported.

Courses

Apart from their content, professional development courses are an opportunity to broaden working relationships beyond your school by meeting experienced teachers from within the education authority, and giving you the opportunity to meet and compare notes with other NQTs. This is not to undervalue the content of the courses themselves. From experience, many NQTs would agree that a very valuable course to attend as early on as possible is one on behaviour management.

The induction file

Newly qualified teachers should maintain an induction file, which is their personal record of the induction period. You have freedom to include what you wish. This is not an exhaustive list but it is useful to have sections on the following areas:

- notes and handouts from training courses attended;
- information and articles that relate to your targets;
- notes made when observing other teachers;
- formal records and notes of observations and assessments made of your teaching; and
- reports written following review meetings.

Being observed

You are normally observed at least six times, one lesson in every half term, during your induction year. The first observation usually occurs during your first four weeks in school. Usually the induction tutor undertakes these observations, but it is likely that other people from within or outside the school, such as the headteacher, subject co-ordinators or a representative from the LEA, will be involved as well. As with your ITT course, the observations are prearranged. After each observation there is a follow-up discussion and usually a written report. As on teaching practice the discussions and reports from the observations should be seen primarily as an opportunity to gain useful feedback which will facilitate your professional development.

Additional Duties

Fêtes worse than death

From teaching practice and from your own experience as a school pupil you will be aware of the existence and importance of extracurricular activities, from school fêtes to musical productions. These are both an extension of your teaching activities and an opportunity to extend social and professional contacts with colleagues, parents and children. They may not be compulsory but there may well be an expectation that you attend and participate in such events.

Some of these activities may be directed towards the pupils' development, others towards the school community as a whole. In the former category are lunchtime and after-school clubs and musical and dramatic productions. In the latter category are fund-raising and other social events which parents often help to organize. In your NQT year you should not be expected to take on burdensome additional responsibilities, but both types of activity are an opportunity for you to demonstrate additional talents, such as running a French club or coaching a sports team.

As with any other occupation, teaching is a mixture of technical, interpersonal and organizational skills. To the NQT, for whom their teaching post is their first 'proper' job, the transition to working life may present challenges in addition to those arising from their teaching role. You may find that there are after-school events during the year, such as a parent–teacher association fund-raising event, which you are expected to attend. This raises two further aspects of extracurricular activities: the public relations aspect or your role as a representative of the school and your own career development.

Meetings

Meetings are often seen as intrusive on a teacher's time, but when properly prepared for and conducted, they can save time in the longer run. You cannot avoid them, so it helps to adopt a positive frame of mind towards them. There are usually cycles of planned meetings, but there are also unplanned meetings, often with parents.

Staff meetings cover organizational matters, housekeeping issues, teaching policy and training for the school staff as a whole. Although an NQT's role in conducting these is usually minimal, your preparation is generally the same as for other members of staff, in terms of reading any necessary papers beforehand or thinking of points or questions to raise. It is important not to be fazed by the contributions of more experienced and well-established members of staff. If you have something to say let your voice be heard. Your contributions to meetings at all levels should be balanced between showing initiative and enthusiasm and being sensitive to your colleagues' greater experience and knowledge. Your responsibility for follow-up action after a meeting is also generally the same as for other members of staff, for example, implementing a new library book procedure or checking on health and safety points. It is advisable that you make a note of any action following a meeting that you are responsible for and the deadline for achieving it.

There are also likely to be key stage meetings and, if there are two or more teachers in a year group, year group meetings. These often cover matters of common interest such as planning or sharing and using resources. Your role in these meetings is probably more extensive than in whole-school meetings, as the agendas will probably have a more direct and immediate impact on your class.

Time Management

The standard principles and techniques of time management apply to teachers as much as to anyone else. These are important not only for your performance as a teacher, but also for your health. Managing your time sensibly can be beneficial to your well-being, and therefore to your longer-term effectiveness as a teacher.

Time management for teachers relies heavily on planning. It helps to plan as far in advance as you sensibly can. This makes your life less stressful. With all the stresses that NQTs can experience, the more unnecessary ones you can remove the better. Planning is a tool you can use to pace yourself over the whole of the first year, not just the first half of a term.

There are peaks and troughs in the workload. There are peaks such as times leading up to and during national tests, parent consultations, report-writing and school visits; you might find it hard to spot the troughs! Since the workload is not evenly spread you need to set yourself a pace that you can sustain at normal levels but can also increase when necessary to cope with particularly busy periods. There is a danger that you get burnt out even before the end of the first term.

You have only so much time, but you can also use the time of others. In fact, you will need to manage the time of colleagues, particularly TAs, as well as your own. This again means good planning, so that their time is used most efficiently and they are not, for example, waiting for you to tell them what needs to be done. You may also be able to benefit from parents' help and again this should be planned for in advance.

Here are some tips about time management:

- Make lists of things to be done and keep notes so you do not overlook things. There is nothing worse than a last-minute panic. Lists will also help you to prioritize.
- Make good use of your non-contact time by, for example, occasionally earmarking some for reports and other essential paperwork.
- Decide when you function most effectively. Do not push yourself when you are overtired. Holmes (2003, p. 234) advises NQTs to 'beware of the law of diminishing returns'. You can reach the point where, for example, an hour's work gives only half an hour's output.
- Keep at least one evening a week free of school work and also limit yourself to only a few hours at the weekend.
- Keep your diary up to date and write in it when particular jobs will be done.
- Take a break at lunchtime even if it is only a short one. Get some fresh air!
- Do not leave things until the last minute and build some flexibility into planning your workload. In teaching, things are always cropping up unexpectedly which can floor even the most organized person.

- Start your report-writing as early as you can. Reports are very time-consuming and there will be an absolute deadline by which to complete them. The first experience of these is very difficult, and you are likely to need a lot of support, especially at the beginning. As your colleagues will also have reports to write, it pays to ask them for help before they begin to feel pressured themselves.
- Consider attending a time management course early in your induction period.

Finally, time management is not just about what you do, but also about what you do not do. Remember there is life after school and you need to get a sensible balance between school and home life. Too much emphasis on work could lead to burnout. It is essential to allow yourself time to unwind, to relax and to give time to yourself, your family and friends. You are not paid to be a 24/7 school teacher!

Help! Sources of Information and Support

Finally, remember, you are not alone. It is important to network and to use as many sources of help as possible including:

- colleagues;
- your induction tutor;
- other NQTs;
- tutors from your ITT institution;
- teachers from other schools;
- LEA advisers;
- professional journals;
- national bodies such as the TTA and the DfES;
- professional associations; and
- the Internet.

Issues for Reflection

Below are some questions for an NQT starting in a new post.

- How do you plan to manage your relationships with your class and with other children in the school?
- How will your classroom express your teaching philosophy and teaching style?
- What strengths do you believe you have as a teacher? How will you exploit these? How will you address any areas for development that you perceive in yourself or that have been identified by others? Do your strengths or development needs relate to classroom activities or to your wider role as a teacher?
- What kind of impact do you hope to make on the school as a whole?

- How will you manage your relationships with colleagues, with parents and with other stakeholders such as governors? What image of yourself do you want to project to these other adults?

Summary of Key Points

- Plan and prepare as far in advance as you can before the autumn term begins and throughout the year. Stay in control.
- Get yourself informed about children, parents, school policies, procedures, the school itself and resources. Do not be afraid to ask questions.
- You are a member of staff as well as a teacher. Think about your relationship and behaviour towards your colleagues.
- Be confident in yourself and with other people you meet.
- Be reflective about your professional development needs.
- Make the most of colleagues' help and network with other NQTs.
- Be organized and manage your time efficiently.
- Look after yourself and balance work with home life. There is, or there should be, life after school!

Suggestions for Further Reading

Books and pamphlets

TTA (2003) *Induction Standards: TTA Guidance for Newly Qualified Teachers.* London: TTA. This is a comprehensive guide to the latest arrangements for induction for teachers in England.

TTA (2003) *Into Induction 2003: An Introduction for Trainee Teachers to the Induction Period for Newly Qualified Teachers.* London: TTA. This pamphlet is a brief and easy-to-read guide to induction and professional development.

TTA (2003) *Career Entry and Development Profile.* TTA: London. This provides guidance on how to use the CEPD to support professional development and to structure the meetings and reviews that take place during induction.

Website

TTA website, NQT induction section, www.tta.gov.uk/induction This site includes a range of materials designed to support those who are involved in induction arrangements. Most of these are also available from the TTA Publications Unit on 0845 6060 323. The site includes a selection of frequently asked questions about induction.

References

In the references below the following abbreviations and acronyms are used:

DfE   Department for Education
DfEE   Department for Education and Employment
DfES   Department for Education and Skills
DoH   Department of Health
GTCE   General Teaching Council of England
OFSTED   Office for Standards in Education
NACE   National Association for Able Children in Education
QCA   Qualifications and Curriculum Authority
TTA   Teacher Training Agency

Books and Articles

Alexander, R. (2002) *Culture and Pedagogy*. Oxford: Blackwell.

Anderson, H., Adlam, T., Coltman, P., Cotton, E. and Daniels, R. (1996) 'Spinning the plates. Organising the early years classroom'. In D. Whitebread (ed.), *Teaching and Learning in the Early Years*. London: Routledge Falmer.

Ashton, Baroness C. (2003) *Report of The Special Schools Working Group*. London: DfES.

Bainbridge, S. (2002) 'Planning, developing and implementing the curriculum for pupils with learning difficulties', Key Stage 3 National Strategy Conference 2002, key note speech.

Barrell, G.R. and Partington, J.A. (1985) *Teachers and the Law*. 6th edn. London: Methuen.

Barrs, M. and Pidgeon, S. (eds) (1994) *Reading the Difference: Gender and Reading in Elementary Classrooms*. Ontario: Pembroke.

Bastiani, J. (1989) *Working with Parents: A Whole-School Approach*. Repr. 1992. London: NFER-Routledge.

Bastiani, J. and Wolfendale, S. (eds) (1996) *Home–School Work in Britain: Review, Reflection and Development*. London: David Fulton.

Bell, D. (2002) *The Annual Report of Her Majesty's Chief Inspector of Schools*. London: OFSTED Publications.

Berger, A. and Gross, J. (1999) *Implementing the Literacy Hour for Pupils with Learning Difficulties*. London: David Fulton.

Berger, A., Morris, D. and Portman, J. (2000) *Implementing the National Numeracy Strategy for Pupils with Learning Difficulties*. London: David Fulton.

Blair, M. and Bourne, J. (1998) *Making the Difference: Teaching and Learning Strategies in Successful Multiethnic Schools*. DfEE Research Report No. 59. London: DfEE.

Blake, N., Smeyers, P., Smith, R. and Standish, P. (2000) *Education in an Age of Nihilism*. London: Routledge Falmer.

Blatchford, P. (ed.) (1989) *Playtime in the Primary School: Problems and Improvements*. Windsor: Nelson.

Blatchford, P. (1994) *Break time and the School: Understanding and Changing Playground Behaviour*. London: Routledge.

Bleach, K. (ed.) (1998) *Raising Boys' Achievement in Schools*. London: Trentham Books.

Bocking, B. (1995) 'Fundamental rites? Religion, state education and the invention of sacred heritage in post-Christian Britain and pre-war Japan', *Religion*, 25, pp. 227–47.

Bolton, A. (1997) 'Should religious education foster national consciousness?', *British Journal of Religious Education*, 19(3), pp. 134–42.

Britton, J. (1992) *Language and Learning*. 2nd edn. London: Penguin Books.

Brown, A. and Furlong, J. (1996) *Spiritual Development in Schools: Invisible to the Eye*. London: The National Society.

Brown, E. (1992) 'A framework for religious education', *British Journal for Special Education*, 19(4) pp. 137–40.

Brown, M. (1998) *D.W. The Picky Eater*. London: Red Fox.

Bruner, J. (1986) *Actual Minds, Possible Worlds*. Cambridge, MA, and London: Harvard University Press.

Bruner, J. (1996) *The Culture of Education*. Cambridge, MA, and London: Harvard University Press.

Burke, C. and Grosvenor, I. (2003) *The School I'd Like*. London: Routledge Falmer.

Bushell, R., Miller, A. and Robson, D. (1982) 'Parents as remedial teachers: an account of a paired reading project with junior school failing readers and their parents', *Journal of the Association of Educational Psychologists*, 5(9), pp. 7–13.

Calvert, M. and Henderson, J. (eds) (1998) *Managing Pastoral Care*. London: Cassell.

Carnie, F. (2003) *Alternative Approaches to Education, a Guide for Parents and Teachers*. London: RoutledgeFalmer.

Central Advisory Council for Education (England) (CACE) (1967) *Children and their Primary Schools.* (Plowden Report). London: HMSO.

Cheetham, R. (2000) 'Collective worship: a window into contemporary understanding of the nature of religious belief?', *British Journal of Religious Education*, 22(2), pp. 71–81.

Cheetham, R. (2001) 'How on earth do we find out what is going on in collective worship? An account of a grounded theory approach', *British Journal of Religious Education*, 23(3), pp 165–76.

Cherland, M.R. (1994) *Private Practices: Girls Reading Fiction and Constructing Identity.* London: Taylor and Francis.

Clark, H. (2002) *Building Education.* London: Institute of Education.

Cline, T., de Abreu, G., Fihosy, C., Gray, H., Lambert, H. and Neale, J. (2002) *Minority Ethnic Pupils in Mainly White Schools.* DfES Research Report 365. London: DfES.

Cockburn, A.D. (ed.) (2001) *Teaching Children 3 to 11: A Student's Guide.* London: Paul Chapman Publishing.

Cohen, M. (1998) 'A habit of healthy idleness: boys' underachievement in historical perspective', in D. Epstein, J. Elwood, V. Hey and J. May (eds), *Failing Boys?* Buckingham: Open University Press.

Cole, B. (1996) *Drop Dead.* London: Jonathan Cape.

Cole, M. (ed.) (2002) *Professional Values and Practice for Teachers and Student Teachers.* 2nd edn. London: David Fulton.

Cooling, T. (2000) 'Pupil Learning', in A. Wright and A.-M. Brandom (eds), *Learning to Teach Religious Education in the Secondary School.* London: Routledge Falmer.

Copley, T. (1997) *Teaching Religion – Fifty Years of Religious Education in England and Wales.* Exeter: University of Exeter Press.

Cowie, H. and Wallace P. (2000) *From Bystanding to Standing By.* London: Sage Publications.

Croner (2001) *The Head's Legal Guide.* New Malden: Croner Publications Ltd.

Cullingford, C. (1997) *The Politics of Primary Education.* Buckingham: Open University Press.

Dainton, S. (1995) 'Collective worship: reaching a consensus', *Resource: Journal of the Professional Council for RE*, 18(1), pp. 11–16.

David, K. and Charlton, T. (eds) (1996) *Pastoral Care Matters in Primary and Middle Schools.* London: Routledge.

Dean, G. (1998) *Challenging the More Able Language User.* London: David Fulton in association with NACE.

DfE (1988) *Education Reform Act.* London: HMSO.

DfE (1994) *Religious Education and Collective Worship.* Circular 1/94. London: DfE Publications Centre.

DfEE (1995a) *The Education (Pupil Registration) Regulations.* London: HMSO.

DfEE (1995b) *Protecting Children from Abuse, the Role of the Education Service.* Circular 10/95. London: HMSO.

DfEE (1995c) *Misconduct of Teachers and Workers with Children and Young*

Rudge, J. (2000) 'The Westhill Project: religious education as maturing pupils' patterns of belief and behaviour', in M. Grimmitt (ed.), *Pedagogies of Religious Education: Case Studies in the Research and Development of Good Pedagogic Practice in RE*. Great Wakering, Essex: McCrimmon.

Rudge, L. (1998) 'I am nothing' – does it matter? A critique of current Religious Education policy and practice in England on behalf of the silent majority', *British Journal of Religious Education*, 20(3), pp. 155–65.

Rudge, L. (2000) 'The place of religious education in the curriculum', in A. Wright and A.-M. Brandom (eds), *Learning to Teach Religious Education in the Secondary School*. London: RoutledgeFalmer.

Rudge, L. (2002) 'Citizens, subjects or souls: the monarchy in the 21st century – a means of defending faith?', *RE Today*, 19(2), pp. 42–3.

Rundell, S. (2001) 'Learning from boys', *Literacy Today*, 28, September p. 22.

Runnymede Trust (2003) *Complementing Teachers: A Practical Guide to Promoting Race Equality in Schools*. Manchester: Granada Learning.

Rutter, J. (1994) *Refugee Children in the Classroom*. Stoke-on-Trent: Trentham Books.

Sammons, P., Hillman, J. and Mortimore, P. (1995) *Key Characteristics of Effective Schools: A Review of School Effectiveness Research*. London: OFSTED.

Sayer, J. (2000) *The General Teaching Council*. London: Cassell.

Schon, D. (1983) *The Reflective Practitioner*. New York: Temple Smith.

School Curriculum and Assessment Authority (SCAA) (1997) *Guidance for Schools: The Promotion of Pupils' Spiritual, Moral, Social and Cultural Development* (draft). London: SCAA.

Scott, C. and Cox, S. (1999) 'The occupational motivation, satisfaction and health of English school teachers', *Educational Psychology*, 19(3), pp. 287–308.

Scottish Executive Education Department (2001) *A Teaching Profession for the 21st Century: Agreement Reached Following Recommendations Made in the McCrone Report*. Edinburgh: Scottish Executive.

Sharp, S. (1996) 'Bullying in the primary school'. In K. David and T. Charlton (eds), *Pastoral Care Matters in Primary and Middle Schools*. London: Routledge.

Sluckin, A. (1981) *Growing up in the Playground*. London: Routledge Kegan and Paul.

Smart, N. (1989) *The World's Religions: Old Traditions and Modern Transformations*. Cambridge: Cambridge University Press.

Smith, J.Z. (ed.) (1995) *Dictionary of Religion*. San Francisco, CA: HarperCollins.

Smith, W.C. (1979) *Faith and Belief – the Difference Between Them*. Oxford: Oneworld Publications.

Stone, M. (1986) 'The education of the black child', in A. James and R. Jeffcoate (eds), *The School in the Multicultural Society*. London: Harper and Row.

Straker, A. (1983) *Mathematics for Gifted Pupils*. Harlow: Longman.

Strauss, G. and Browne, A. (1991) *The Night Shimmy*. London: Jonathan Cape.

Suschitzky, W. and Chapman, J. (1998) *Valued Children, Informed Teaching.* Oxford: Oxford University Press.

Swann, M. (1985) *Education for All: The Report of the Committee of Inquiry into the Education of Children from Ethnic Minority Groups.* (Swann Report). London: HMSO.

Teece, G. (2001) *A Primary Teacher's Guide to RE and Collective Worship.* Oxford: Nash Pollock.

The Times (1893) *Times Law Report Williams* v *Eady.* London: *The Times.*

The Times (1990) *Porter* v *Barking and Dagenham LB and Another, The Times,* 9 April.

Thompson, D. (ed.) (1992) *The Pocket Oxford Dictionary.* Oxford: Clarendon Press.

Thatcher, A. (ed.) (1999) *Spirituality and the Curriculum.* London: Cassell.

Times Educational Supplement (*TES*) (2001) 'Warning to cool the test frenzy', *TES,* 2 November p. 8.

Titman, W. (1994) *Special Places, Special People: The Hidden Curriculum of the School Grounds.* London: Learning Through Landscapes.

Tizard, J., Schofield, W.N. and Hewison, J. (1982) 'Collaboration between teachers and parents in assisting children's reading', *British Journal of Educational Psychology,* 52, pp. 1–15.

Torrington, P. (1998) 'Spirituality – the practice in primary schools', *SPES Magazine* (8), p. 35.

Troyna, B. (1984) 'Multicultural education: emancipation or containment', in L. Barton and S. Walker (eds), *Social Crisis and Educational Research.* London: Croom Helm.

TTA (2003a) *Induction Standards: TTA Guidance for Newly Qualified Teachers.* London: TTA.

TTA (2003b) *Into Induction 2003: An Introduction for Trainee Teachers to the Induction Period for Newly Qualified Teachers.* London: TTA.

TTA (2003c) *Career Entry and Development Profile.* London: TTA.

Watson, B. (1993) *The Effective Teaching of Religious Education.* Harlow: Longman.

Watson, J. (2003a) Preparing spirituality for citizenship, *International Journal for Children's Spirituality,* 8(1), pp 9–24.

Watson, J. (2003b) *Citizenship Education and its Impact on Religious Education.* Norwich: University of East Anglia.

Webster, D. (1982) 'Awe in the curriculum', in University of Exeter School of Education *Religion, Spirituality and Schools: Perspectives 9.* Exeter: University of Exeter.

Webster, D. (2000) 'Collective worship', in A. Wright and A.-M. Brandom (2000) *Learning to Teach Religious Education in the Secondary School.* London: RoutledgeFalmer.

Williams, D. (2002) 'Gender dominates the school agenda', *The Guardian,* 18 May, London.

Wilson, G. (2003) *Using the National Healthy School Standard to Raise Boys' Achievement.* London: DoH.

Wolffe, J. (ed.) (1993) *The Growth of Religious Diversity: Britain from 1945.*

London: Hodder and Stoughton.

Wright, A. (1999) *Discerning the Spirit, Teaching Spirituality in the Religious Education Classroom*. Oxford: Culham College Institute.

Wright, A. (2000) 'The Spiritual Education Project: cultivating spiritual and religious literacy through a critical pedagogy of religious education', in M. Grimmitt (ed.), *Pedagogies of Religious Education: Case Studies in the Research and Development of Good Pedagogic Practice in RE*. Great Wakering, Essex: McCrimmon.

Wright, A. (2003) 'Freedom, equality, fraternity? Towards a liberal defence of faith community schools', *British Journal of Religious Education*, 25(2), pp. 142–52.

Websites

The following websites, referenced in the text, were consulted during the period April to August 2003. Addresses and details were correct at the dates of consultation but may have been subject to subsequent change.

Alternatives in Education website, www.AlternativesInEducation.co.uk

BBC Schools website, www.bbc.co.uk/schools

Birmingham Grid for Learning website, www.bgfl.org/bgfl

Britkid website, www.britkid.org

Centre for the Study of Inclusive Education website, www.inclusion.uwe.ac.uk/csie/csiehome.htm

Croner CCH Edinfo-Centre website, www.edinfo-centre.net

DfES website, www.dfes.gov.uk

DfES website, Ethnic Minority Achievement section, www.standards.dfes.gov.uk/ethnicminorities

DfES website, Special Educational Needs section, www.dfes.gov.uk/sen

DfES website, Standards Site, Primary section, www.standards.dfes.gov.uk/primary

East Riding Intranet for Learning website, www.eril.net/home2

European Roma Rights Center website, www.errc.org

Farmington Institute for Christian Studies website, www.farmington.ac.uk

GTCE website, www.gtce.org.uk

Governornet website, Information for School Governors, www.governornet.co.uk

Kids Health website, www.kidshealth.org

McGraw Hill website, Multicultural Supersite, www.mhhe.com/socscience/education/multi

Multicultural Pavilion website, www.edchange.org/multicultural

NACE website, www.nace.co.uk

National Association for Special Educational Needs website, www.nasen.org.uk

National Confederation of PTAs website, www.ncpta.org.uk

National Curriculum website, Gifted and Talented Guidance, www.nc.uknet/gt

National Grid for Learning website, www.inclusion.ngfl.gov.uk
Norfolk Esinet for Learning website, www.norfolkesinet.org.uk
National Statistics Online website, www.statistics.gov.uk
Norfolk Traveller Education Service,
  www.norfolkesinet.org.uk/pages/viewpage.asp?uniqid=1298
NRICH website, nrich.maths.org.uk
Optimus Publishing website, www.optimuspub.co.uk
Parent Centre website, www.parentcentre.gov.uk
Professional Council for Religious Education website, www.pcfre/org.uk
Pyramid Educational Consultants UK Ltd website, picture exchange commu-
  nication system, www.pecs.org.uk/html/pecs.asp
QCA website, Curriculum and Assessment section, www.qca.org.uk/ca
Raising Boys' Achievement website, www-rba.educ.cam.ac.uk
Random House website, www.randomhouse.co.uk
Religious Exchange Service website, www.re-xs.ucsm.ac.uk
Ride Foundation website, www.ridefoundation.org.uk
Runnymede Trust website, www.runnymedetrust.org
Teacher Net website, www.teachernet.gov.uk
TEACCH website, www.teacch.com
The Guardian Education website, education.guardian.co.uk
The Guardian website, GTCE/Guardian/MORI 2003 Teacher Survey,
  education.guardian.co.uk/micrsite/gtc
Times Educational Supplement website, EAL section,
  www.tes.co.uk/your_subject
TTA website, NQT induction section, www.tta.gov.uk/induction
University of East Anglia Keswick Hall Centre for RE website,
  www.uea.ac.uk/edu/religion
C: MACNT indxltd primteach 8–03-2004 8:46.45 am

Index